Fatal Fortnight

Fatal Fortnight

Arthur Ponsonby and the Fight for British Neutrality in 1914

DUNCAN MARLOR

Foreword by

LORD PONSONBY OF SHULBREDE

Frontline Books
London

Fatal Fortnight:
Arthur Ponsonby and the Fight for British Neutrality in 1914

This edition published in 2014 by Frontline Books,
an imprint of Pen & Sword Books Ltd,
47 Church Street, Barnsley, S. Yorkshire, S70 2AS
www.frontline-books.com

ISBN: 978-1-47382-286-3

CIP data records for this title are available from the British Library

For more information on our books, please visit
www.frontline-books.com, email info@frontline-books.com
or write to us at the above address.

Printed and bound by CPI Group (UK) Ltd, Croydon, CR0 4YY

Typeset in 11.2/14 pt Minion Pro

Contents

Illustrations

Acknowledgements

The genesis of this book goes back over more than a decade and a large debt of gratitude is owed to many people. First and foremost I must thank the Ponsonby family for its unfailing support, especially Laura Ponsonby and Kate Russell, Arthur Ponsonby's grand-daughters, both for their generous hospitality at Shulbrede Priory and their considerable help with the Shulbrede archives, and valuable suggestions, including the diary of Sir Hubert Parry, which had not occurred to me but which turned out to be priceless. Also I must thank Frederick, Lord Ponsonby of Shulbrede, great-grandson of Arthur Ponsonby, for the foreword that he has kindly provided, which gives a present day parliamentarian's perspective on his ancestor's story.

I thank Robin Dower, grandson of Sir Charles Trevelyan, for his kind help with details of the Trevelyan family; Wallington Hall, Northumberland, especially Lloyd Langley; and the Robinson Library, Newcastle University, especially Geraldine Hunwick, Archivist and Special Collections Librarian, for help with Trevelyan family archives and visual material and to the Trevelyan Family Trustees for their permission to use this.

Thanks are due to Mark Outhwaite, great-grandson of Robert Leonard Outhwaite, for help in respect of details of the Outhwaite family; and to Edward Milligan, former Librarian of Friends House for his assistance, insights and personal memories regarding Thomas Edmund Harvey.

I am grateful to David Kynaston for reading through the material and for his helpful suggestions. I thank Sir Tam Dalyell, former Father of the House of Commons for his interest over some years and for sharing family insight into Sir Edward Grey.

Special thanks also are due to Colin Harris, Superintendent of Special Collections at the Bodleian Library, Oxford, for his kind help over some years regarding the Ponsonby Papers and other collections. In thanking him I thank the many librarians and archivists who have made possible the researches on which this book is based.

At Frontline/Pen and Sword I would like to thank Michael Leventhal, Kate Baker his assistant, and their colleagues, for their support for this project and their excellent work and guidance in bringing the book to publication.

Foreword

By Frederick Ponsonby,
4th Baron Ponsonby of Shulbrede

———————

DUNCAN MARLOR'S ACCOUNT of the lead-up to the First World War tells the story of the role of backbench MPs in the parliamentary debates that led up to war. Arthur Ponsonby, my great-grandfather and at the time a Liberal backbencher, led the fight for British neutrality. The book challenges the sense of inevitability and unity of purpose which political leaders of the day, pro-interventionist newspapers and many historians sought to present to subsequent generations. As Duncan Marlor says, there was real drama in the parliamentary debates and votes that set Britain on course for war.

In writing this foreword some 100 years later and with memories of parliamentary debates on recent wars in my mind, it is interesting to try and draw some comparisons. I shall limit myself to three.

The first is a question of the scale of the proposed wars: while in 1914 few could have predicted the true horror of the war to come it was nevertheless true that the British government and British people were ready to sustain losses far higher than would ever be contemplated today. Senior officers and many MPs would have fought a number of wars in their careers and while there had not been a general war in Europe involving Britain since Napoleonic times, they would have been steeped in the military history of large-scale European wars. They would have considered that war was to protect British interests through its empire and maintaining the balance of power in Europe. Contrast that with today's wars where the fight is not between nation states acting in alliance to protect their own interests but between coalitions of states, led by America and acting in defence of human rights as defined by international treaty. The interpretation of UN resolutions is central to the justification for today's wars.

My second comparison is between public opinion then and now: the thrust of Duncan Marlor's narrative is that there was far more anti-war feeling in the lead-up to the First World War than has hitherto been acknowledged. Whilst this is true and he presents a compelling argument, it remains the fact that most of the anti-war rebels lost their seats in the 1918 general election. It also remains true that there was plenty of pro-war sentiment and even violent opposition to peace rallies, something which would be unthinkable for any of the wars undertaken in recent years. I would suggest that being anti-war in 1914 took greater courage with greater risk of being socially ostracised than being anti-war today. This is probably because the sense of threat was far greater; the very existence of Britain as an independent country was in question in 1914 whereas none of the wars in recent years threatened the state itself.

My third comparison concerns the status of Parliament and follows on from the public mood as perceived in 1914 and now. It is as true today as it was in 1914 that a simple reading of a parliamentary debate could lead a reader to an erroneous conclusion. It is often the case that there are many more speakers against a government's position than for it. This is simply because government Whips want to get on with the business of the day and do not need the government's position repeated again and again. It was also true in 1914 as it is today that Parliament was seen as the national cockpit at a time of crisis. Then as now opponents of government war policy believed Parliament had been knowingly misled in an attempt to secure the support necessary for action. They would agree with Arthur Ponsonby's dictum that 'the first casualty of war is truth'. Procedurally the parliamentary route to war has changed little. Whether the vote is on War Credit as in 1914 or endorsing the government's pro-war position as with Iraq in 2003 matters little. What is unprecedented, as far as I know, is for a government to be knocked off its course towards military action by a parliamentary vote as was the case with Syria in 2013. It remains to be seen whether this should be interpreted as parliamentary strength or governmental weakness.

Duncan Marlor's book brings alive the political personalities, the passions and debates in the 'fateful fortnight' in 1914. Every parliamentarian today will recognise the tensions between their own principles, loyalty to constituents, party and country and embarking on a war with unknown consequences.

Frederick Ponsonby

Introduction

————————

THE BRITISH DECISION to participate in the war which began in 1914 is heavily worked soil. The approach of the hundredth anniversary has prompted a chorus of historian affirmation, some of it quite strident, of the necessity of going in. The war justifiers regret the prominence of the anti-war poets such as Wilfred Owen, shake their heads indulgently about the simplifications of *Oh, What a Lovely War!* and *Blackadder Goes Forth* and declare sadly but categorically that Britain simply had to stop the Germans. Germany, they say, was aiming at domination of Europe and posed a perilous threat to the vital interests and security of Britain and its Empire; Britain had either to fight or become a client or vassal state of a Greater Germany. There has also been a vigorous re-working of the 1914 moral justification: Britain was fighting to resist lawless German aggression against Belgium. The case for British neutrality has had a minority run – from an imperialist perspective. This argues that had Britain kept out and not squandered its resources, the British Empire would not have declined so drastically. Meanwhile the evolution of the British decision to go in has been investigated in close detail, with the papers of Cabinet ministers and other members of the ruling circle trawled through. The British ground has, one might think, been covered. In fact there are serious gaps.

Firstly, there is the lack of any narrative from the perspective of Parliament – of how Britain's emergent parliamentary democracy was kept in the dark by the executive and protests were bundled aside. Most mentions of Parliament scarcely get beyond the big speech with which the Foreign Secretary, Sir Edward Grey, pitched for war on 3 August 1914. Here an old tale is reheated. In it Sir Edward is listened to intently (with thoughtful murmurs of assent) and then cheered heartily (but in dignified fashion) by all the MPs, except the Labour Leader Ramsay MacDonald – a solitary voice of disagreement, the story goes, in a House otherwise united in the will for war. The shades of the owners and editors of those pro-war newspapers who coined this patriotically pleasing mythology must be content with its durability.

Then there is the burying of the *real* drama. The Foreign Secretary had to have the majority of the House of Commons with him by vote or acclaim, or there would be no British war: hence the knife-edge suspense, especially as it was not known when Sir Edward stood up what he was going to say. By its response to the Foreign Secretary Parliament made its decision. To some MPs, it was a disastrous one. One Member, speaking in the House a year into the war, looked back on 3 August 1914 as 'the fatal afternoon'.

Often blanked out of the history completely is the evening of 3 August following the Foreign Secretary's speech, when backbenchers debated the war and most of the MPs who spoke, called with passion for Britain to stay out. The absence, in most of the accounts, of these intense parliamentary hours, as Britain hung between peace and war, would do credit to Kremlin air-brushers. Further, there is the War Credit debate of 6 August when the Government had to apply to Parliament for the first of a series of loans, without which Britain's war could not have been fought. In this the Government had to set out its case to Parliament for going to war. The House of Commons heard what were among the angriest exchanges in its long history, but the debate has left almost no imprint on the pages of the history of the nation gearing up for the conflict.

But the biggest omission is the story of the band of MPs who battled for British neutrality, led by a backbench Liberal whose father had been Queen Victoria's Secretary, and who had ridden in a coach as the Queen's pageboy. Their arguments read as wide-ranging, moving, sharp, often surprising, and they are not imperialist ones. These MPs were mostly anti-imperialist Radical and Labour. No imperialist case for neutrality in the European war was heard in the House of Commons.

Most of us have some particular interest in the Great War. Mine is my great-uncle. He was Duncan Marlor (1880–1926), of a hat-manufacturing family in Denton, Manchester, a railway clerk at the outbreak of the war. As chief claims officer at a station of the Great Western Railway, he had decent prospects. He was by all accounts a bright and personable young man. He enlisted in the Army as a private in October 1914 and served with the Grenadier Guards and the Welsh Guards. He became a machine-gunner on the Western Front. He was wounded and came home on leave to convalesce. Because he was deemed not to have reported back quickly enough, he was returned to France under close arrest. After that his letters home ceased. His family's desperate attempts to trace him after the war were unsuccessful. Later research discovered that he died in 1926, living in lodgings in Liverpool, still fairly young. Duncan was not one of the fallen, but he was one of the war's unnumbered other victims. This book is dedicated to his memory.

Prologue

ON 17 OCTOBER 1914 the *Stirling Observer* published a letter from the local Member of Parliament, Arthur Ponsonby. It made depressing reading:

> Eight nations are at war and this number may be increased as time goes on ... Carnage is proceeding on a scale without a parallel in the world's history and thousands of lives are sacrificed daily. Vast tracts of country are being reduced to ruin and desolation. The ravages of destitution, misery and starvation increase every day as the war continues. The hopes of reform and social amelioration must be abandoned for our lifetime. Modern civilisation has crumbled to the ground. Barbarism reigns triumphant. For this soldiers and sailors are not responsible. It is the work of governments, statesmen, diplomatists and monarchs ...[1]

Two months earlier no one could have foreseen the world which was now taking shape.

Ponsonby was right to predict that more nations would join the war. The number of belligerent nations would more than double and the conflict would run for another four years. Even the spluttering end after vast loss of life, with 'victory' for some and exhaustion for most, would not be the end of the malignity. There were the deep physical, psychological and economic scars. And dragon's teeth had been sown. In later years these would sprout grotesque new forms of tyranny and a re-run of world war – in effect a continuation of it –with aerial destruction of civilian populations, genocide and slavery. And civil wars would erupt as long-term consequences of 1914–18 right down to our own times.[2]

Consolations of the First World War are frequently claimed for Britain, notably increased work opportunities for women and female enfranchisement. Certainly the war speeded the loosening of social restrictions on women, but the process was already happening. One has only to glance at the newspapers of the summer of 1914, before war came, to see that socially Britain was buzzing and that change was already on the way. Female suffrage had already reached the point of inevitability by 1914. When it came, during the war, women under the age of thirty were excluded. The wartime workplace gains for women were soon clawed back when the men returned. The history of war as a catalyst of progressive reform is, to say the least, a doubtful one.[3]

Could the calamity of 1914 have been averted? Could Britain realistically have stayed out? Let us return to a Monday at Westminster in late July of that year.

1

Spectators Only?

Monday, 27 July 1914

IN LATE JULY 1914 Arthur Ponsonby, 43-year-old Liberal Member
of Parliament for Stirling, was looking forward to getting away from
London. The House of Commons was as congenial as anywhere when
the capital was hot, thanks to its air conditioning and ingenious use of
ice blocks for temperature control, but most MPs, Ponsonby included,
were ready for the recess. It had been a political summer of frayed
tempers and stress.[1]

As the last week of July opened, Arthur's special attention was on
a bill which he himself had had devised. One of its provisions would
enable the disclaiming of inherited titles. As things stood, an heir to a
peerage had no option but to become a Lord in the event of 'an accident
of death', as the MP put it. A Member inheriting a peerage had to give
up his seat in the House of Commons and join 'the deliberations of the
moribund assembly at the end of the corridor'. The bill was intended to
change this.[2]

Ponsonby was an expert on aristocratic behaviour. Of that class himself (though relatively impoverished), with numerous lords among his
ancestors, he had penned two critical books, *The Decline of Aristocracy*
and *The Camel and the Needle's Eye*. At Question Time on Monday, 27
July he was set to ask Liberal Prime Minister Herbert Henry Asquith
to make time for his bill. Sponsoring it he had seven Liberals and one
Labour Member.

Most attention lately was on Ireland. The Government's Irish
Home Rule Bill had produced a crisis. It was now seriously threatening
to spark civil war. With the two main parties in the House, Liberals
and Conservatives, practically equal, the Government's majority
depended upon the Irish Nationalists. The Nationalists supported the

Government in return for the promise of Home Rule. The Government bill provided for a modest measure of devolution but it was the subject of political frenzy. The conflict between Catholic Nationalists in the south who wanted it and Protestant Unionists in the north who did not, had reached deadlock. The struggle was suffocating politics. It was not just an Irish issue. The conflict between Protestant landowners and Catholic tenants brought in more widely the politics of haves and have-nots. The Ulster opposition to Home Rule was ferociously backed by the Conservatives (known mostly at this time as 'Unionists').

It was escalating. A hundred thousand anti-Home Rule Ulster Volunteers were drilling under arms. A large Irish Nationalist counter-militia was being gathered. The news which had kept the country agog the previous week had been a last-ditch attempt at peace-making with a conference at Buckingham Palace hosted by the King. This had ended in failure on the Friday.

Arthur Ponsonby was always glad of his weekend escape. His home, Shulbrede Priory, deep in the border woods of Sussex and Surrey, was built out of the remains of an Augustinian Priory. Part dated back to the twelfth century. Arthur was a talented artist. He enjoyed sketching his ancient homestead and its surrounds. The Prior's Chamber had early-sixteenth-century wall paintings of birds and animals with their sounds turning into Latin on Christmas Day (the duck: *quando? quando?*; the bull: *ubi? ubi?*). On 27 April Ponsonby had recorded in his diary, 'garden quite inexpressibly beautiful, masses of blossom, tulips and fresh green'. It was balm after the bickering of the House of Commons. The MP reflected that, 'the weekend at Shulbrede is the one thing that helps to set me straight'. The household comprised Arthur, his wife Dolly (Dorothea), his thirteen-year-old daughter Elizabeth and his ten-year-old son Matthew, along with several servants.[3]

Arthur arrived in London on this last Monday morning of July to find that the Irish trouble had taken a turn for the worse. On Sunday at Bachelors Walk in Dublin there had been an incident. A large crowd had been jeering and throwing stones at British soldiers who had been trying to seize arms collected by the Nationalist militias. Guns were fired by British troops. Three civilians were killed and thirty-two wounded. Civil war was closer.

Ponsonby was dismayed by his Government's apparent bias: 'This is in Dublin while the Ulster volunteers paraded openly armed through the streets of Belfast. I am not sure that the Government had not better go now.'[4]

In February, at the start of the session, he had expressed his frustration in his journal:

> The consciousness of my incompetence and the futility of my inaction grows and yet smouldering deep down there is still an unquenched fire of determination for action and an undying and increasing hatred of conservatism, arbitrary authority and privilege.[5]

The political climate of the summer, as the Irish crisis worsened, was recalled in the memoirs of a friend of Arthur Ponsonby, Richard Denman, a young Liberal who sat for Carlisle. Denman recalled the occasion when Conservative MP Leo Amery walked with him up and down the lobby outside the library, telling him that if the Government compelled Ulster to accept an Irish Government, he would join them in armed resistance. Amery was one of the drivers of the Conservative–Ulster alliance.[6]

The Ireland situation was indeed dangerous. In March the Prime Minister had had to sack his War Minister for permitting Army officers in Ireland to leave their posts if they had Ulster connections. The so-called 'Curragh Mutiny' had great reverberations. Army officers were closely linked to the social aristocracy. Some people wondered whether the Army was an impartial instrument of the elected House of Commons. The Home Rule bill threatened to break the control wielded by the English establishment in Dublin and a highly indignant ruling class was not prepared for this. The animosity spilled into the social 'Season' as Tory hostesses 'cut' the Liberals and their womenfolk.[7]

The ruling classes were tightly knit. While the parties were heaping invective on each other in the House of Commons, their leaders were often to be found socialising in each others' grand houses. But in 1914 the political fury was not synthetic. The dominance of the aristocracy had been severely jolted by the 'Peers versus People' battle which produced the 1911 Parliament Bill. This removed the right of the House of Lords to block legislation. Ulster versus Home Rule was a continuation of the conflict.

July 1914 was certainly crisis month for British politics. It meant that not much attention was paid to Europe. But there was always plenty that needed to be watched. The great European powers were armed to the teeth. They were fearful of each other and mutually suspicious. Military conscription provided them with enormous armies. Europe was unstable. There was the ever-present risk of Britain being sucked into general war. If so this would destroy for a generation or more the hopes of progressive reform. 1914 had brought some relative calm in Europe, but now there was serious trouble.

The new crisis was in the Balkans, where the rickety Ottoman and Austro-Hungarian empires battled with nations on the rise, notably the Serbs. In the Balkan Wars of 1912 and 1913 the Balkan League (Greece, Serbia, Bulgaria and Montenegro) fought to liberate Serbs under Ottoman rule. But then Serbia, Bulgaria and Greece fought again over the spoils of Macedonian territory. The wars were contained but the Balkans remained unsettled. A special worry was Bosnia-Herzegovina. This had previously been a protectorate of Austria-Hungary but in 1908 it had been annexed into the Austro-Hungarian Empire. Many of its people were Serbs and this was seen as an affront to Serb pride. It dangerously pitched against one another the rival nationalisms of Serbs, with a desire for South Slav unity, in a Greater Serbia or a Yugoslavia, and of Germans who wanted to expand eastwards. Serbia meanwhile was giving covert support to a terrorist Serb liberation organisation called the 'Black Hand'.[8]

On 28 June, the heir to the throne of the Austro-Hungarian Empire, Archduke Franz Ferdinand, had made his ill-fated visit to the capital of his Bosnia-Herzegovina province, Sarajevo, where he fell to a bullet to the jugular fired by a pro-Serbia nationalist, trained and armed by the Black Hand. Would there be a Third Balkan War? If it happened there was the real risk of Russia and Germany getting into a Slav versus Teuton showdown. This would be liable to pull in France and maybe Britain too. Last time it had been averted. What about this time? Chancellor of the Exchequer David Lloyd George declared that while 'you never get a perfectly blue sky in foreign affairs' (a truism if ever there was one) he thought that Europe would 'pull through'. The British social establishment anyway was preoccupied at this time of the year with its Season – racehorses, boats and fashions. But then, on Thursday 26 July, came what was called the 'Austrian Note to Servia [Serbia]'.[9]

It was sent by the government of the Austro-Hungarian Empire. It demanded that Serbia should admit onto its territory representatives of

Austria-Hungary to investigate the Archduke's murder. What if Serbia, egged on by Russia, said no? The Note had a list of requirements and was couched in terms so humiliating that it appeared to invite rejection. Would this be the Balkan war that pulled in the big powers? It was a very serious possibility. In Britain the Prime Minister was one of those whose mind was working ahead. Asquith had a girlfriend called Venetia Stanley. His copious and indiscreet correspondence with Stanley provides a daily political commentary which is a historian's treasure trove. An Asquith letter of Friday, 24 July sets out the doomsday scenario of Germany supporting Austria and Russia and France supporting Serbia in a European war. His view was that: '. . . we are within measurable, or imaginable, distance of a real Armageddon, which would dwarf the Ulster and Nationalist Volunteers to their true proportion'.[10]

Europe had two big blocks: the Triple Alliance of Germany, Austria-Hungary and Italy; and the Triple Entente of France, Russia and Britain. '*Entente*' was supposed to mean a special friendship, short of an alliance. In 1904 Britain's Entente Cordiale with France was instituted, and in 1907 there was the Anglo-Russian Convention. France and Russia were both countries against which Britain had been accustomed to fight. The Triple Entente was an arrangement which aimed to avoid conflict between its member states and to provide security for them.

But was the Triple Entente in reality a military alliance? Government ministers denied it but some on the backbenches had suspicions. The blocks had become the system. Would the much-prophesied war of the alliances happen now over Serbia? Germany had given Austria a 'blank cheque' to send whatever ultimatum it wanted to Serbia and had agreed to provide support for Austria if Russia intervened.

The European power-tussling was viewed with much apprehension by some in the British Parliament. The nations in the power game all feared being militarily overhauled and beaten in war. Germany felt hemmed in by Russia and France. Russia had been rocked by heavy defeat in its war of 1904–5 with Japan but had lately revived. It was expanding its industrial capacity and its military firepower. The 'balance of power', a phrase that Ponsonby and his friends abominated, had for a while favoured Germany but was seen as likely to topple over the other way. Germany's aggressive military establishment thought that an early strike was needed before it was too late. Meanwhile in Russia there was strong Pan-Slav pressure for war if the new crisis developed.

The concern on the Liberal backbenches and in the Labour Party (and on the part of a few Conservatives) about what arrangements or expectations might be hidden from Parliament went back a long time. Foreign Secretary Sir Edward Grey was deep in the Foreign Office mode of secrecy. He was not disposed to publish 'Blue Books' (Government information) on what was happening with the Entente.

Were Britain's Entente chickens about to come home to roost? The Prime Minister apparently did not think so. He reassured Venetia Stanley that if the big war did happen, 'Happily there seems to be no reason why we should be anything more than spectators.' He called it, however, 'a blood-curdling prospect'. But *would* Britain be able to stay out? If not, the prospects for social reform would plunge. Resources would be re-directed from slum-clearance to ships and shells. It was the last thing that progressive MPs like Arthur Ponsonby wanted.

Ponsonby's family was in the aristocratic soldiering tradition. His grandfather was Major General Sir Frederick Cavendish Ponsonby, a nephew of Georgiana, Duchess of Devonshire. Fred Ponsonby, a conspicuously brave officer with Wellington's army, had a memorable Waterloo. As he was staggering to his feet injured in both arms and with a blow to the head, a French lancer rode up, yelling at him, '*Tu n'es pas mort, coquin?*' ('Aren't you dead, you rascal?'). He drove his lance between Ponsonby's shoulder blades and through a lung. Despite the attentions of battlefield plunderers, including one of the allied Prussians, Fred Ponsonby survived. It was the kindness of an officer on the enemy French side, who gave him a swig of brandy and placed a knapsack under his head, which saved his life.[11]

Sir Frederick's son, Sir Henry Ponsonby, served in the Crimean War. He was at the siege of Sevastopol. He was shocked by war's savagery. He became Queen Victoria's Private Secretary, an 'advanced Liberal' in a Conservative court. He was the discreet fixer, managing with adroit tact the Queen's friendship with her Scottish servant John Brown. Henry's third son, Arthur Augustus William Harry Ponsonby, was born in 1871 at Windsor Castle. He was appointed pageboy to the Queen. He would ride to Buckingham Palace in a red coat and white breeches, enjoying getting off school. But, as he wrote later, he was unimpressed by regal and aristocratic pomp: 'I took it all quite naturally because my family with all their faults were never proud of their position and if anything looked down on rank and grandeur.'[12]

After Eton came Balliol College, Oxford. A fellow-undergraduate here was Herbert Samuel, in 1914 a Government minister. When Samuel invited one of the leaders of the 1889 London Dock Strike to speak to students, Arthur was not among those learning about the conditions of working men and their families. He was outside the room jamming the door with coffin screws because he disapproved of the visit. There was no indication at this time of a career in progressive politics.[13]

But Arthur was no mindless hooray-Henry. A serious thinker, he fretted about whether he had free will. His special interest lay in drama. In a university production of Aristophanes' anti-war play *The Frogs* he played The Corpse and met his future wife Dolly, daughter of Sir Hubert Parry, composer (later) of the 'Repton' tune for 'Dear Lord and Father of Mankind' and of 'Jerusalem'. Parry composed some music for the play. At Oxford Arthur also played to some acclaim in *She Stoops to Conquer*, as Tony Lumpkin, the upper-class playboy enjoying the company of the lower-order alehouse crowd.

Ponsonby's sport with the English class system came easily to one who felt detached from its pretensions. He went with the play to Queen Victoria's Osborne House retreat on the Isle of Wight, to perform before the Queen, with two princesses joining the cast. It was here that he met the man who would shape the direction of his life. Sitting next to the Queen in the council room audience was a member of Gladstone's Liberal Government as Minister-in-Attendance. This was Sir Henry Campbell-Bannerman.[14]

Thespian sparkle ran in the family. Arthur's mother, Mary Bulteel, was a smart charades performer in her young days, a recommendation when Queen Victoria appointed her as a maid of honour. Arthur enjoyed his Oxford dramatics. He was a stage natural. He even contemplated becoming a professional actor, selecting a stage name. But 'Arthur Brooke' never trod the boards.[15]

Arthur was at first intended by his family for the Army, following his father and his two brothers, but his mother had many friends in the diplomatic service and Arthur was guided in. He served at Constantinople and Copenhagen, copying telegrams, docketing papers, composing despatches and also enjoying some leisure and travel. He then moved into the Foreign Office establishment, serving under the Permanent Under-Secretary, Sir Thomas Sanderson, who was known as 'Lamps' because of the fascinating thickness of his spectacles. A good linguist, Ponsonby did well enough, but the rigid structures of the Foreign Office cramped his desire for creative contribution. Ponsonby was developing a political conscience and turning to the socially progressive wing of the Liberal Party. He shifted direction by joining the party organisation and went on to serve as private secretary to Sir Henry Campbell-Bannerman, now Prime Minister, 1905-8.

Arthur's decidedly left-wing outlook affronted his brother Frederick (Fritz), who was Assistant Private Secretary to the well padded Edward VII. Fritz's memoirs describe a luncheon which the Prime Minister gave to the King and Prince Ferdinand of Bulgaria at Marienbad, which Arthur Ponsonby organised: 'It was a magnificent repast and Arthur dropped being a rabid socialist and became the diplomatist with good manners and talking German and French perfectly.'[16]

But Arthur wanted to be a politician. Despite the special connections of his family he was more interested in the development of European democracies than in Europe's monarchs and their relations and entourages. His special interest in politics was the Foreign Office and the diplomatic service, which from his personal experience he felt to be in need of democratic reform.

Political life suited him. His mother said to him, 'You understand people.' Mary Ponsonby, of diminutive stature like the Queen, was his major influence. As Arthur was growing up, his mother was still at court, a friend of the Queen. Court life did not inhibit her progressive views. She was the feminist who knew when to be discreet. Mary's son was following in the family's reformist traditions. Arthur's great-grandfather Charles (Earl) Grey was the Prime Minister who put through the Great Reform Bill extending the Parliamentary franchise.

Arthur aimed to get into Parliament. He had been adopted as Liberal candidate for Tory-held Taunton in 1903. A 1904 Taunton photograph shows him moustached and in a jaunty summer outfit. Life at Shulbrede Priory, the rough-hewn residence blissfully discovered two years previously and destined to be a lifetime home, was agreeable, though Liberal Party organisation chores kept Ponsonby in London during the week. He lost his first contest (fairly narrowly) at Taunton in the 1906 General Election Liberal landslide – getting a whiff of the bribery of the times which was used against him by the supporters of the successful Conservative lawyer – but two years later when the seat of Stirling fell vacant on the death of the Prime Minister, he was adopted as Liberal candidate and this time he was elected, with a good majority. Ponsonby was the radical MP with the aristocratic vowels, generally popular as he settled into the House of Commons.

He set out his political stall early. He was firmly against the aspirations of Winston Churchill, First Lord of the Admiralty, to reconstitute the Liberal Party to attack socialism. He wrote in his diary, 'there are many of us who would not consent to attack Socialism. I for one am more convinced of the truth of it as an ideal than ever.' Ponsonby worked closely with members of the working-class Parliamentary Labour Party, which had been formed after the Labour breakthrough in 1906. Discretion was needed in cooperation between Liberal and Labour MPs, since the ambitious new Labour Party was prickly, but Ponsonby was one of those who saw common purpose. A copy of a 1909 Labour group photograph at the House of Commons was labelled by Dolly: 'Labour Members and AP'. Arthur must be one of the figures in the background looking on. The titling of the picture is playful but it picks up where Arthur stood politically.[17]

Ponsonby's arrival in Parliament was in time for the 1909 'People's Budget' of Chancellor Lloyd George, who was trying to use this means to drive through reform blocked by the House of Lords. Amid the contention of that year there were debates deep into the night. During one of these Arthur slipped out of the Commons to get some air. There was enough light on the Thames Embankment for the MP to catch shocking sight of London's deprived by night. He was inspired to do some research, which he would turn into his book, *The Camel and the Needle's Eye*, on the grim struggle of the poor for basic survival. He described in the book what could be seen by visitors to the Embankment at night-time:

> They can see the ragged and filthy bundles of humanity lying around the parapet at the foot of Cleopatra's Needle, or the rows of wretched caricatures of men and women lined along the wall under the shelter of the bridges. If they go late enough there is a strange silence which at first gives the impression that the place is deserted. But it only means that these waifs and strays, these wretched outcasts, are enjoying the few hours' reprieve given even to them by the blessed oblivion of sleep.[18]

It made a big impression. It confirmed Ponsonby's determination to work for a fairer society.

Arthur's diary for 27 July 1914 does not mention Europe. The letter which he wrote to Dolly (who was preparing for son Matthew's tenth birthday celebrations the following day) has only a passing reference: 'European war I hope may still be prevented.' There might be a war in Europe but the idea of Britain being pulled into a conflict arising from a quarrel between Austria and Serbia was preposterous.[19]

Arthur had met up for lunch with a former colleague of his Campbell-Bannerman days. Among the topics was the education of the young Matthew. The child was sensitive and his parents were concerned about how he would fare in the rough and tumble of public school. Arthur had enjoyed his own five and a half years at Eton, where he was house captain and elected to the school's elite society Pop, which caused him to recall: 'Nothing in life can quite come up to it. Swaggering about with a cane in stick-up collars, childishly self-conscious of the impression I was making seemed a great joy.' But Matthew was not the confident sort, hence the parental worries. The boy was presently at a small school in nearby Haslemere run by a Mr Oldaker who was said to be kinder to the day boys because they would report straightaway at home any unpleasantness. Ponsonby's ex-colleague enthused about Bedales School in Hampshire. This coeducational school with a liberal ethos was a popular choice of Radical MPs for their children.[20]

After 'a most delightful luncheon' the MP made his way to Parliament for the usual 2.45 p.m. start of business.

A familiar television image today, the House of Commons in 1914 was an occasional artist's impression in picture papers like the *Illustrated London News*. It was destroyed by a German air raid in 1941 but rebuilt as a replica after the war, tradition winning out over improvement. A time-traveller would find the chamber of the Commons surprisingly familiar. The benches were a darker shade of green and of course there were no microphones, but the fundamentals were the same: Government and Opposition on opposite sides of the chamber, each side being divided by its gangway half way along, with the Government and Opposition front benches 'above' the gangway. At the top of the chamber was the Speaker, in his ornate chair. The human vista of the Commons in 1914 was of course all-male. Members generally wore sober garb, apart from the loud checks occasionally to be seen on Labour jackets.[21]

Then as now the Commons was adversarial in its design. Two sides faced each other in the debating chamber across the dividing aisle. It was occasionally remarked that it was very different across the Channel, where the French Chamber of Deputies was shaped like a theatre, with political groups shading into each other.[22]

The 1914 Commons today would be called 'a hung Parliament'. Roughly, the totals were: Liberals and Conservatives 270 each, Irish Nationalists 80 and Labour 40. The Liberal Government ruled with Nationalist and Labour support. The Liberal Party – a combination of liberals and Radicals – occupied the Government side of the chamber, along with the Labour Members. Arthur Ponsonby and his Radical friends sat below the gangway, behind the two Labour benches at the front of this section. On the Opposition side – together in geography but not in spirit – were the Conservatives and the Irish Nationalists.

Today MPs were trying to cope with an overload of news. A Liberal, Christopher Addison, wrote in his diary that even Ireland was 'now overshadowed by this Austro-Servian affair and the horrible fear of European complications'.[23]

Addison, as a doctor in the teeming East End of London, had seen the link between poverty and disease before going on to be a lecturer at the Royal College of Surgeons. He sat for the London seat of Hoxton, a by-word for Dickensian slums. He had been a backer in Parliament of the National Insurance Bill. Threats to the peace of Europe were a highly unwelcome distraction.

More news had come in. Serbia had returned a grovelling response to the Austrian note, conceding most of its demands, but crucially rejecting Austrian intervention in its internal justice. It was mobilising its troops. Austria had severed diplomatic relations and ordered partial mobilisation against Serbia. Ominously, Russia and Germany were lining up with their allies Serbia and Austria respectively. On the Sunday, Germany had threatened mobilisation if Russia did not halt the partial mobilisation which it had begun. Ireland had unusually serious competition for top of the news.

Among the MPs looking at the double crisis of Ireland and Europe was the junior Education Minister (Under-Secretary), Charles Trevelyan, MP for the Elland division of West Yorkshire. At forty-three a year older than Arthur Ponsonby, Trevelyan was another promoter of progressive reform whose background was in Britain's social elite.

On this Monday Charles wrote his political survey in his letter to his wife Molly (Mary):

The papers are horrible reading this morning. This bloody business in Dublin will raise such a sense of injustice that our people will be lashed to fury. As to Europe I think there will be a great war. But I don't think that we shall be drawn in. At any rate all my energies have to be devoted to urging my Cabinet friends not to let themselves be involved in the smallest degree.[24]

Trevelyan's family was a rung below that of Arthur Ponsonby in the hierarchy of aristocracy, but the Trevelyans were wealthier. They were illustrious in literary and radical political circles. One ancestor was the historian Lord Macaulay; Charles's father was Sir George Otto Trevelyan, who had been a Cabinet Minister under Gladstone, including serving as Secretary of State for Ireland. Charles himself had experience of the British administration at Dublin Castle. Thirty years earlier as a young man he had done a spell as an intern – private secretary to the Lord Lieutenant of Ireland. He recalled later that he noticed over the gates 'the figure of Justice, but looking inward with *her back turned to the people*'.[25]

Trevelyan had two houses. One was on his family's Northumberland estate, where his wife and their four young children were at present, and another in London in Great College Street near Parliament. This had the enviable benefit of a bell linked to the Westminster system to summon him to voting divisions. The MP appreciated his social good fortune, but saw his role as trying to make a more just society. The 'Edwardian Radicals' have suffered some historians' scorn for the contradiction between their social status, and use of its channels, and their politics but, for Trevelyan at least, to have detached himself from his resources and contacts would not have helped his causes. At all events he managed without too much trouble to square his privileged position with his left-wing politics.[26]

He had been outspoken in denouncing the National Service League's campaign for conscription. Prussia's defeat of France in 1870 and the unification of Germany in 1871 had produced a powerful new nation. Germany's growing strength had prompted in Britain a crusade for National Service. It was fronted by Lord Roberts of Boer War fame, with strong Tory backing. It saw compulsory military training as needed to defend against the Teutonic threat to British imperial dominance.

Conscription would pull Britain into the continental military system. As Sir John Keegan observed in his Reith Lectures, 'by the end of the nineteenth century most European states had taken draconian powers to extract service from young male citizens'. France had recently made its national service term three years, like that in Germany. Charles Trevelyan had written a pamphlet against conscription. The Liberal publication department had refused to produce it and it had to come out under the auspices of the Young Liberals at the MP's own expense. The Liberal leadership was careful not to upset the social establishment.[27]

In Trevelyan's constituency, the weekly *Brighouse Echo* had a report of a speech of his at a Halifax garden party during the weekend. In it he had called for victory over social reaction in the continuation of the Peers versus People battle. Like Arthur Ponsonby, Trevelyan was one of the 'New Liberals' who included socialist-type state intervention on their political agenda. On Serbia, he had remarked in his speech that, 'we might be on the eve of a catastrophe for great countries in the east of Europe', but it was 'a quarrel that by no conceivable possibility could involve England'.[28]

The MP had probably read this day's *Times*. Its editorial saw matters differently. It talked about Britain working to preserve peace but only as a preface to a declaration about 'our friendships that guarantee the balance of power in Europe':

> We shall be found no less ready and determined to vindicate them with the whole strength of the Empire, than we have been found whenever they have been tried in the past. That, we conceive, interest, duty and honour demand from us. England will not hesitate to answer their call.[29]

'Honour' meant a nation's standing and reputation.

This *Times* article was the start of Britain's move towards war. It was inspired by the permanent chiefs of the Foreign Office. Sir Arthur Nicolson, the Permanent Under-Secretary of State, was happy in a letter to a friend two days later to take the credit. In it he remarked that 'it would be difficult, if not impossible, for us to stand outside a general European conflagration'.[30]

The Times was more than a distinguished newspaper. It was a significant player in Britain's governing establishment. The 1913 book *Common Sense in Foreign Policy* by Sir Harry Johnston, a friend of

Arthur Ponsonby, assessed that during later Victorian times in all major developments in foreign and colonial policy *The Times* was consulted by Government, or 'at any rate informed a little in advance of the public or the foreign chancelleries'. Johnston in his career as a colonial administrator had seen the establishment at close quarters. By 1914, with the surge in recent years of mass-market popular papers, *The Times* had competition for influence, but it was still the voice of the social establishment, especially on foreign policy. It was currently owned by press magnate Alfred Harmsworth, Lord Northcliffe (who also owned the big circulation *Daily Mail*). MPs noted its editorials.[31]

In all 670 Members were elected in the December 1910 General Election. Most were from the well-to-do classes (164 being landowners). About half had attended public school. A recently elected MP found the experience of arrival in the House of Commons like that of a new boy at public school. Some 213 Members had attended Oxford or Cambridge University. Confusingly, there were some 'Lords' in the Commons – members of aristocratic families, some of them heirs to great peerages, who had courtesy titles.[32]

There was the usual fair sprinkling of MPs with a military background, including veterans of Army (and occasionally Navy) Empire service – Boer Wars, Zulu Wars, the Anglo-Egyptian War, the Nile Expedition, Afghanistan (the 'Great Game') and so on; and some were officers of the fairly new home defence Territorial Force. Conservative entries in *Dod's Parliamentary Companion* were peppered with Army ranks, but a few of the military men were Liberal.

The continental crisis was making some waves. The previous forty years had seen a big leap in literacy with the revolution of free and compulsory elementary education and with the availability of 'the cheap press'. Harry Johnston's book had observed the results: 'Foreign affairs are in the street now, are discussed in the "tube" and the suburban train, on the 'bus, in the factory – even in the slum.'[33]

The voting franchise had been greatly expanded in the later Victorian period. Voters expected their representatives to have some awareness of the wider world. Plenty of MPs, including on the backbenches, did have some interest in foreign policy, in some cases expert knowledge. The last half century had brought change. Harry Johnston considered that his book on foreign policy would have 'savoured of indiscretion or impertinence' had he written it back in the 1850s or 1860s, the days when the foreign policy of Britain and its Empire was still 'shaped by a small camarilla, consisting of the Sovereign, two Cabinet ministers, the Permanent Under-Secretary of State for Foreign Affairs and perhaps one representative of "la plus haute finance"'.[34]

But change was not moving anything like as fast as some would have liked. The Foreign Secretary and the Prime Minister were happy to keep foreign policy discussion within the ruling inner circle. Full-scale foreign policy debates in the House of Commons were rare. But with the risk of major war, newspaper readers on the tube, Clapham Omnibus, or wherever, would expect their Members of Parliament to know what was going on. At any time now the new larger democracy might be put to the test. Who would determine where Britain stood? Would it be Parliament or a cosy establishment coterie?

The first item of business on this Monday, after prayers read by the Speaker's Chaplain, was Questions. The Commons started at 2.45 (12 on Fridays) and sometimes sat on until well into the night. The timetable enabled the many businessmen MPs to attend to the finances of their coal mines, railway companies, textile mills or whatever, without missing key votes. And the lawyers could look to their practices and still oblige the party whips. There were 148 barristers and solicitors. They moved comfortably between the courts and the law-making Commons, presided over by the be-wigged Speaker.[35]

Being an MP was generally not viewed as an occupation. The Liberal Government had been obliged in 1911 to introduce salaries for MPs (£400 per annum) in order to gain the backing of Labour MPs, whose financial support from trade union funds had been blocked by legal action in the House of Lords. But MPs generally either had a profession outside Parliament or private means. Parliament was a part-time activity. Arthur Ponsonby was a writer, with an output of books and articles on historical, social and political subjects.

Today at Question Time MPs would be listening with unusually close attention. There was Ireland of course, but now Europe also had MPs sitting up.

The reason was the big continental alliances. How Britain had got involved was a murky business.

When Britain's Entente Cordiale with France began, in 1904, the Conservatives were in power and the Foreign Secretary was Lord Lansdowne. The Entente aimed to address the recent big jolt suffered by the British Empire, the globally dominant power which controlled nearly a quarter of the world's territory. In the Second Boer War of 1899–1902 the Dutch-descent Boer settlers in South Africa had embarrassingly given Britain the run-around, with their impudent guerrilla tactics. Gone now was British complacency. Now Government felt the need for friends on the continent of Europe. There was also the large threat of the alliance between France and Britain's imperial rival Russia. The Entente was designed to build bridges with traditional foes and to give Britain and its Empire some security in the new century.

Anglo-French relations had certainly needed attention. It was not so long since colonial rivalry had almost sparked a war. The 1898 'Fashoda incident' in eastern Africa had seen the British and French fleets preparing for battle stations. When in 1901 the *Boys' Friend* comic ran a 'Britain Invaded' story, it was the French who were knocking down Westminster's Big Ben on the cover picture. Anglo-French relations had been improved by the Entente, but what exactly was it? What most MPs did not know was that from the start there were military commitments. These were not formal but they were real because of the expectations created. Britain supported France's stake in Morocco in return for France backing that of Britain in Egypt. France gave up fishing rights in Newfoundland in exchange for Britain giving France an uncontested colonial run in West Africa, while spheres of interest in South-East Asia were allocated between the two nations.[36]

The understood military commitment started early. 'Conversations' were held between French and British military representatives. When the Liberal Government came to power in 1905, the Entente Cordiale was continued. The Government's foreign policy was conducted by Sir Edward Grey, who had been one of the organisers of the 'Liberal League', the right-wing Liberal supporters of the Boer War. The Liberal Party had been deeply divided on the Boer War – its Radicals hated it. When the Anglo-French Entente was instituted there was some Radical support (because France was a parliamentary state) but the Radicals decidedly did not want the Entente to become a military alliance. However, the new Liberal Government stepped up the military cooperation. The hypothetical planning was for France and Britain to fight together should there be a continental war.

What happened was documented by the Liberal journalist Francis Hirst (editor of *The Economist*), based on notes written by Arthur

Ponsonby on his time as private secretary to Prime Minister Campbell-Bannerman. These demonstrated how Sir Edward Grey and Richard Haldane, the War Minister, developed the Entente into what amounted to an implicit military alliance with France behind the backs of most of the Cabinet. The Prime Minister was not properly aware of what was happening, the account claims. The exclusion of Campbell-Bannerman (whom Arthur Ponsonby liked) from blame is perhaps generous.[37]

Backbenchers certainly were told nothing. One Liberal critic who did know what was happening was the former Prime Minister Lord Rosebery. He prophesied that it would eventually lead to war with Germany. The theoretical planning progressed. If the big war happened, a British Expeditionary Force would cross over to the continent to fight alongside France.[38]

In 1907 came the signing of the Anglo-Russian Convention, with Britain now the formal friend of the old enemy the Russian Bear. So it was that Britain in the Triple Entente belonged to what amounted to a three-power military alliance in opposition to the Triple Alliance of Germany, Austria-Hungary and Italy. Entente-making aimed to halt the decline in British global dominance. Britain's land army was the smallest among the European big powers. The British Empire was protected by the Navy, the biggest in the world, but in recent years the build up of Germany's fleet was challenging British naval supremacy. The Triple Entente would prevent the British fleet being capped by an alliance of other fleets. Russia, instead of threatening in central Asia, would, along with France, afford protection against Germany's military ambitions. This was the theory.

The Entente was supposed to bring security without entanglement. Britain would not be likely to want to support France in a war to recover Alsace and Lorraine, which Germany had taken in the Franco-Prussian War, or Russia in a Balkan war. But Britain's partners thought that Britain could not have its cake and eat it. Nor did Sir Arthur Nicolson at the Foreign Office make any bones about it: he wanted to harden the Entente into an acknowledged alliance. So did the Conservatives. On the backbenches, Liberal Radicals, along with the Labour Party, were utterly opposed to a three-way military tie-up in which Britain was a partner of the loathed regime of Tsarist Russia.[39]

The Tsar's rule caused indignation in British progressive circles, which viewed a backward and barbaric regime, with the masses kept under the heel, protests and uprisings crushed, and the Duma (parliament) having only feeble powers and liable to be suppressed if the ruler and his ministers found it getting troublesome. Tsar Nicholas, like the Kaiser in Germany, was a cousin of Britain's King, but Edward VII was a modern constitutional monarch within the parliamentary system. Now, however, Britain was an *entente* partner of Russia. British Radical circles watched warily. They did not like what looked like cosy rapprochement between King Edward and his autocratic Russian cousin. In June 1908 there was fury that Edward was going to visit Nicholas at Reval when 'the hangman of Russian liberty' was in the news for his latest repressions. In the Commons Labour's Scottish veteran Keir Hardie was made to withdraw the word 'atrocity'. Arthur Ponsonby went into the Labour protest lobby. The King was not impressed and Ponsonby was banned from the Buckingham Palace Garden Party.[40]

Sir Edward Grey, on the Liberal imperialist wing, had been Foreign Secretary since the Liberals took office in 1905. The Foreign Office enjoyed considerable autonomy within the Government. While Grey's foreign policy went down well with the Conservative Opposition, it received some sharp criticism from backbench Radicals in his own party. Liberal backbench suspicions about Entente implications ran deep. The Foreign Secretary did, however, have some peace-keeping credit in recent years, even with his backbench Liberal detractors such as Arthur Ponsonby. The Balkan Wars which could have led to a great European conflict, had been contained.

While the Entente tightened, relations between Britain and Germany were vexed. Admiral Tirpitz, the German Navy chief, was pushing hard Germany's challenge to Britain's naval supremacy. Germany had to be watched. The erratic Kaiser had more power than did his British cousin (though much less than their Russian cousin Nicholas). The German military establishment was aggressive, chafing at what was seen as the threatening encirclement of the Franco-Russian alliance. In Britain popular newspapers fuelled excitement over super-warship 'dreadnoughts', the cry being, 'We want eight and we won't wait!'. But Sir Edward Grey was trying to calm things and to put Anglo-German relations on a friendlier footing. In 1912 Britain had responded to German overtures with a ministerial visit to Germany led by Richard Haldane. The mission broke down; while the Germans were prepared to end the naval race in return for a guarantee of British neutrality in a

European war, Britain was only willing to undertake to remain neutral if Germany were attacked.[41]

In recent years there had been signs that Sir Edward Grey was becoming uneasy about where the Triple Entente was going. He was, as one historian has recently put it, 'not irrevocably ententiste'. The revival of Russian power after 1912 increased the potential threat of Russia to Britain and too close involvement with Russia could be hazardous. Germany was now prioritising its land armies in order to hold off Russia. It would not overhaul the global leadership of the British Fleet. The Foreign Secretary had come round to favouring detente with Germany. Improvement of German relations and a cooling of the closeness with Russia made some sense. The Conference of Ambassadors in London which Grey convened in 1912 at the end of the First Balkan War showed him, if anything, leaning towards Austria and Germany in the settlement. His aim was for better Anglo-German relations. He wanted to strengthen the Concert of Europe, that is to say inter-regulated harmony among the nations of Europe, a system which dated back to the Congress of Vienna of 1815. But what if the new Serbia crisis tipped Europe over the edge? It might be too late for Britain to get out of the implications of the Triple Entente. A tense time was in prospect.[42]

Arthur Ponsonby, in his place after his good lunch, asked at Questions for provision of time for his bill. Stepping forward was H. H. Asquith, aged sixty-one and into his seventh year as Prime Minister. Asquith had a background in law and a sharp brain, though he enjoyed the social life of his position and the edge had lately been taken off his political drive. The front page of the *Illustrated London News* in February, when this year's parliamentary session opened, had a drawing of him at the Despatch Box in a crowded House of Commons: tailcoat, starched wing-collar, hair combed in distinguished grey curls, lips purposefully pursed, looking like a man in control. Asquith's crisis management in bumpy times did give him some statesman prestige, but Conservatives jeered at 'Wait and See Squiff'. 'Wait and see' was his supposed catchphrase; and he was fond of a drink. Arthur Ponsonby was not one of the Prime Minister's social circle. He had, however, dined at 10 Downing Street on 15 April, having been invited by Violet, the Premier's daughter, to her birthday party. His diary has: 'talked chiefly to Elizabeth and Violet Asquith – politics an exciting game'.[43]

Ponsonby argued that, since so far there had been no opposition to or criticism of his bill, it should be regarded as 'non-contentious'. Asquith's response was dusty: the bill was not unopposed, he said. That, as it turned out, was the end of Ponsonby's project. Title inheritance reform would be swept aside, like much in domestic politics, by a tsunami of events as yet unimaginable. A facility to disclaim peerages was instituted forty-nine years later, with the 1963 Peerages Act, after the campaign of Tony Benn.[44]

The Stirling MP also asked about a hunger-striking suffragette. Arabella Scott had been imprisoned in Perth the previous year for nine months for attempting to burn down Kelso racecourse, and had been on the 'Cat and Mouse' yo-yo, whereby a woman on hunger strike would be released to recover and then re-imprisoned. Ponsonby wanted to know whether Arabella was being strapped down and force-fed, a savagely brutal procedure. The Secretary of State for Scotland admitted the force feeding, denied the strapping down and argued that the woman had been uncooperative with the terms of her release licence. He said that Miss Scott had now been released again.[45]

From his bench Arthur Ponsonby had a good view of the mixture of Conservatives and Irish Nationalists opposite. His family had Irish connections. The parliamentary seat of Kilkenny had been more or less a Ponsonby family possession in the early part of the nineteenth century. Fred Ponsonby had been MP (Whig) for Kilkenny while serving with Wellington. Both Kilkenny seats were now held by Irish Nationalists. The sympathies of Arthur Ponsonby were with the Nationalists. He now watched John Redmond, the Irish Nationalist leader, rising in his place on the top bench next to the gangway to put a question about the Dublin incident.[46]

The responding minister, Augustine Birrell, a man of educated wit, struggled today. The shooting, he said, had been on the instructions of an official who had been suspended. John Redmond's brother William punned that the official 'should be hanged!' and Conservative Lord Robert Cecil yelled back that it was ministers who should be hanged. Arthur Ponsonby took a poor view of the treatment of the Nationalist Volunteers. He wrote to his wife: 'The fact remains that the Govt cannot move the Army when they want to and cannot stop the Army moving when they do not want to.'[47]

Ponsonby had only a single sentence about Europe in his letter to Dolly: 'European war I hope may still be prevented.'

The Leader of the Opposition, Andrew Bonar Law, as expected, questioned the Foreign Secretary about Serbia. Bonar (rhyming with honour) Law was a brisk Glaswegian. He quickly got to his point:

> I rise to ask the Foreign Secretary whether he would communicate any information to the House as to the situation which exists between Austria and Servia?[48]

Sitting among the junior ministers behind the front bench, Charles Trevelyan was listening intently. An hour or so earlier he had been perturbed by an encounter with Edward Grey. He wrote later:

> I was in the lobby before prayers were over. Grey was there ... I went up to him and asked him for news. I said something quite politely about the matter concerning us not at all, and that I assumed we should be strictly neutral. He replied in an extraordinarily hard, unsympathetic way. He seemed to be coldly angry with me and insisted on perverting my words into the meaning that under all circumstances we should necessarily stand aside. So obvious was it that he disliked the idea of neutrality that I got extraordinarily uncomfortable, without knowing what it all meant. It created a profound distrust in my mind.[49]

The Foreign Secretary had no definite news on Serbia, but he did have a peace proposal of his own to report. This was for a four-power conference in London of Britain, France, Germany and Italy (the powers which were not involved in the dispute) to try to get Austria, Serbia and Russia to resolve matters peacefully. So far he had not received complete replies. He then made an observation:

> It is, of course, a proposal in which the cooperation of all four Powers is essential. In a crisis so grave as this, the efforts of one Power alone to preserve the peace must be quite ineffective.[50]

Sir Edward reflected that if the conflict did spread beyond Austria-Hungary and Serbia:

> It can but end in the greatest catastrophe that has ever befallen the Continent of Europe at one blow; no one can say what would

be the limit of the issues that might be raised by such a conflict; the consequences of it, direct and indirect would be incalculable.

Charles Trevelyan was now thoroughly worried. He wrote another letter to Molly:

I don't believe that peace will be kept in Europe. But I shall work my hardest to keep us out of the war. If we seem to be getting entangled I should resign.[51]

The law-robed Clerk of the House read out the Orders of the Day. The main item was Naval Estimates. It was good timing. There had just been an eye-popping Grand Review of 180 warships at Spithead near Portsmouth, including the steam turbine-powered dreadnoughts. Sailors cheered the King in salute. The mighty naval assembly should have dispersed afterwards. But First Lord of the Admiralty Winston Churchill, the Cabinet's energetic ex-Tory, countermanded the instructions. He wanted the Fleet kept together for possible action. He was frankly excited about the possibilities. His attitude was with that of *The Times* editorial writers.

The House of Commons was used to hearing about the 'sure shield' of the Royal Navy, which enabled a quarter of the world map to be coloured red. It was also used to complaints from Radical Liberal and Labour MPs about the high costs of Empire. Imperial policy was also seen by some MPs as unethical because of the diversion of money from social reform at home and because the subject peoples suffered from profiteering settlers.

Parliament had to vote the money, hence Supply Debates. Radical opposition to naval expenditure was tempered: among Radicals there had always been support for a policy of naval defence. It was better than a huge land army and military conscription. 'Britons never shall be slaves' could be taken in two senses.[52]

Defence was one thing. The arms race was another. In the last five years arms expenditure by the six largest European states had risen by 50 per cent. In 1911 Arthur Ponsonby was one of the two tellers for the Ayes on a motion of protest against the 'enormous increase during recent years in the expenditure on the Army and the Navy'. In the debate Ponsonby called for dreadnought money to be re-directed into improving the quality of life of the nation's poor:

It is want of money that has always kept us back. We want to clear away the tax on the breakfast table; we want to see slums that disgrace our great towns taken down and destroyed; but we are always held back by want of money, while all the time we are spending superfluously vast sums on arms and engines of perfect finish and wonderful invention. For what purpose? For the destruction of human life.[53]

The Admiralty debate on 27 July 1914 was shortened because of the Irish crisis. Unimpressed was retired Admiral Charles Beresford, Conservative Member for Portsmouth. Beresford had commanded a gunboat at the bombardment of Alexandria in the Anglo-Egyptian War of 1882, disregarding instructions in Nelson fashion and capturing a heavily armed fort. He was said to have a tattoo of a fox-hunting scene down his back. In recent years his warnings about the build-up of German naval power had kept him in the public eye. *Punch*'s cartoonist depicted him shinning up a pillar in the Commons with his spyglass, keeping an eye on Winston Churchill.[54]

Beresford was in a cleft stick. He wanted 'to make strong criticism of the general policy of the Admiralty' but felt that it would be unpatriotic to show up naval weaknesses at a time like this. The Admiral did not like alliances and balance of power. In the debate on the Navy Estimates on 18 March he was scornful:

When we had command of the sea and trusted to our own right hands we wanted no ententes and alliances and the British Fleet was a factor for peace.[55]

Balance of power promoters saw a balanced Europe as allowing the Royal Navy to get on with ruling the waves. But Beresford saw European alliances as the politics of fear: the wide extent of Britain's imperial interests was possible because of the 'Splendid Isolation' policy of avoidance of entanglement in European affairs. He viewed the Triple Entente as certainly leading to war. He greeted each new day with the words, 'Good morning, one day nearer the German war'. There was some support for his views within the Foreign Office, one of whose members, Sir William Tyrrell, had written to a friend in 1907 about the 'weakness of a policy which looks upon treaties and agreements as substitutes for armies and navies'. Tyrrell was now Sir Edward Grey's private secretary.[56]

The naval debate on this day heard about the wages and work conditions of mechanics, boiler-makers and others in the naval dockyards, but nothing about military alliances.

What would be in store for the sailors and dockyard workers if Asquith were to be wrong about Britain being just a spectator in a European war? They would expect MPs to be properly informed about where Britain stood regarding military alliances. The previous month Joseph King, Member for North Somerset, had asked at Question Time:

> Whether any naval agreement has been recently entered into between Russia and Great Britain; and whether any negotiations, with a view to a naval agreement, have recently taken place or are now pending between Russia and Great Britain?[57]

Sir Edward Grey testily reminded the questioners that they had asked about this the previous year and that:

> The Prime Minister then replied that, if war arose between European Powers, there were no unpublished agreements which would restrict or hamper the freedom of the Government or of Parliament to decide whether or not Great Britain should participate in a war. It remains as true today as it was a year ago.

Plenty had happened since then. Grey told Parliament nothing of it. Questioners like Joseph King were fobbed off with bland reassurances. The French and Russian governments wanted closer Anglo-Russian ties. The Russian Foreign Minister, Sergei Sazonov, was pursuing a naval agreement as the next best to an alliance, which he knew the British Parliament would not permit. Grey was uneasy. He shared the disquiet of Sir George Buchanan, the British Ambassador at St Petersburg. The recent growth of Russian power had changed the international situation. The Cabinet had decided that the naval conversations with Russia should not commit Britain and postponed the talks until August. But still the effects were there. The Germans foresaw the possibility of a coordinated naval campaign against Germany from the Baltic and the Atlantic and their fear of encirclement was intensified.[58]

The big political interest today was whether the Irish Nationalists would vote against the Government over the Dublin shootings. In an emergency debate John Redmond spoke of a 'monstrous attempt to discriminate' between Nationalist and Unionist volunteers, but he held off from full confrontation.

Arthur Ponsonby was one of a sizeable number of MPs on both sides of the House who sought an Irish solution within a federal Great Britain of devolved democracy. It was an idea which the Prime Minister himself favoured. But its time was not yet. It was still the locked horns of the Irish Home Rule struggle. In March Winston Churchill had remarked in the Commons that the great quarrel on Ireland would only be set aside in favour of 'what I will call a higher principle of hatred'. This did not take much working out.[59]

The last Commons business of the day was finance. The Government had taken shares in the Anglo-Persian Oil Company and the arrangements were being debated. This was one of those occasions when MPs became a 'Committee of the Whole House', presided over by the Deputy Speaker. An observer would have spotted the Sergeant at Arms shifting the position of the mace on the table.

The decision to go for Persian oil was already made. The Admiralty was designing its warships to be powered by oil not coal. The large expense had pushed up Winston's Churchill's Naval Estimates and the Cabinet battle between Churchill and Lloyd George over these had dominated the early months of 1914. Churchill won. The fuel change meant dependence on foreign oil rather than Britain's own coal fields. The Persian oil was seen as timely for Britain's naval needs. Oil meant speed and a better chance of sinking enemy ships. But exploitation of it in Persia meant cooperation with Russia's plans for the area and that meant locking Britain in further with Russia. There was a political price to pay.[60]

The Persian oil was in a buffer zone between the British and Russian sectors of dominance. Securing the oil would require Britain to get closer to Russian methods – carving up Persia rather than helping with its national development. Arthur Ponsonby had slammed the policy in the debate on the Anglo-Persian Oil Company on 17 June:

> We know that ever since the Anglo-Russian Convention of 1907 we have been weakening the government of Persia. We think in our arrogance that British capital and British enterprise can do nothing but confer an immediate benefit and advantage to a backward state as the Persian Empire. That may or may not

be the case but Persia had a complete civilisation when we were walking about in skins.[61]

Honourable Members shouted 'Woad!' Perhaps the 'Tory bloods' were having some sport. Perhaps the bars had been doing a good trade.

Now, a month on, the political price for closeness with Russia could be about to be called in. Russia, like France, would have expectations of its Entente partner in the event of European war if it came to that. If Britain were pulled in with Russia it would be fighting as an ally of the Tsar and would have to support the military purposes of his socially backward regime.

In the previous century Britain and Russia had had troubled relations over territories, such as Afghanistan, which lay between Russia and Britain's Indian Empire. They had opposed each other in the Crimean War. The House of Commons veterans of that grim conflict on the Black Sea were all dead or gone by now but there were several MP survivors of the Anglo-Afghan Wars of 1878–80.

A Liberal who attended the oil finance debate, Christopher Addison, commented in his diary, 'No one took much interest.' The buzz was in the lobbies. Addison's diary records mounting anxiety after the Foreign Secretary's statement. He noted that by the end of the evening 'things seemed to look very bad'.[62]

Reports were circulating. The prospects for peace seemed to have improved in the afternoon when the German ambassador, Prince Lichnowsky, told Grey that the German government accepted in principle his four-power mediation idea. But Lichnowsky had it wrong. The German Government was rejecting the conference. Grey hoped that he could repeat his peace-making success, which had contained the Balkan Wars from escalating into a European war. Had a conference been held now it is probable that matters could have been resolved successfully. But 1914 was not 1912. The German refusal of the conference was ominous.[63]

One Liberal, Richard Holt, Member for Hexham and a Liverpool ship-owner, looking back a week later in his diary, admitted that at first he and had his friends had 'thought not much' about the European troubles. But late at night on Monday at Westminster, as the news of the failure of the peace conference proposal started to get around, there were the first serious anxieties about what it might mean for Britain.[64]

Business finished at several minutes after midnight and the Commons echoed to the traditional cries from the policemen and door-keepers of 'Ho-o-o-o-ome!' which harked back to the days when MPs going home travelled in groups to ward off possible attacks by footpads and highwaymen.

Arthur Ponsonby made his way to his rooms at Lincoln's Inn Fields, a popular pied-à-terre for MPs. He was the chairman of an unofficial backbench group, the Liberal Foreign Affairs Committee. If the European crisis deepened, this could bring him into prominence. But at present, despite the mounting worry, the Stirling MP felt that the risk of British involvement in war over Serbia was small. Britain's crisis was Ireland.

2

A Balkan War Begins

Tuesday, 28 July 1914

NEXT DAY ARTHUR PONSONBY wrote to Dolly: 'European war seems rather more likely and that may have a steadying effect on us here.'[1] He had heard the news of the failure of Sir Edward Grey's conference proposal.

Domestic upheaval was on Arthur's mind. The family was going to stay at the home of Dolly's father at Rustington on the Sussex coast. Dolly was in a whirl of shopping and packing and had been busy with Matthew's birthday. She reported that the delicate child was 'very tired and looks most fearfully drawn in the face'. Arthur was set to join the family at 'Rusty' for the weekend. He would be happy when life was back to normal at Shulbrede, though he got on well with his father-in-law.[2]

Hubert Parry had composed some music about the family into which his daughter had married. In *Shulbrede Tunes* (1913) Arthur Ponsonby was 'Father playmate'. Parry explained to an enquirer in 1917 that his son-in-law was, 'all sorts of delightful things – a great companion to the children as well as a great politician and deeply interested in Art and Music as well'. Parry's biographer describes the tune as representing Arthur's 'writing, his capacity for fun, his interest in history and the archaeology of his home, his love of discussion, politics, and art'.[3]

A worrying Westminster week was unfolding. On this morning Arnold Rowntree, a Liberal who sat for York and was a member of Ponsonby's group, was on a committee looking at enabling local authorities to provide holiday dinners for malnourished children. Rowntree, forty-one, belonged to a famous Quaker family. He was a director of its Cocoa Works, which employed 4,000 people in York, with progressive arrangements: five-day week, occupational pension, works council, doctors and dentists. Cocoa went with the non-conformist strand of Liberal/Labour – anti-alcohol as well as anti-war. In his daily letter to his wife Mary, Arnold assessed the Europe trouble: 'very uncertain but I think there is no doubt that the chance of keeping European peace is distinctly better than yesterday, though I fear Austria will fight Serbia'. The MP did not know that the Foreign Secretary's big power conference scheme had failed.[4]

For Arthur Ponsonby, the day began with breakfast with his older brothers, Fritz and John. Both followed the family military tradition. Johnnie was a Coldstream Guards lieutenant colonel of nearly thirty years' Army service, including Uganda, Matabeleland (the Zulu War) and the Boer War. He was now stationed in England. Fritz, who was a lieutenant colonel in the Grenadier Guards, had also served in the Boer War. He viewed his brother's politics with some scorn. In 1912, after newspaper articles suggesting that Arthur might make a good leader of the Liberal Radicals, he was sarcastic:

> I have no doubt you are a necessary scourge and that your views which are a good hundred years ahead of your time have some effect on public opinion. No answer as you must be inundated by letters from half-witted people![5]

The Ponsonby family exemplified the history of the British Army in the last hundred years – grandfather and grandfather's cousin fighting the French at Waterloo; father fighting the Russians in the Crimea; present generation serving in the Empire.

Fritz was Secretary to the King as Keeper of the Privy Purse. The breakfast on this Tuesday morning was at his accommodation at St James's Palace. Arthur went on from there to the London Library in St James's Square to do some research. His first published book, at about the time he entered Parliament, was *Spiritual Perfection*, an alarmingly pious-sounding title but actually a lively dialogue, reflecting Arthur's philosophical side. He took a pseudonym for this book: Thomas Clune was one of Shulbrede's medieval priors.

Then Ponsonby made his way to the weekly 'Nation lunch'. This gathering each Tuesday at the offices of the *Nation* weekly newspaper (a forerunner of the *New Statesman*) was a Liberal institution. It was hosted by the paper's editor, the celebrated radical journalist H. W. Massingham – 'men of all classes and creeds from Prime Ministers downwards', as Liberal MP Charles Masterman, doyen of Liberal progressives and now in the Cabinet, put it. But the lunch was below par this week: 'rather wild and without focus as Massingham was not there', Arthur explained to Dolly.[6]

Ponsonby's next port of call was a meeting with 'Federalist Tories'. Some Conservatives supported the idea of Irish Home Rule as part of 'home rule all round' taking in the dominions of the Empire. It could tie in with the Scottish Home Rule campaign of Scottish Radicals. (A bill had passed its Second Reading the previous year, with Government support.) There were plenty of cross-party currents. But the mood for cooperation was waning and there was little optimism on Ireland now. Arthur reflected ruefully to Dolly, 'I cannot see how we can help matters much.'

But Ireland was no longer the only crisis. At Commons Questions the Prime Minister was asked by the Conservative Lord Hugh Cecil about the Austrian ultimatum to Serbia: could he say 'if hostilities have broken out'? Asquith's reply that, 'we have no definite information about that', suggested that war might indeed have begun.

Cecil and his brother MP Lord Robert Cecil were sons of the Marquess of Salisbury, three times Prime Minister. Members will have recalled the electric charge of Hugh Cecil's pronouncement in March 1913 in the Debate on the Address, following King George V's opening of that year's session. He put it thus:

> There is a very general belief that this country is under an obligation, not a treaty obligation, but an obligation arising out of an assurance given by the Ministry in the course of diplomatic negotiations, to send a very large armed force out of this country to operate in Europe.[7]

Where would Britain get the men? Cecil spelled it out: 'compulsory military service' if 'the voluntary system' broke down.

The Prime Minister announced a debate for Thursday on the Irish Home Rule 'Amending Bill'. This aimed at a compromise by taking Ulster temporarily out of Home Rule. The tide, however, was moving against a peaceful settlement of Ireland. Leo Amery had predicted August or September as likely dates for the start of civil war. Thursday's debate could send up starter flares. Now Austria and Serbia added to the worries.[8]

Tuesday saw the appearance of *Punch*. This week's magazine had a cartoon showing a cockerel, labelled 'Servia', facing unflinchingly an Austrian eagle hovering with menacing talons. Lurking behind a rock was the reason for the smaller bird's perky confidence – a bear wearing a Russian cap. Elsewhere the magazine's star cartoonist Bernard Partridge had the lead drawing – a young Irishwoman with a harp looking despairingly for the dawn across a dark sky. Partridge was already working on the next week's lead. It would appear on 5 August under the title 'Mutual Service', with Britannia clasping the hand of a dove-clutching Peace and beseeching her: 'I've been doing my best for you in Europe: please do your best for me in Ireland.' Never would a topical cartoon be rendered so redundant by events between drawing and publication.[9]

Rising now to give an account of the crown colonies and protectorates was Lewis 'Lulu' Harcourt, the Colonial Secretary. Harcourt was a high-living socialite. His father, Sir William, had been Gladstone's Chancellor of the Exchequer. There were family connections with the Ponsonbys. William had once been engaged to Mary Bulteel. William's son Lewis followed his father's anti-militarism and was against continental military entanglements. But he was no 'New Liberalism' progressive. He had been against the welfare spending proposals of the 'People's Budget'. He was also an anti-feminist. In 1912 suffragettes tried to set his house on fire. He was friendly with Arthur Ponsonby, though Arthur did not think much of him. He was useful as a contact regarding what was going on in the Cabinet, though not a particularly reliable one.[10]

Topics raised in the colonial debate included the British protectorate of Somaliland in the Horn of Africa, where Sir Gilbert Parker, a Conservative who wrote romantic fiction, was worried about lawlessness. In the interior was the Dervish state ruled by Mohammed Abdulla Hassan, known by the British because of his religious fervour as 'The Mad Mullah'. This ruler was famous in Britain and featured in P. G. Wodehouse's 1909 novel *The Swoop or How Clarence Saved England* as one of an improbable collection of simultaneous invaders of Britain, which included the Swiss Navy. This was Wodehouse's dig at the craze for 'invasion novels', the newspaper serialisation of one of which had been advertised by sandwich-board men walking the London streets wearing Prussian-type spiked helmets.

The Somaliland Expedition of 1903–4 had been the most recent war in which any current Member of Parliament had participated. There was one Commons veteran of this, the Conservative Lord Alexander Thynne, who was almost a contemporary of Arthur Ponsonby at Balliol. He would be killed in action in France in September 1918.

Parker was followed by Edmund Harvey who, like his brother-in-law Arnold Rowntree, was a Yorkshire Quaker. Harvey, thirty-nine, sat for Leeds West and was another Ponsonby committee man. A former Warden of the East End settlement Toynbee Hall, he was much involved with slum alleviation campaigns.

Harvey said that in this debate he was going to talk about 'the welfare of the natives, particularly in British East Africa'. Parliamentary concerns about British involvement in Africa went back a long way. In 1894 Sir Charles Dilke, elder statesman Liberal MP for the Forest of Dean and unofficial leader of the Radicals, who was deeply sceptical about colonial development, spoke of 'disturbance of native institutions, appalling loss of life and complete absence of advantage to the survivors', adding that:

> I should be inclined to say that the only person who has up to the present time benefited by our enterprise in the heart of Africa has been Mr Hiram Maxim.[11]

Maxim was the inventor of what had become known as the machine gun. This device kept shooting as long as a soldier squeezed the trigger and it could fire 500 rounds a minute. The *Army and Navy Journal*'s assessment was that the gun was 'specially adapted to terrify a barbarous or semi-civilised foe'. Few could have imagined then that a generation later Europeans would be blasting each other with this weapon on the continent of Europe.[12]

Since then the railway construction from Mombasa to Lake Victoria, a colossal project dubbed by some 'The Lunatic Express', had opened up British East Africa to white settlers. Of 30,000 labourers shipped over from India, 2,000 died in the gruelling and dangerous railway construction work and 7,000 had to be invalided back to India. The moral objection by some MPs to the cheapness of lives in the development of imperialism was reflected in debates like this. British East Africa and Uganda were protectorates. To the south lay the protectorate of German East Africa (later Tanganyika, then Tanzania). There had been trouble over the mistreatment of the native population in both German and British territory, the problem being grasping and exploitative European settlers, who took advantage of the limited resources and structure of the imperial authority.

Edmund Harvey had been reading the report of the Native Labour Commission. He had been shocked by the catalogue of abuses in the scramble by settlers for land and labour. They had been finding ways of compelling the natives to work for them and the legal system was being used against the natives. Harvey declared that:

> I think that we have very great reason to see that we take away this reproach now being made against our rule that while we talk very much about shouldering the white man's burden, we take great care to secure for ourselves the black man's land.[13]

African colonial development and the power rivalry in Europe were closely tied up. In the 'Scramble for Africa', between about 1880 and 1910, France, Britain, Portugal, Belgium, Holland and Dutch-descent Boer settlers, and Germany (which came late to the Scramble), competed for territory.

The debate heard also about the hardships and sufferings of the native black population in the Union of South Africa. South Africa had been the war theatre where most of the House of Commons military veterans had served. The Second Boer War was the big British war of recent times. Twenty-five of the MPs now sitting in the House of Commons had participated. They were mostly Conservatives but there were three Liberals. There was also an Irish Nationalist – who had fought on the Boer side.

In this debate one MP raised the ethical issue of military versus social priorities in expenditure. Conservative Boer War veteran, Rowland Hunt, who sat for Ludlow, complained about the morally dubious acceptance by the British Government of a present to Britain of a dreadnought battleship from the Sultan of the Malay States when the money spent on it could have been used to improve hospitals and sanitation in his realm.

Next up was Education Estimates. On duty for the Government was President of the Board of Education, Joseph (Jack) Pease, one of the Commons' seven Quakers and director of several colliery companies. Pease was President of the Peace Society. At the time of the Boer War

Quaker chocolate manufacturers who produced special chocolate packs for the troops refused to make a profit on it because they disapproved of the war.

Dramatic, if not unexpected news had been spreading. At 11 o'clock there was a special question from Andrew Bonar Law to Sir Edward Grey. The Conservative leader asked about 'the present position in Europe'. Grey's reply confirmed the rumours:

> The only information I can give is the simple matter of fact that we have official confirmation, both from Vienna and Nish that war has been declared.[14]

Nish (Niš) was the seat of government in Serbia (moved from Belgrade for safety some days earlier). European war had started.

Tuesday was one of the House of Commons' frequent late nights. The announcement on Austria and Serbia was followed by two hours of debate on tubercular infection in cows and the hazards for milk. Concentration on the finer points of milk was an effort tonight. Among those in the chamber was Christopher Addison, who as a doctor had particular concern regarding the health risks of milk. He recorded in his diary that the European situation was 'even blacker than yesterday' and that nobody was very interested in the Milk and Dairies Report.[15]

At 1 a.m. there was a division in which Arthur Ponsonby was among about 200 MPs who voted. Probably not many had been in the chamber listening to the arguments. Thoughts were on the war between Austria and Serbia and whether it would activate the big alliances. The battle to keep Britain out of the war was starting. Arthur Ponsonby would have to summon his committee as soon as possible. When the Sergeant at Arms removed the mace from the table shortly after 1.30 a.m., there was already a sense for some that their world was about to be altered.

3

'Close the Ranks'

Wednesday, 29 July 1914

THE LIBERAL FOREIGN AFFAIRS COMMITTEE was a ginger group. It was formed in November 1911, with around eighty members. It was a response to Liberal backbench concerns after the war-threatening Agadir Crisis, which featured the Moroccan port, French troops and a German gunboat named *Panther*. The episode was remembered in British politics for a startling occurrence. David Lloyd George, famous opponent of the Boer War, and champion of social reform who brought in old age pensions and national insurance, made a full-bloodied jingo speech warning off Germany. Agadir gave some inkling of the reality of the unspoken military commitments between Britain and France, which had been kept from the House of Commons. Liberals were disturbed. A friend wrote to Arthur Ponsonby that, 'Grey is hated by the Liberals and ought to go. Our foreign policy is based on an alliance with burglars.' The backbench agitation against the concealment of Foreign Office policy from Parliament did not impress *Punch*. A cartoon showed a couple of scruffy MPs (Radical or Labour) demanding that Sir Edward Grey, portrayed as a suave card player, should show his hand to his opponents.[1]

The secret articles in the Anglo-French Entente were published by the Government after revelations in a French newspaper. The details turned out to be innocuous, but this did not put an end to the disquiet. The British Government had backed France in the two Morocco crises (the first being 1905–6) in its dispute with the Sultan of Morocco and with Germany. The unanswered question was: what British military commitment to France was *implied*? What were France's expectations? The Liberal backbench group aimed to try to monitor what the Government was up to. It represented Liberal international conciliation traditions. War was inimical to the social reform which they were in politics to promote. Not all members of Arthur Ponsonby's committee were Radicals but it generally represented that quarter of the House. On foreign policy, the Government was much closer to the Conservative Opposition than to Radical Liberal backbenchers.[2]

Arthur Ponsonby became chairman in 1913. He wanted to see ministers more accountable on foreign policy and the processes of the Foreign Office less secret. He felt that there should be a closer relationship between the Government and the Liberal Party which kept it in power. There were many aspects to foreign policy reform. There was the class-bound diplomatic service. Arthur Ponsonby was one of a number of MPs who wanted to see an end to the caste system of entry depending on social rank and wealth. He submitted a memorandum to the Royal Commission on the Civil Service in the early summer of 1914. More generally, he raised the question before the Select Committee on House of Commons Procedure in 1914 of undemocratic conduct of foreign policy. His campaigns struck a chord in the radical press.[3]

Suddenly foreign policy was a compelling issue. Arthur Ponsonby wrote in his diary: 'War between Austria and Servia has broken out. It seems only too probable that other powers will be drawn in.'[4]

Ponsonby's group had been largely inactive lately. It existed to monitor foreign affairs and in that respect 1914 so far had been relatively uneventful. Now, with the eruptions in Europe, the committee needed to declare a position on behalf of rank and file MPs of the party of Government. Ponsonby sent out invitations to a meeting to take place before dinner.[5]

There was now some urgency. *The Times* had stepped up its call for British involvement in European war should it happen. The newspaper had its usual advertisements for European hotels for when society decamped from London, but this year readers would be thinking twice about travelling as they read reports about war in the east of Europe.[6]

The paper conjured the horrors of general war in Europe for the first time since the Napoleonic conflict, 'carried on by all the dreadful engines which science has since devised'. The leader writer might have elaborated on this. There had been the devastating machine guns used by the colonial powers in Africa, and in the Boer War there had been the Boers' Mauser rifles and automatic weapons which had inflicted grievous casualties on British troops. But the paper, while urging the importance of conciliation, evidently wanted Britain to be in any general European war. Though Britain had no direct interest in the Austria–Serbia dispute, it was a member, the writer reminded readers, of the Entente with France and Russia: 'To that Entente we shall remain faithful in the future, come what may, as we have been faithful to it in the past.'

The leader was entitled 'Close the Ranks' – a telling metaphor. *The Times* was calling off its followers for the moment from the great fight over Ireland. It wanted a temporary settlement: Home Rule but excluding the whole of Ulster. All the British energy and emotion currently focussed on Ireland must now be switched towards Europe. No spelling out of the message was required. The paper wanted Britain to fight with its Entente partners against Germany and its partners. The manifesto for national unity in the face of European enemies even took in cricket. The final of the three leading articles was entitled 'Pride of County'. The Middlesex batsmen had recently been bowled out cheaply by Kent's star bowlers Frank Woolley and Colin Blythe. The competitive passions of county against county, argued the writer, underlined pride in the nation. Sadly, Colin Blythe would be one of those who fell at Passchendaele.

At Commons Questions the Prime Minister, in reply to the Conservative Leader, was giving little away about how the Government saw the crisis:

> The situation at this moment is one of extreme gravity. I can only say, usefully say, that His Majesty's Government are not relaxing their efforts to do everything in their power to circumscribe the area of possible conflict.[7]

Bonar Law had no comment. This silence left the correspondent of *The Times* wondering. Next day's edition commented:

> One thing seemed to be wanting. In times of international crisis it is usual for the Leader of the Opposition to make it plain, if only in a single sentence, that the British Government speaks and acts for a united Parliament and country. This afternoon one waited for Mr Bonar Law to make that statement, but he chose to let it be taken for granted.[8]

It was a sharp nudge to the Conservative Leader. Ireland was still his agenda when it should have been set aside. Bonar Law believed firmly in a British commitment to fight with France and Russia should there be a war between the big alliances. However, he was not *yet* disposed to go with what *The Times* wanted. Of Ulster Protestant descent, he was heavily engaged with the anti-Home Rule campaign.[9]

What about his party? The debates and discussions among Conservative MPs around the lobbies, bars and restaurants of Westminster would be likely to generate a feeling one way or the other.

Questions today included road deaths in the London area. Home Secretary Reginald McKenna disclosed that during the first six months of the year 55 deaths here were down to horse-drawn vehicles, while 197 unfortunates were despatched by motors. Modernity on the roads exacted a toll. What, it might be wondered, would be the mortality rates of the new modes of warfare if conflagration blew across Europe?

Question Time regulars included the Foreign Affairs Committee's Sir William Byles, Member for Salford, who was proprietor of the *Bradford Observer*. Byles was a 'Lib-Lab' Member. The Lib-Labs were the small number of working-class Liberal MPs. The Salford MP was himself middle class but he associated himself with them and with the Labour Party. Today he had a question for the Home Secretary about a boxing match:

> Whether his attention has been directed to the inquest held at Maidenhead on the body of William Walter England, who received fatal injuries at a boxing match, advertised as a champion fight for £25 a side, which took place at the Maidenhead Hippodrome last Wednesday night? Whether the Home Office has the power to prohibit these exhibitions?[10]

McKenna was not minded to intervene. There was a parting shot from Sir William: 'Then, the sport of cock fighting is prohibited, and the sport of man fighting is encouraged?'

Byles, seventy-five, was a veteran campaigner for social reform, his causes including full suffrage, female as well as male, the abolition of the death penalty, and an improved quality of life for the working classes. He had been active in the Inter-Parliamentary Union for Peace and Arbitration for twenty years. He was one of those who fretted about the risks of the Entente. On 24 March 1913 he had asked the Prime Minister:

> ... whether he will say if this country is under any and, if so, what obligation to France to send an armed force under certain

contingencies to operate in Europe; and if so what are the limits
of our agreements, whether by assurance or by treaty, to the
French nation?[11]

There was the usual cheerful reassurance that British independence
was untrammelled. Now, with the assembling clouds making fast work
of Lloyd George's blue sky, the validity of Despatch Box pledges that
there was no military alliance with France might soon be put to the test.

Down the corridor in the chamber of the red benches, a viscount
was being promoted to earl. Field Marshal Horatio Herbert Kitchener,
of Khartoum and Boer War fame, was on leave from his post as
British Consul-General in Egypt. Kitchener was a hero. The fact that
he originated the term 'concentration camp' – in the Boer War (with
the strategic driving of civilians including women and children into
disease-ridden enclosures, with heavy mortality) had seemingly not
sullied his role-model status. His title derived from the 1898 Battle
of Omdurman (Khartoum) which secured the British re-conquest of
Sudan. Winston Churchill, there as a young subaltern, witnessed the
machine guns of the British wreaking butcher's shop slaughter on the
hapless Dervishes, killing 10,000 and wounding many more of their
bigger but poorly equipped army, with the loss of less than fifty. He saw
'brave men destroyed, not conquered, by machinery'. He was shocked
by Kitchener's instruction for the desecration of the tomb and the body
of the Mahdi, Muhammad Ahmad, in revenge for the slaughter of the
garrison and the killing of General Gordon in 1885. This had prompted
Liberal protests in Parliament, but Churchill noted that, 'All the Tories
thought it rather a lark.' Now Kitchener was in London. He would be
available should he be needed. It was felicitous or ominous depending
on perspective.[12]

Several years before, Kitchener had predicted that Germany could
'walk through the French army like partridges'. Would Britain be
expected to bolster the French Army against the Germans? There had
been big developments in British Army organisation in the last decade,
which had caused some MPs to wonder whether European military
involvement was in prospect.[13]

One of these was Sir William Byles. His un-military appearance
provoked sport among the Tory wags when he spoke on military issues.
His attitude to the arms race was expressed in a debate on defence
estimates on 28 February 1907:

> I think the whole conception of our military system – the whole
> scale of the military defences – is out of all proportion to what
> is really necessary if only we cultivate a friendly policy with the
> nations of the earth instead of destroying one another.[14]

Byles was one of those whose voices were raised when War Minister
Richard Haldane instituted an Expeditionary Force of 160,000 men
(six divisions of infantry and one of cavalry). It was supposed to be a
'striking force' for Empire purposes, but the Salford MP wanted to know
why, since the Empire did not need a strike force. The Expeditionary
Force, though modest by the standards of the conscripted continental
war states with their armies of millions, still seemed enormous. The
MP commented on 4 March 1908: 'To be asked in the House for an
expeditionary force of such magnitude is certainly depressing to the
friends of peace.'[15]

The creation of the Expeditionary Force was in reality with a view
to Britain going to the help of France in a European war and there
was detailed planning for this in the 'conversations'. Parliament was
fobbed off with Empire policing as the reason, but backbenchers like Sir
William Byles went on probing.

As the day's debates began, with Scottish Agriculture, eleven MPs
made their way upstairs to the committee corridor. The Ponsonby group
turn-out was hardly a great demonstration of Liberal backbenchers'
determination to keep Britain at peace. MPs were not used to Europe as
an urgent concern.

Among those who appeared was Arnold Rowntree. During the
morning the York MP wrote to his wife that the meeting was 'important'
and that the European situation was 'very grave'.[16]

Also present was the previous chairman. Philip Morrell, forty-
four, sat for Burnley. At Eton and Balliol he had overlapped with
Arthur Ponsonby (Morrell being one year older) but his was a very
different story from Ponsonby's. He had three unhappy years at Balliol,
culminating in a nervous breakdown. Philip's wife, Lady Ottoline, was
one of the Bloomsbury Group of avant-gardes. Bloomsbury writers,
poets and artists frequented the Morrell Bedford Square home. Philip
was another upper class radical identifying with the interests of the
disadvantaged. His area of specialism in the Foreign Affairs group was
one which Ponsonby himself shared, Persia and Russia.[17]

For some years Persia had been a touchstone cause. Persia in British progressive protest was somewhat akin to South Africa and Chile in the 1970s. In 1906 the Shah had agreed to a constitutional monarchy and a parliament had been elected. But the big powers moved in to squash the hopes. Britain had abandoned Persia's democrats. Oil had much to do with it. Philip Morrell had spoken in a debate on Persia on 17 June on the British Government's proposed acquisition of share capital in the Anglo-Persian Oil Company. He and his friends were opposed to Britain's involvement in Persia with its Russian Triple Entente partner. They saw heavy international dangers. Morrell argued that it 'seriously threatened the independence and integrity' of Persia.[18]

Of a staunchly Conservative family, Morrell was a solicitor before he entered politics. Literature and history were more his natural field than the knockabout of the Commons but his wife encouraged him to seek a Liberal seat. Money came from the Liberal League, a quirky circumstance given that Morrell turned out to be left-wing and anti-war. Philip was never comfortable with the public spotlight. But sometimes a compulsive inner drive to speak out overrode inhibition. Afterwards there could be mental turmoil. The June debate on Persian oil seems to have been one of these occasions. Ottoline, in a letter to Bertrand Russell, related that her husband had arrived home after 'a horrible and awful experience'. In making a speech in the Commons he had 'said all sorts of things he had not meant to say'. It 'upset him too dreadfully'.[19]

Arthur Ponsonby also spoke in this debate. In his speech he likened the Persian oil policy to storing 'gunpowder near some furnace': 'The furnace for the present is smouldering and does not show any sign of activity but at any moment it may blaze up.'[20] Morrell, however, probably did not know that Ponsonby was also self-critical about his performance:

> Spoke on Persian oil yesterday. I very much doubt the wisdom of this step – fresh obligations, fresh responsibilities in one of the most dangerous corners of the world. I was allowed only ¼ hr and spoke badly.[21]

What Morrell said at Arthur Ponsonby's committee meeting is not known. Its outcome was a letter to Sir Edward Grey, which Ponsonby composed. After a fulsome assurance of confidence in the Foreign

Secretary, he commented on press coverage of the European crisis:

> The tone of some of the newspapers and the somewhat alarmist
> reports of the mobilisation of our forces have very much upset
> Liberal members and grave fear was expressed lest public
> opinion become inflamed . . .[22]

Then there was a statement of the meeting's feeling:

> It was decided that everything possible should be done to
> counteract the influences which already seem to be working for
> our participation in what may prove to be a general European
> conflict. It was the feeling of the meeting that we could not
> support the Government in any military or naval operations
> which would carry this country beyond its existing treaty
> obligations. It was felt that if both France and Russia were
> informed that on no account would we be drawn into war even
> though they and other European powers were involved it would
> have a moderating effect on their policy.

What were Britain's 'existing treaty obligations'? If Germany
moved against France, invasion through Belgium was overwhelmingly
probable, given the heavily fortified border between France and
Germany. There was a multi-power 1839 treaty on Belgium, to which
Britain was a signatory. *Was* Britain committed by this to fight an
army trying to pass through Belgium in a war between the big powers?
Arthur Ponsonby and probably the majority of his group would say No,
since the treaties were about the neutrality of Belgium, and Germany's
purpose would be getting at France rather than taking over Belgium.
The autobiography of Sir Edward Grey recalled an argument with
an unnamed Liberal MP about the middle of the week. Grey asked,
'Suppose Germany violates the neutrality of Belgium?' The MP replied,
'She won't do it'. This was head in the sand. The Ponsonby group had
no such illusions. In a general European war a German invasion of
Belgium as its opening move was standard military theory. It was going
to be a big problem for the British neutralist cause.[23]

Arthur Ponsonby's letter to the Foreign Secretary floated the idea of
a full meeting of the party. However, there was stress on a desire not to
embarrass the Government with premature publicity. The committee's
resolution was enclosed:

That this meeting having had its attention drawn to statements in *The Times* and other organs of the press that this country may be involved in the war which has broken out in the east, desires to express its view that Great Britain in no conceivable circumstances should depart from a position of strict neutrality and appeals to His Majesty's government to give effect to this view while continuing to offer its good offices in every promising way to secure the restoration of peace.[24]

Arthur Ponsonby had included Sir Edward Grey in a 1913 Cabinet 'report': 'His House of Commons manner has been a great service to him. It is very simple, very sincere, dignified and direct ...' What follows inspires less confidence:

He is out of touch with the party. I don't suppose he knows more than a score of them by name. He has a great reputation in the country especially among Tories ... He is rather aloof and unapproachable which makes a certain mystery that attracts. He trusts the opinion of his permanent officials more than his own judgement and is therefore capable of making serious mistakes.[25]

The permanent officials were the likes of Sir Arthur Nicolson, the Permanent Under-Secretary and the Assistant Under-Secretary, Sir Eyre Crowe.

Sir Arthur Nicolson was deep in the conservative establishment. In conversation with Paul Cambon, the French ambassador, in 1912 he lambasted the Government as 'this radical–socialist Cabinet' which he thought could not possibly last. He was married to the sister-in-law of the Marquess of Dufferin, one of the big Ulster landlords, and the Government's Irish Home Rule programme was anathema to him.[26]

Sir Eyre Crowe, Nicolson's deputy, had been born in Leipzig. He still had traces of a German accent. He was an admirer of much in German life but a vigorous proponent of vigilance over German military ambition and the vital needs of the Triple Entente and of keeping up British naval strength. Recently, in the light of Germany's shifting of priorities towards its land armies to face Russian expansion, he had been coming round to a view of possible realignment of Britain and Germany. But any rapprochement with Germany was now being overtaken by events. In this crisis Crowe was arguing strenuously for standing with France against Germany.

Would Sir Edward Grey keep Britain clear of war? One who had doubts was Charles Trevelyan, who wrote to his wife during this day:

> I find at the bottom of my heart that I distrust Grey, though I am sure he will do his best to keep peace. But I don't think he sees the utter wickedness of our being drawn in under any conditions and therefore may get dragged along by circumstances. A man is not to be trusted who does not at least say to *himself* whatever others may do we cannot go to war. If any overt act of military preparation took place, I should have to consider resigning at once.[27]

An entry in the diary of Cabinet minister Charles Hobhouse (Postmaster General) indicates that at this time the Foreign Secretary was convinced by the German Ambassador, Lichnowsky (who was an Anglophile), that Germany, and especially the Kaiser, was working hard for peace. On that basis Grey was inclined to remain neutral. But the Ambassador was being kept in the dark by his Government. Grey was incensed when he discovered.[28]

Usually it was Grey and his staff deciding Foreign Office matters, subject to being responsible to the Prime Minister. But now the European crisis had brought in the wider Cabinet with its radical elements like Lloyd George. If great decisions should need to be taken, it remained to be seen whether the regular circle would get its way. Grey was working every sinew this week to avert a terrible clash of the big European alliances. But would the Triple Entente manoeuvrings which he had kept from Parliament land Britain in the big war anyway? Back in 1906 Grey had written, 'If there is war between France and Germany, it will be very difficult for us to keep out of it.'[29]

In the chamber the agriculture debate was opened by Glasgow Liberal Member, Alexander MacCallum Scott. A youngish barrister, Scott was the son of a clergyman. On 12 February he had set out in his journal, as the new session began, a list of nine topics from which he aimed to get '6 good speeches'. There was no comment in his diary yet about the European crisis. This MP was hardly likely to want Britain to get drawn in. He had been a leading figure in the League of Liberals Against Aggression and Militarism.[30]

During the evening Arthur Ponsonby received a summons to a meeting with Sir Edward Grey, in response to his committee's communication. He made a careful note of the points which the Foreign Secretary made at this, including that:

> We were absolutely free and working for peace.
>
> The movements of the fleet were only necessary moves and in no way preparatory.[31]

Grey had been at a Cabinet meeting in the morning, which had looked at the prospective situation of Belgium in a European war. In the 1839 Treaty of London, guaranteeing Belgium's neutrality and independence, the signatories were Britain, France, Austria, Russia and Prussia. Germany had taken over from Prussia. On what Britain should do if the crisis did turn into a general European war including a German invasion of Belgium, opinions were divided. No decisions were made except that the French and German ambassadors would be told by the Foreign Secretary that Britain was unable to give any advance pledge either on standing aside or on joining in.

Arthur Ponsonby and his colleagues desired a statement of British neutrality but they were not going to get this. Grey's argument was that such a statement would be counter-productive for keeping Russia and France pacific: it would help negotiations to keep them in doubt. But he did say that he would show the Ponsonby committee's communication to the Prime Minister.

What of the just under forty Labour MPs? They had been at the forefront of the objections to increases in military expenditure, and Labour MPs had been among those interrogating Ministers about the military implications of the Entente. Missing from Parliament today was Labour's most famous Member. James Keir Hardie, MP for Merthyr Tydfil, was in Brussels as a British representative at a meeting of the International Socialist Bureau. The ISB was the central committee of the worker solidarity Second International, founded in 1889, whose greatest challenge might now be approaching.

It was not seen that way. There would be dangers, it was thought, but the new Balkan war would be contained as had the previous ones. There was, however, no holding of breath that in Austria and Serbia workers would magnificently down tools to halt the wars of the capitalist rulers.

The last month had given no fillip to worker solidarity against war. The delegates from the conflict zone reported glumly that there was nothing which could be done against the patriotic flag-waving and that anti-war demonstrations would bring risk to life. Nothing had been possible in the previous Balkan Wars. Now it was the same. Preparing for an international strike as a weapon against war was a longer-term project. Keir Hardie was one of its strongest promoters. The celebrated French socialist Jean Jaurès another. But the Germans had been less keen. The grand scheme was awaiting discussion and possible ratification at a big ISB Congress scheduled for Vienna. This was now brought forward to 9 August and the venue moved to Paris. Hardie had not wanted the date interfered with. To him, ratification of the anti-war strike principle was more important than a demonstration against the Austria-Serbia war, which might pass.[32]

Keir Hardie was the delegate of the Independent Labour Party. The ILP pre-dated the Parliamentary Labour Party and had seven MPs within the Labour group. Hardie's story could already fill a book of Labour history, but these days he was rather an isolated figure in the Commons and no longer held the House when he spoke. Lately he looked more to the socialist movement in the country and to international socialism than to the House of Commons. But, with his shock of white hair, he was still capable of rousing passions.

Back in the House of Commons the agriculture discussions dragged on. Supply debates could be stamina-sapping, giving rise to the 'Bores of Supply'.[33] Tonight the real story was taking shape outside the chamber – in the lobbies, the dining rooms and the bars – where the conversations of MPs were determining rank and file feeling on European war.

Next there was a debate on naturalisation of aliens. It was 1 a.m. when the last clause of the bill in question was reached. Consideration was heard of a proposal by Willoughby Dickinson, Liberal, St Pancras North, who had earlier been at Arthur Ponsonby's meeting. Dickinson, a lawyer, was a House of Commons champion of women's suffrage. He belonged to a British–German inter-church body and he was the founder of a journal called *The Peacemaker*. In this debate he asked for the removal of the words which deemed a wife to be a British citizen if her husband opted so to be (or an alien if that was what her husband decided). Why should women not have the right to choose for themselves? In support, another Liberal remarked that some Members were prepared to fight a civil war against Irish Home Rule and yet were happy to refuse women the right of choice on nationality. But the move was seen off heavily at the vote.[34]

In the war, Austrian gunboats on the Danube were shelling Belgrade. By the end of the day there had been time for MPs to digest the implications of a potential clash of the big European alliances. Where were Conservative emotions? Resistance to Home Rule had occupied passions on this side of the House recently. But would imperial and military-minded Conservatives now be switching their campaigning energies to push for Britain to seize the opportunity to take on Germany and remove it as an imperial competitor?

There was still another debate – on an Inebriates Bill clause which would see persons brought before the courts for drunkenness liable to be committed to a reformatory for two years if they breached an undertaking to abstain from any intoxicating liquor, sedative, narcotic or stimulant drug. The proposal was slammed by Josiah Wedgwood, Liberal Member for Newcastle-under-Lyme.

> The fact is I hate this bill. It is one of a trio of Bills, the others being the Mental Deficiency Bill and the Criminal Justice Administration Bill, all being directed to take in the unfits and misfits – those who do not fit into our civilisation – and put them into institutions in order to turn them into more useful citizens to the possessing classes.[35]

The bills were part of the eugenics culture. Josiah Wedgwood, a member of Arthur Ponsonby's committee, loathed this. In 1912 he had successfully led the opposition to a proposed bill to incarcerate 'mentally defective' people, supposedly for their own good and to prevent them from breeding. The Mental Deficiency Act of 1913 was less sweeping but it still had powers to detain and in certain cases to control procreation. Wedgwood turned his familiar scorn on the breach of conditions provision of this bill, observing that the expression 'intoxicant' was wide enough to include consumption of Mother Siegel's Soothing Syrup as grounds for confinement in an institution. The present bill received its Second Reading, with not many joining Wedgwood's opposition, but the Home Secretary did later agree to meet the MP. In the event the bill was one of those which would be knocked out by events.[36]

Shortly after 3 a.m. a hundred or so weary Members trooped off home. Arthur Ponsonby had left before then. He was making no trouble for the party leadership, but there was some influence which he could attempt to exercise behind the scenes. He would make a start with Winston Churchill.

4

'That Hateful Medieval Survival'

Thursday, 30 July 1914

WINSTON CHURCHILL WAS SEEN by some as a dangerous hazard to peace. Edmund Harvey, writing to his father on this day, assessed that 'the great majority of the Cabinet are absolutely sound on keeping England out of the war', but he noted apprehensively that 'there is a minority of a different view and one dreads the influence of Churchill'.[1]

Arthur Ponsonby had written of Churchill: 'At the Admiralty he is intent on some great coup – that great coup may be war which he would enjoy immensely as he fancies himself as a strategist . . .'[2]

There had been a time when Churchill was with those who were against the spiralling naval expenses. That was before he went to the Admiralty. Now Churchill revelled in being in charge of the most powerful fleet in the world. He was the man of modernity, a keen flyer who was busily developing a Naval Air Service along with much other innovation. He was frankly exhilarated at the possibilities of the new turn of events. On Monday, when Grey's idea of a conference seemed likely to come off, Asquith told Venetia Stanley that the Admiralty chief had 'exclaimed moodily' that it 'looked after all as if we were in for a "bloody peace"'. Was it really worth trying to enlist the help of such a war buff?[3]

Ponsonby felt that it was. Personal relations were friendly. In the letter which he now wrote to Churchill, he urged the Admiralty Minister to 'use all your influence towards moderation'.[4]

The Times reported the war between Austria and Serbia. There were maps and accounts – fighting on the Danube, a bridge blown up, but not much detail yet. There was some self-congratulation on how the previous day's editorial appeal to the politicians at Westminster to 'Close the Ranks' had gone down. It had, said the paper, been well received:

> Members are deeply impressed by the seriousness of the European crisis, and the appeal of *The Times* for a settlement in the face of grave national peril found many echoes in the Lobbies.[5]

Settlement of Ireland, that is. There is some evidence that what *The Times* wanted was happening. In the Conservative Party there was a gathering mood to switch focus from Ireland to Europe. Edmund Harvey, in his letter to his father, commented:

> The overwhelming mass of the Tory party seem to regard war as inevitable and some seem to be eager to take the chance of smashing Germany. Bentinck and a few others are for peace, but I am afraid they would be swept away by the rest of their party if they tried to protest.[6]

Lord Henry Cavendish-Bentinck was MP for Nottingham South. He was the brother of Lady Ottoline Morrell. He collaborated with Philip Morrell on reform issues such as improving factory conditions.[7]

Frustration was getting to Alexander MacCallum Scott. He wrote in his diary:

> Negotiations should be secret, but not policy. If the Government will not declare its policy it is for this house to do so. If the leaders will not lead then it is for the party to declare its views.[8]

The MP was disgusted by the collusion between his Government and the Opposition leadership. He was 'not going to be blindfolded by the two front benches'. Scott's view of the conflict in Europe was plain: 'This country must not be involved.'

The signs were disconcerting. The Conservative Party's back-benchers were swinging towards the war line of the right-wing newspaper editorials. More evidence of what was happening among the Conservatives is to be found in a letter written on this day by Arnold Rowntree to his wife. Conservative MPs and the *Pall Mall Gazette* (a forerunner of the London *Evening Standard*), he told Mary, were 'urging the Government to state publicly at once that if Russia and France are brought into the conflict, this country will be behind them'.[9]

The editorial which Rowntree had read spoke of 'the enormous influence which British sea-power must exercise'. It blew a martial trumpet:

> Our most vital interests absolutely forbid us to run the risk of seeing France crushed or to permit any violation of the neutrality of Belgium or Holland. Antwerp is not less 'a pistol pointed at the heart of England' now than it was in Napoleonic times, but rather more.[10]

Here, with Napoleon quoted, was the national security and national interest invocation that was pulling the Conservative rank and file at Westminster into the war camp. Rowntree was right to be alarmed. If Conservative newspaper editors and backbench Conservative MPs were signalling that they were up for war, war could be on the way. The argument that Germany must not be allowed to win a European war and dominate Europe, since the security and prosperity of Britain and its Empire would be damaged, was set to play powerfully.

That Thursday Westminster was abuzz. On this day of the big Irish showdown the galleries were crowded, with opponents of Home Rule arriving in large numbers. Irish deadlock was stubborn. The Unionist side was prepared to go along with Home Rule provided that the whole of Ulster was *permanently* excluded. The Nationalists were ready to accept the *temporary* exclusion of those counties in Ulster which expressed a wish for it. The Government was preparing its 'Amending Bill' to fix the boundary and to specify the arrangements and length of time for exclusion. Working out the boundary line was fraught. It had come down to a few parishes of Tyrone and Fermanagh, but there was no breakthrough.

In the Cabinet Room the Prime Minister was poring over population statistics of Protestants and Catholics. He was interrupted by a telephone call from the Leader of the Opposition. Bonar Law wanted him to come to his Kensington home. Sir Edward Carson, the fiery lawyer who sat for Dublin University, who was leading the resistance to Irish Home Rule, would be present. Asquith obliged. What transpired was an Opposition request to put the Amending Bill on hold in the light of the international situation, so as not to advertise domestic dissensions.

Carson admitted that it had been a great wrench for him to support this. Asquith, after consultation with Lloyd George and Grey, assented.

The change had come. It was impossible for the time being for Bonar Law and Carson to sustain the Ulster fight. With Europe taking a grip on Conservative emotions, the campaign was being suspended. It was a move of necessity. If a general European war came and if Britain should join it, civil war over Ireland would hugely help Britain's enemies. Already Germany had been supplying weapons to both sets of volunteers in Ireland. The side which gained advantage from the turn of events was the Irish Nationalists. When Asquith saw Redmond afterwards, the Nationalist leader proposed putting off the Amending Bill until the next session (the current session being due to end in several weeks) and putting the Home Rule Bill on the statute book but inoperative until the Amending Bill could become law. This was the course which was followed.

The Opposition Leader's scheduled question for the Foreign Secretary on the European crisis was intently awaited. Bonar Law asked Grey simply whether he had any information. Sir Edward confirmed that his diplomatic initiative had failed. He reported Russia's partial mobilisation. *The Times* next day would have the headline 'Waning Hopes'.[11]

The debating chamber of the House of Commons was strictly male: function, style, ambience, everything. And yet there were women present. They could not be seen but they were able to watch the proceedings. They were the occupants of the Ladies' Gallery. Their view was hampered by a grating on the front, a sort of metal trellis, called 'the grille'. It prevented MPs from being distracted by glimpses of watching females and it preserved the masculine aura. Alexander MacCallum Scott was an opponent of votes for women but thought that the grille was an abomination. He called it in a 1911 debate 'this remnant of the zenana and the harem, this relic of barbarism'.[12] Behind it today was a large attendance of women who had come to watch what was expected to be the determining moment in the struggle over Irish Home Rule.

They were mostly supporters of the Ulster cause. Violet Asquith, who was there with her stepmother Margot, described the scenes. The ladies were set for war, having taken Red Cross classes in bandage making. They gasped with astonishment when the Prime Minister announced that he did not intend to proceed with the motion which stood in his name. The Amending Bill was postponed.[13]

What followed was anti-climax: another Milk and Dairies debate. It examined the problem of contamination of milk in churns at railway stations (where 'extraordinary practices' went on).

Charles Trevelyan wrote to Molly:

> I have ceased to care about Ireland. The bigger question overshadows it utterly. On the whole English people are so far keeping their heads. But there is much too much current belief that we are under an obligation to help France in case of war, and a feeling that honour, that hateful medieval survival, at least would compel us.[14]

The Ponsonby committee met again at 6 p.m. The turnout was bumped up to twenty-five. It included Christopher Addison, who wrote in his diary that, 'everything was overshadowed by the foreign situation'. The mood was heavy. Arnold Rowntree, who was present, wrote to his wife that, 'Matters are terribly grave'.[15]

Arthur Ponsonby's record is brief: 'Chairman reported conversation with Grey. Instructed to write to PM and put down private notice question to Grey.'[16]

The letter to Asquith sharpened the committee's line:

> The postponement of the Amending Bill, the deplorable tone of *The Times* leading articles and the alarmist rumours which are being circulated all contribute to making Liberal Members very desirous of expressing in the most emphatic way possible the strongest possible conviction that Great Britain on no account should be drawn into a war in which neither treaty obligations, British interests or even sentiments of friendship are at present in the remotest degree involved . . .[17]

Again it was necessary to include a hedge – 'at present'. What was unspoken was the likely Belgium route should Germany attack France. This could undermine the neutralist solidarity of the committee. The group played its card of speaking for the party. Ponsonby pointed out that the meeting was larger; he claimed that 'there are many who are anxious to join us'. He told the Prime Minister that, while the Foreign Affairs Committee had again decided against publicity for the present so as not to disturb negotiations, feelings were running strongly. He warned clearly what would happen as far as the committee was concerned if the Government opted to enter a European war:

> I was asked to write to you so that the Cabinet may know how deep and sincere this feeling is and that any decision in favour of participation in a European conflict would meet not only with the strongest disapproval but with the actual withdrawal of support from the Government . . .

Ponsonby told the Prime Minister:

> I may not yet be able to speak actually for more than 30 members. But they are representative men and nine tenths of the party are behind us in my opinion and before long we may see fit to ask them all to express this opinion openly . . .

Nine-tenths was pushing it, but certainly Ponsonby did speak for most of the Parliamentary Liberal Party on keeping absolutely out of European war. The problem was that whatever the feeling in the ranks of the party, the Foreign Secretary and his fellow Liberal imperialists would be likely to quit the Government if it did not support France.

The letter ended: 'If you would care to see me tomorrow I would be ready to come at any time convenient to you.'

Backbench diaries chart the rise of anxiety. Willoughby Dickinson wrote on this day:

> War is very near. It seems almost impossible that Russia and Germany will not collide. But this is no reason for us to join in. It will be a national crisis if Great Britain gives a single man to back up Russia in her attempt to safeguard Servia. Whatever Austria may have done Servia has no claim now upon humanity.[18]

Serbia was not well regarded by British Radicals. Charles Trevelyan had used the term 'Servian swindler' in one of his letters earlier in the week. Serbia was the guilty party in the row with Austria-Hungary. Its intelligence agency encouraged the Black Hand organisation which inspired the assassination of the Archduke. The Balkan Wars had been a time of sharp lesson-learning for some British progressives. The first of the two bouts had prompted some of them to support a war which touched a nerve of crusading for liberation. But the rejoicing at victory for the aspiring nations gave way to disgust when the second war broke out over the spoils of victory. In September 1913 Arnold Rowntree (who had not been one of crusaders) reported grimly to his wife on having heard 'a ghastly account of the result of the war in the Balkans'. As well as the suspicions about Serbian links to the demise of the Archduke, the case for Serbia was even less attractive given the close association of Serbia with Tsarist Russia.[19]

There was plenty to discuss at dinner.

In the debating chamber there was an 'Expiring Laws Continuance Bill' looking at whether shot-firing in coal mines could be made safer. It was a worthy cause, but thoughts were increasingly turning to 'What now?' speculation.

The Parliamentary Labour Party now made its first move. Its MPs were convened by its Leader (Chairman), Ramsay MacDonald, the Scot who sat for Leicester. There was no need to argue out a position. The party was united on Britain keeping out of war and in supporting a British role of acting for peace and conciliation. A resolution hoped that 'on no account will this country be dragged into the European conflict, in which as the Prime Minister has stated, we have no direct or indirect interest'. The declaration continued:

> The party calls upon all Labour organisations in the country to watch events vigilantly so as to oppose if need be in the most effective way any action which may involve us in war.[20]

Ramsay MacDonald, forty-seven, was a man of charisma flavoured with mystery. Born in extreme poverty, at Lossiemouth, he had married into the upper middle classes. The death of his wife Margaret in 1911 affected him deeply. As his biographer David Marquand puts it, 'part of MacDonald died with her'. The Labour Leader dreamed of his group of working-class MPs breaking out of class limitations into a great left-of-centre party, which he would lead to power. But Labour was fraught with rifts and rows. Suspicions of collusion by MacDonald with the class enemy Liberals had caused a rumpus in the party earlier in the year.[21]

MacDonald had been Leader since 1911 of what was a federation of Labour groups. There were the union blocks (the Miners' Federation of Great Britain being by far the biggest), the ILP, and one Member from the British Socialist Party. It could have been ramshackle and discordant but the Leicester MP had a firm grip, despite spats with the economic spokesman, Philip Snowden, over dealings with the Liberals. Snowden was currently in the United States on a fact-finding world tour, having left Britain in mid-July when, so says his autobiography, 'there was not a war cloud on the horizon'.[22]

War could bring a big shake-up in British politics. C. P. Scott, the editor of the *Manchester Guardian*, had built his newspaper into a position of influence in British progressive politics. He feared that the Liberal Government would ditch Liberal principles and the wishes of its backbenchers. In his diary on Monday 27 July he recorded a conversation with Percy Illingworth, the Liberal Chief Whip. Scott had read that morning's *Times* editorial and suspected correctly that it was inspired by the Foreign Office. If the Government did call for war entry, Scott was contemplating using the *Guardian*'s influence on the left to get it turned out. There would be 'an end to the existing Liberal combination', that is to say a break-up of the Liberal Party, which consisted of liberals and Radicals in alliance. Scott said to Illingworth that 'the next advance would have to be based on Radicalism and Labour'. If Asquith and Grey tried to take the country into a Conservative war, their Government would have to go. Arthur Ponsonby was no doubt one of the MPs whom Scott had in mind for his new alliance.[23]

During the day Ponsonby had a letter from Churchill. Its tone was guarded. The Navy Minister agreed that 'Balkan quarrels are no vital concern of ours' and assured Ponsonby that he and the Government would continue to do their best to keep the peace. But a German attack on Belgium or France, Churchill said, would engage 'other issues' than the present ones and 'it would be wrong at this moment to pronounce finally one way or the other as to our duty or our interests'. Ponsonby did not know that Churchill was putting out feelers to Conservative lawyer MP, F. E. Smith, who had his finger on the Tory pulse.[24]

This was not a late night for the Commons. A few minutes before 9 p.m. the Speaker proposed the adjournment. But there was an emergency question from MacCallum Scott. Something on the tapes of the corridor teleprinter had caught the Glasgow MP's eye. The Special Reserve and the Territorial Force were being called out. Scott was once described by *Punch* as 'one of the most pertinacious inquisitors of the Treasury [Government] Bench', but he did not make any progress today. His request for an explanation was batted away by John Gulland, Liberal Whip: notice of the question had not been given. But Scott's concern was pertinent, since there was evidently major home defence activity about which the Commons was not being informed.[25]

Though he did not know it, the MP had picked up a step towards putting Britain on a war footing. The Government had activated its War Book's 'Precautionary Stage'. The Glasgow MP was not alone in being disturbed by the Territorial development. The Government hastened to print a notice in the newspapers, reassuring the public that Britain was not mobilising: the orders given were 'purely precautionary and of a defensive character'. In Asquith's letter of the previous day to Venetia Stanley he reported attending an Army Council meeting at which the precautionary period was explained: 'rather interesting because it enables one to realise what are the first steps in an actual war'. MPs were not informed that Britain was taking the first steps of what could turn out to be transition to war.[26]

The War Book, an annual publication of the Committee of Imperial Defence, listed what had to be done, stage by stage, in the event of the Foreign Secretary telling the Cabinet that he foresaw 'the danger of this country being involved in war in the near future'. If the War Book's stages advanced to actual war, there would be a raft of measures including, among much else, censorship; and Parliament would see the arrival of a bill for the control of aliens. Scott's question about the item on the tapes had picked up the start of a process.[27]

During this day there was major diplomatic activity, of which Parliament generally was unaware. Venetia Stanley by contrast was kept well briefed. Asquith in his Thursday letter informed her of 'a rather shameless attempt on the part of Germany to buy our neutrality during the war by promises that she will not annexe French territory (except Colonies) or Holland and Belgium'.[28]

The offer came from the German Chancellor, Bethmann-Hollweg. Sir Edward Grey, according to his secretary Francis Acland, was 'in a white heat of passion' about it. He telegrammed Edward Goschen, the British Ambassador in Berlin, that 'it would be a disgrace to us to make this bargain with Germany at the expense of France – a disgrace from which the good name of this country would never recover'.[29]

British democracy was sidelined. The Liberal Radicals, the Labour Party and the remaining Conservative neutralists, did not get the chance to react to the German offer. Some MPs would certainly have been strongly in favour of negotiations on the basis of the offer, or using the offer as a starting point. Britain could have put itself into a position to look after the interests of neutral countries, like Belgium, and of France too. And Britain could have protected its own vital interests by ensuring that Germany did not occupy the French or Belgian coasts. But the British Government did not report the offer to the Commons because to do so would have meant admitting the expectations of France that had been set up by the Anglo-French military arrangements, which had been kept from Parliament. While war and peace and the future of Britain and Europe were discussed in closed inner circles, the House of Commons was left to debate milk-marketing arrangements.

Another meeting of the Liberal Foreign Affairs Committee was scheduled for the next day.

5

'Many People Seem to Have Gone Crazy'

Friday, 31 July 1914

AS FRIDAY OPENED, Charles Trevelyan, writing to his wife, was inclined to optimism: 'I have nothing to say about politics but what is in the papers. As yet no great war movement is manifest. The tone is all the other way ...'[1] Trevelyan had apparently not been listening to the conversations of the Conservative rank and file which had disturbed Edmund Harvey and Arnold Rowntree.

Friday's *Times* had a typical 'Servant Problem' feature, offering assistance to mistresses struggling to staff their houses as expanding industry offered alternatives to young lower-class women. Everywhere there were signs that women were breaking out of their social confines. There was a report today of a suggestion of women police. But the paper also had clear signals that domestic issues might soon be relegated. There was dense description of the Russian mobilisation. Mobilisation was of great significance. In a big European war no potential participant could allow another to steal a march by starting their run up earlier.[2]

Charles Trevelyan had been reading the speculation in the papers of how the war would affect Europe's ability to feed itself. He wrote to Molly:

> The more financial tension and collapses in the city there are in poor old Europe, Canada must continue to feed a starving world and will not be invaded by Germans, except as immigrants ...

Canada was known as 'Britain's granary'. The Navy provided Britain with great world power but two-thirds of Britain's food was imported.

Britain's island population had become urbanised and industrialised. The disruption of world trade could have serious consequences.[3]

Trevelyan added: 'But so far the Cabinet are acting sanely.'

The Conservative newspapers were pushing their message that Britain must go in. The *Pall Mall Gazette* called for Britain to be 'prepared to use our sea power to uphold our honour and protect our interests'. Readers could conjure the picture of the dreadnoughts about to go into action.[4]

For Charles Trevelyan, Friday was the day when his perceptions changed. His Personal Record has:

> On Friday July 31st I began to be really alarmed. Walter Runciman was telling me as much as he reasonably could about what was going on. It seemed to me extraordinarily unsatisfactory. One thing was clear: that Grey was insisting on keeping our hands free . . . I could see that something was going very wrong. But all was absolutely secret, only that the Harmsworth press was beginning to shriek for war.[5]

Walter Runciman, Agriculture and Fisheries Minister, lived next door to Trevelyan in Great College Street. If Britain should get into war, Runciman would have the responsibility, along with the Trade Minister, for seeing that the nation was fed. The Harmsworth Press was Lord Northcliffe's *Times* and *Daily Mail* and the pictorial paper the *Daily Mirror* of his brother Harold (who became Lord Rothermere).

What happened to 'really alarm' Charles Trevelyan? The big development at Westminster of the day was a rumour which swept the House of Commons during the morning, when MPs arrived ready for the Friday mid-day start. Christopher Addison reported in his diary 'rumours of an astonishing German proposal with respect to Belgium'. Even junior Ministers such as Trevelyan were in the dark about the German offer of the previous day.[6]

Keir Hardie took the chair at the British National Committee of the Second International, which met to consider the results of Brussels. Remarkably, the committee decided to protest over the bringing forward of the date of the International Congress. However, activity was quickening in the ILP organisation, which responded to the Labour Party appeal. Anti-war demonstrations were arranged. There were forty-three of these in the last days of July. Now there were the makings of an organised demand for neutrality. The weekend anti-war showpiece was to be a Labour rally in Trafalgar Square. It was a closing of the ranks in the opposite way to what *The Times* wanted.[7]

Visiting the House of Commons was the distinguished social scientist Graham Wallas (one of the founders, twenty years earlier, of the London School of Economics). He and the radical economist J. A. Hobson (a critic of imperialism as a cause of international conflict) had met at the National Liberal Club during the previous afternoon to discuss their fears that Britain might treat the Triple Entente as a binding alliance requiring war. They cancelled all their Friday engagements and set up the British Neutrality Committee.

Wallas wrote a letter to the *Manchester Guardian* and with Hobson and a few others drafted a declaration calling for British neutrality. He talked to MPs, including members of Arthur Ponsonby's committee. But his own committee did not come into formal existence for several days. It was assumed that the next week at least would be available for organising a campaign and engaging with Government, politicians and people.

There was also the Neutrality League of Norman Angell. Angell was a proponent of the theory that the world had become too inter-connected for nations any longer to be able to fight each other. The doctrine in a later age would be dubbed 'the golden arches' (that countries each with a MacDonald's do not fight each other). Angell had talked to Arthur Ponsonby's committee at the House of Commons earlier in the year. His book *The Great Illusion* was a best-seller, translated into twenty-five languages. It argued that there were no winners from war and that military conquest brought no benefit. But Europe now looked set to plough on into war anyway. Angell decided to do something. On Thursday evening he and several friends had founded the Neutrality League.[8]

During Friday morning Charles Trevelyan went to see him:

> I found him preparing for a press demonstration next week in favour of neutrality. He was buying up whole sheets of news-papers for advertising neutrality.[9]

There was big money behind this campaign. Norman Angell's views had plenty of backing in the financial world. Charles decided to help. He summoned his younger brother, George.

In the House of Commons MacCallum Scott was starting to fear that the Government would take the country to war in defiance of the wishes of its followers. He tried to work out a line of action. How about a motion that the House 'will not grant supply for the purpose of warlike intervention in Europe'? Without supply (the money) there could be no British war. Or he could put a question to the Foreign Secretary to remind him that Britain had no interests of its own directly at stake and should be playing the part of 'disinterested mediator'. Scott racked his brains for two hours and gave up.[10]

His feelings at this time were echoed by a later comment of Christopher Addison that 'we felt helpless as rats in a trap'.[11]

Arthur Ponsonby heard from Sir Edward Grey's private secretary, Sir William Tyrrell, that the Foreign Secretary could not be in his place at noon to answer his question. A remark in Tyrrell's letter to Ponsonby is perhaps revealing: 'The "new style" and line of The Times makes me fairly sick.'[12]

Ponsonby would not have known that Tyrrell had been all set, but for events, to make a clandestine trip that summer to Germany to have talks with the German foreign secretary, Gottlieb von Jagow, who, like Sir Edward Grey, wanted to improve relations.[13] Tyrrell was not part of the strategy of using The Times to whip up feeling for war against Germany. A diary of 1918 recalls it having been common currency at the Foreign Office that in the 1914 crisis Tyrrell was in favour of British neutrality.[14] He and Ponsonby might have found common ground had there been any opportunity but Tyrrell could offer no more than a sympathetic word. Presumably the Ponsonby question to Grey would have sought to prompt the Foreign Secretary to make a definite statement to counter newspaper noise about Britain and the Entente allies standing together in a European war. But it was never asked.

The Liberal Foreign Affairs Committee convened before the start of Commons business. There was no progress for the chairman to report in getting a clear Government statement of neutrality. Two Members who signed the register did not stay long at the Commons. Willoughby Dickinson and Allen Baker left to travel to Lake Constance in Germany for a conference of the Associated Councils of Churches for Fostering Friendly Relations between the British and German Peoples. The timing of this trip could hardly have been worse, but Dickinson and Baker, as conference organisers, had to go. Baker, MP for East Finsbury, a Quaker, was chairman of a big engineering firm in Willesden.

Towards midday there was drama. The tapes were reporting that the

Stock Exchange was closed. The gravity of the international situation could not be more starkly underlined. Almost half of the world's foreign investment passed through Britain. 'Managing the finances of globalisation' was, as one historian has put it, 'the only area in which Britain remained splendidly dominant.' The jitters now began. The news spread round the lobbies. MPs piled into the chamber expecting an announcement. The benches were much more crowded than might be expected for the usual Friday Question Time. Surely there would be some statement from the Government? What was happening in Europe? What did it mean for Britain?[15]

There was no statement. The Cabinet was in session, which was presumably why Sir Edward Grey could not deal with Arthur Ponsonby's question. Grey was telling his Cabinet colleagues about the German bid for British neutrality. Churchill was pushing for war but generally the mood was cautious. Jack Pease's diary summary was that 'British opinion would not enable us to support France – a violation of Belgium might alter public opinion, but we could say nothing to commit ourselves.' The only decision was that the Foreign Secretary should approach both Germany and France to ask about their attitude to Belgian neutrality. Meanwhile in the Commons the Under-Secretary for War H. J. (Jack) Tennant, brother-in-law of the Prime Minister, fielded a query about the shortage of affordable housing in the vicinity of Salisbury Plain Army establishments. There was nothing on the European crisis. Members drifted back to the lobbies. They were left to speculate on rumours. The House of Commons would be put in the picture when it suited ministers. Informed Parliamentary democracy was theory rather than practice.[16]

Arthur Ponsonby received a formal reply from the Prime Minister to his committee's letter. Asquith said that he had 'brought its contents to the notice of the Cabinet'.

After the Cabinet meeting Sir Edward Grey saw the French ambassador, to tell him that the Cabinet could not guarantee military intervention in support of France. He would have liked to do so, in line with the understandings of the Entente, but with most of the ruling Liberal Party against war in support of France and Russia and the Ponsonby group reminding the Government of this, he was not able to deliver Cabinet support. The policy of tacit military alliance was that of the Government but not of the backbenchers whose votes kept it in power. If Germany invaded Belgium the situation could change. Such an event was probable but there was no knowing exactly when it would happen. But European war was coming. Grey now faced the failure of his *entente* policy and the prospect of having to argue the case for British entry into war.[17]

A member of Arthur Ponsonby's committee not at the Commons on Friday was Richard Denman, who was in insurance as a 'Lloyd's Name'. Usually Denman left his Lloyd's underwriting to his clerk partners but today he felt he had to be there himself. He later recalled finding turmoil. No one knew what was going to happen to the insurance of cargo in wartime. There was no knowing even which countries would be belligerents in a week's time while goods were travelling. Denman was one of the few who took on the risks. He did not expect that Britain would be among the early belligerents. Such was his volume of business that he did that he was able to buy a substantial hall in Cumbria out of his share of the profits.[18]

In the afternoon's main Commons debate there was an attempt to put a new clause in the National Insurance Amendment bill, to allow workers who were unemployed because of strike action to be paid benefit if their group of workers was not that which took the action. There were some brisk exchanges. As a Conservative company director was speaking, the lone British Socialist Party MP, Will Thorne, interjected one of his one-liner yells: 'Starve them: that is what you mean!' In 1910 it was suggested by *Punch* that obstreperous Labour MPs like Thorne, educated in the elementary schools, missed the social conditioning of public school beating. It asked whether 'in sparing the rod you may spoil the Member of Parliament?' Actually, Thorne had not attended an elementary school. He had no formal education to speak of. He started work at the age of six, turning a wheel for a rope maker. He was one of the organisers of the 1889 London Dock Strike. In 1908 in Parliament he proposed unsuccessfully, on behalf of the BSP, a Citizens' Army Bill, to make military training compulsory for males between eighteen and twenty-nine. The socialist flavour of the conscription would be that the soldiers would elect their officers. A little militarism, so long as it was working-class based, did not come amiss with the BSP strand of Labour.[19]

During the debate Liberal MP William Pringle, a Glasgow lawyer and rising star of the Liberal left, pounced on an observation by Liberal right-winger Handel Booth, an ironmaster. Booth did not want strikers cushioned by unemployment benefit. He was showing pleasure at finding himself in alliance with both the front benches in saying no to benefits for employees of works shut down by strike action. Pringle was withering:

> I view with suspicion any alliance between the two front benches. But I think there is occasion for even more suspicion when we find a triple alliance between the two front benches and the honourable member for Pontefract.[20]

The MP disliked the way collusion between the Government and Opposition front benches shut out the viewpoint of Liberal Radicals. Pringle had been at a Liberal rally in London on Wednesday, which filled two venues. This had shown that party emotions were still solidly with the drive for domestic reform and Home Rule for Ireland. The message was that the Government must see its legislative programme through. This included further electoral reform. The electorate was still well short of the full adult male population. Some of the economically disadvantaged could not vote and some businessmen had more than one vote, as did some university graduates. The cry was that the great battle for democracy must be won. At the meeting Pringle had declared: 'Ulster is the last ditch of the British aristocracy. They know now that even in that ditch they are beaten.'[21]

Pringle's radicalism, it should be said, was selective. He was in some respects a traditional Liberal – and he was an opponent of women's suffrage. This rally was targeted by suffragette disrupters.

That was Wednesday. Now, just two days later, the Liberal battle was on hold, pushed aside by the rush of events in Europe. What now? With Conservatives wanting to go into the European war, might the alliance of the front benches take the country to war in defiance of the wishes of Liberal MPs on the backbenches? There was much to watch.

There was again more stir in the lobbies and corridors of the Commons than inside the debating chamber. The tape machine was chattering. Shortly after 3.00 it had double sensational news. The Bank Rate was raised to 8 per cent (days earlier it had been 3 per cent) and Germany was announced to be mobilising.[22]

Among those walking through the voting lobbies when a division was called on the National Insurance clause was A. F. (Freddie) Whyte, Liberal MP for Perth, who was Parliamentary Private Secretary to Winston Churchill. Whyte pencilled some notes on House of Commons paper about the events of this time and put these together into a type-script account, which now rests in the papers of Charles Trevelyan. It includes a conversation with Churchill at 3.38 p.m. on this day as the two passed an alcove while walking through the No Lobby:

W.S.C. Tell me, Freddie, what's the temper of the party about Grey's statement yesterday and the day before?

A.F.W. They're uneasy –

W.S.C. (Interrupting) Do they realise that we are on the brink of war?

A.F.W. Many of them don't; many of those who do don't like it; and only those in the know, realise that we probably can't avoid it.

W.S.C. Please nose around, Freddie, and tell me later what you find . . .[23]

There was the regular voting routine of the two tellers each for the Ayes and the Noes, who counted up, and the announcement of the result. The proposed National Insurance clause was heavily defeated. If MPs could have known that the familiar division bells would not ring again for nearly eight months, they would have shaken their heads in bewilderment.

It was about 5.00 when the day's debates ended. News had gone round that a statement was going to be made by the Prime Minister.

Asquith's announcement did not take long. It was to report, on the basis of news from Germany, that Russian mobilisation had gone from partial to full and that if it proceeded, German mobilisation would follow. The tapes had got it wrong about Germany mobilising, but Members could infer that this was likely to happen soon. (It did the following day.) The Prime Minister declined to take questions and the House adjourned till Monday.

The Commons did not know that the news of Russian general mobilisation had caused Sir Arthur Nicolson and General Sir Henry Wilson, Director of Military Operations at the War Office, along with Sir Eyre Crowe, to call for immediate British mobilisation and for solidarity with France. The view of the Foreign Office establishment was that Britain must go in with France and Russia.[24]

Arthur Ponsonby quickly re-convened his committee to consider the Government statement. The resumed meeting had to be brief. He had a train to catch within the hour. His wife was relying on him to appear at Rustington. Arthur would be met at Arundel Station by Dolly and the chauffeur. Dolly found it stressful when the household shifted to her parents' place. Arthur had written to her early in the week to say that he hoped that, 'you will not find Rusty too trying'. She needed her husband's support.[25]

Ponsonby decided not to change his domestic plans. He trusted the Government to stick to a role of conciliation. His committee men adjourned at 5.15, having scheduled their next meeting for the early afternoon of Monday before Parliamentary business commenced. That would be the start of a week of being vigilant to make sure that the Government was not pulled into military adventures, and of looking for ways of helping ministers to make peace in Europe. Meanwhile, though Europe would be heavy on his mind, Ponsonby could turn his attention to his family weekend by the coast, where his father-in-law's yacht, *The Wanderer*, with its tall masts, would be the centre of attention and possibly there would be a trip out to sea.[26]

Freddie Whyte went from the Commons to the post office, where he found a letter from his Perth Liberal Chairman saying that he hoped Britain would not be 'drawn in'. Many in Perth were prepared to sign a neutrality petition to Parliament. Whyte telegrammed back urging against this. He had been getting Liberal feedback for Churchill. He warned his minister that 'scores of our fellows below the Gangway are really supporters of neutrality at heart'. He predicted that the Government 'may have a difficult passage next week'. 'The Gangway' was more than just a feature of House of Commons geography. Liberal MPs who sat below the gangway were more likely to be dissenters than those above the gangway, who were generally more solidly loyal to the Government. Whyte will have been left in no doubt about the strength of feeling here against British involvement in the war.[27]

Charles Trevelyan had another unsettling encounter with Sir Edward Grey. He was walking back home late in the evening from Brooks's Club:

> On the path down to the bridge across the St James Park water,
> Grey came by. We stopped and talked. He spoke quite calmly
> of the severity of his work. I had then no certainty that he was
> going to take us into war. But I was beginning to doubt him.

> Knowing his views I felt he would have spoken to reassure me if he had any sympathy. I felt how hard he was, nothing but cold distance. I remember a feeling coming over me as he spoke that he was of a different world, and that I almost regarded him as an enemy. I parted from him sick with the feeling that he was concealing things that I would hate.[28]

The bridge across the lake in St James's Park had a view of the buildings of the Foreign Office on one side and of Buckingham Palace on another. Grey cannot have been thrilled to bump into a Radical junior minister at this time. His coldness was nothing new. He was always distant from all but a few Members of Parliament. It did not mean that he was scheming to take Britain into war. But had his previous policies locked Britain into it? Whatever Grey was thinking at this point – and he will not have given much away – Trevelyan was justified in his deep unease.[29]

Arthur Ponsonby was by now with his family. He would have had plenty to think about as his train rattled through the Surrey and Sussex countryside. Russia would not halt its mobilisation and therefore Germany would mobilise and these two powers would fight each other. France would join in alongside Russia. British neutrality would come under severe pressure.

Let us pick up Ponsonby's arrival at Rustington at the house of Hubert and Maud Parry. Hubert's diary casts some light on Arthur Ponsonby's view of the crisis:

> Dolly went to meet Arthur at 7.45 and when he came he gave us interesting accounts of war fevers and universal war preparations. He is very busy as chairman of a section of the Liberal Party opposing our being drawn in. He spoke with the warmest admiration of Edward Grey, of his coolness and patience, and clear headedness. But many people seem to have gone crazy.[30]

These warm words for the Foreign Secretary explain Arthur Ponsonby's decision to head for the station even after the Prime Minister's statement. He felt that though many had 'gone crazy' there was no risk of the Government following them. Charles Trevelyan, after his chance meeting with Grey by the park bridge, was not so sure.

6

'The Crime and Folly of Joining in'

Saturday, 1 August 1914

THE HOUSE OF COMMONS was in weekend abeyance. There would be no reports from ministers at the Despatch Box until Monday. Would there be a debate on Monday? With the country agog over the eruptions on the continent and influential newspapers shouting for Britain to take up arms, the House of Commons had so far been discussing anything and everything but the war.

One MP was rudely shaken on Saturday morning. Josiah Wedgwood had collected his four children early from Bedales School in order to cycle with them home to Staffordshire for the holidays. He recalled in his memoirs that as his party rode through Farnborough they encountered 'a khaki battery in full kit on the move – then another'. War was evidently on the way. The MP could not believe it. He had been one of those who thought that 'international finance would not allow it'. Wedgwood would not have been surprised to know that the Governor and Deputy Governor of the Bank of England were aghast at the idea of Britain getting into a European war, predicting that it would wreck the credit system and cause riots and violence. In the House of Commons in 1911 Wedgwood, while remarking on the influence for peace of the internationalism of labour, added: 'Finance is becoming international too, and finance also as it becomes international is the strongest bond in favour of peace.'[1]

Whitaker's Almanack for 1914 agreed, telling its readers that, 'The influence of finance tends to preserve peace.' Even arms manufacturers like Krupp in Germany had no interest in a big European war.[2]

In *The Times* the intervention call was playing loudly this morning. Commitment to Belgium was now joining national interest in the argument. The *Pall Mall Gazette* declared that whether or not there was anything in writing, Britain was 'deeply pledged' to Belgium 'morally and for the sake of our own security'. And the editorial spoke of the 'certainty' that British sea power would be 'cast into the scale'.[3]

Despite the queues outside the banks and other manifestations of financial crisis, there was no general sense of an approaching great national decision. While many of the Conservative rank and file MPs were eager for Britain to take on Germany, for the Conservative leaders, weekend pursuits beckoned. Andrew Bonar Law was playing tennis at a hall near Henley. Other Tory leaders were boating. As United States President Wilson's envoy Colonel House had recently found, in Britain nothing could disturb the summer routines of Society.[4]

Arthur Ponsonby was also on a boat. He took Matthew and Elizabeth to a show at Littlehampton in the afternoon and then had tea on *The Wanderer*. Hubert Parry was a keen sailor: he liked 'wild weather'. After tea his skipper started up the motor and took the boat out to sea. It will have been a refreshing diversion for Arthur, but the rush to war in Europe could not be forgotten for long. Parry's diary records that over dinner there was 'much discussion about the crimes of war'.[5]

This was turning into a painful time for Ponsonby's father-in-law. Parry was an admirer of German culture and music. He loathed jingoism. He had composed the musical accompaniment to the Oxford University Dramatic Society's 1913 production of Aristophanes' satire on the folly of war, *The Acharnians*. For Aristophanes, the warring sides were the Athenians and the Spartans and his targets were the military men and politicians who stirred up war fervour. The production was topical, since Parry's music evoked Britain and Germany. Twenty-three centuries, it might be said, had failed to move the world on from war enthusiasm. A boastful Athenian general was given music reminiscent of the big themes of Elgar's 'Pomp and Circumstance' marches, referred to in the programme notes as 'a parody of some patriotic effusions'. The overture, with its strains of 'Rule, Britannia', 'The British Grenadiers' and 'We Don't Want to Fight but By Jingo If We Do' was obviously satirical. It was greeted rather uneasily by the audience at a subsequent production at Bournemouth, Parry commenting in his diary that it was, 'as if they were afraid it wasn't quite proper'.[6]

The world of 1914 with its exciting modernity was bursting with the dynamics of change. Arthur Ponsonby was in politics to try to harness some of it for progressive reform. But now, as Ponsonby and his family and the Parrys discussed around their Sussex dinner table the latest events, it appeared that war on a continent-wide scale and of an unknown nature was about to enter the system. But there was still hope that Britain would not be one of the belligerent nations.

Arthur Ponsonby must have wondered how his two committee men were faring on their inter-church mission to Germany. We know from a diary kept by Willoughby Dickinson. He recorded the stresses of travelling across a continent plunging into war. When he and his colleague reached the French–German frontier on their train journey, they had to take a long and circuitous route to Lake Constance, since the rails were cut. They travelled without food. Civilised life was closing down.[7]

Up in Charles Trevelyan's constituency, readers of the weekly *Brighouse Echo* were only now catching up with the local MP's speech there a week previously. Then he had declared that there was 'no conceivable possibility' of Britain becoming involved in a European conflict. A few days had changed that.

Trevelyan went along to Norman Angell, 'the only man who seemed to have much initiative', he thought. The Neutrality Committee of Hobson and Wallas was merely gathering names and 'did not know how to act furiously in an emergency', Trevelyan recalled, adding: 'I of course could do nothing overt, as being in the Government, but helped to warn and stir up.'[8]

There was much newspaper analysis. A *Manchester Guardian* correspondent reported that: 'I estimate that four-fifths of the Government's supporters associate themselves informally with the position of Mr Ponsonby and his colleagues.'[9]

Richard Holt certainly did, writing in his diary this Saturday that, 'it is almost impossible to believe that a Liberal Government can be guilty of the crime of dragging us into this conflict in which we are in no way interested'. For the Liberal rank and file there was no conceivable reason why Britain should be dragged into a quarrel between Austria and Serbia.[10]

In the Labour Party there was shock over the newspaper calls for war. MPs Keir Hardie and Arthur Henderson (the Labour Secretary) called a meeting of the British section of the International and issued a manifesto against 'the governing class and their Press who are eager to commit you to cooperate with Russian despotism'. Hardie wrote to the *Daily Citizen* calling for an international strike against war.[11]

Charles Trevelyan now had his brother George with him. During the day he wrote to his wife: 'I am so disgusted at the inactivity of the mass of people that I am staying in London to try to manufacture a large system of protest ...'[12] He predicted to Molly that it would be 'a very dangerous moment when France declares war on Germany'. He feared the hazards of 'a Jingo moment', but added that 'there is comparatively little Jingo feeling in spite of the villainy of the Harmsworth Press'. His surmise was that:

> There is no danger of war at once. We are not going in with France. But the danger will come when and if Germany defeats France and a popular outcry arises. There may also be great difficulties over Belgian neutrality.

He wrote again later:

> George and I have been occupied most of the day in getting a Neutrality Committee started. It will be useful if war begins on the continent and there is a period of violent agitation for a war.[13]

During the afternoon French mobilisation was ordered. Germany implemented general mobilisation in the early evening and a couple of hours later declared war on Russia. The entry of France into the war was only a matter of time. Whether it was France or Germany which declared war on the other did not make much difference: France was going to be in, in accordance with its alliance with Russia. It would bring matters to a head for the British Government. A better piece of news for neutralists was the announcement by Italy that it would be staying out of the war.

In Germany, Bethmann-Hollweg, the Chancellor, had reached an accommodation with the Social Democratic Party (SPD) to keep the representatives of the working classes onside in the event of war. The socialists were squared, apart from a minority. Earlier in the week there had been a huge anti-war rally in Leipzig, but on this Saturday the same main square was packed with a crowd yelling for war, among them many SPD members. The war party was in the ascendant. It was the original partial Russian mobilisation which had started the chain of events off which turned the Austria–Serbia crisis into a Europe-wide one, but it had given the German war hawks the opportunity which they wanted and they had taken it.[14]

German politics were unstable. It was never quite clear between the Kaiser, the Chancellor, the elected Reichstag and the military as to who was in charge. The military party in Germany had been very active this summer. President Wilson's envoy, Colonel House, who had been trying to bring about closer relations between Germany and Britain, had found in Berlin an atmosphere which he described as 'militarism run stark mad'. Now in this crisis the war party in Berlin had grabbed the initiative. Since mid-week any hope of a diplomatic settlement had stood little real chance.[15]

Meanwhile the international socialist movement was rocked by news of the murder of Jean Jaurès by a nationalist fanatic in a French cafe. The ILP's Bruce Glasier, editor of the *Socialist Review*, wept. He called it in his diary 'a calamity to our movement'.[16]

The Cabinet met on Saturday morning. There were no decisions except not to ask Parliament to approve the sending of the Expeditionary Force to France. Winston Churchill, as described by Asquith to Venetia Stanley, was 'very bellicose', but the general feeling was against going into the war simply to support France. This day did, however, see a movement in the direction of British intervention: the Fleet was mobilised. Meanwhile Grey made an offer to the German ambassador that the British Government would guarantee French neutrality if Germany did not attack France. This would mean Britain ditching the troublesome Russian alliance. The Kaiser was in favour of accepting and concentrating on the war in the east. But General Moltke, Chief of the Great General Staff (Army), was strongly against and the offer came to nothing. In any case it turned out that Lichnowsky's reporting to his government of the offer was not quite correct: he omitted the stipulation that Germany should not redeploy troops from the west to the east.[17] It was also completely wishful thinking on the Foreign Secretary's part that France would consider breaking with its alliance with Russia.

The Foreign Secretary was under heavy pressure. A number of times during these days he repeated unsuccessfully his proposal for a conference. Meanwhile the French Ambassador, whom he met after the Cabinet meeting, was pleading for British support. Grey agreed to raise the question of the French coasts in Cabinet the next day. He also said that if the Cabinet permitted it, he would ask the House of Commons on Monday for an affirmation that Britain would not permit the neutrality of Belgium to be violated.[18]

The Liberal newspapers were still neutralist. The *Manchester Guardian* had 'The crime and folly of joining in'. The *Nation* magazine was also batting strongly for non-intervention. This week's edition, which came out on Saturday, declared that, 'it is everywhere recognised that a Minister who led this country into war would be responsible for a war as causeless and unpopular as any war in history'.[19]

On this day a ginger group went into action. The previous day Conservative MP, George Lloyd, a Yeomanry officer, had overheard Asquith saying in quiet tones to the Speaker, 'But, Sir, this is no concern of ours.' When news of the Prime Minister's remark was relayed, some Conservative backbenchers were dismayed. An action group was formed. It included Lloyd and Leo Amery. Until well into the week Amery had been deep in the Ulster campaign. Now his drive was switched to making sure that Britain took on Germany. He was dismayed, as he wrote in his diary, to find that there was no Army involvement in the Government's consultations and that the Committee of Imperial Defence had not been summoned. The Conservative group worked its privileged contacts. Lloyd went to see the French Ambassador. He found Cambon in angry despair, saying that France regarded itself as 'completely betrayed': that Sir Edward Grey was refusing British military assistance despite France having moved all its ships south on British advice. The Ambassador was declaiming bitterly about 'honour'. Grey's stated intention to raise the matter of Belgian neutrality with the House of Commons evidently did nothing for Cambon. It was not about Belgium. What the French ambassador wanted was Britain's support for France in the war.[20]

The Lloyd group now had its ammunition. A telegram was sent to try to raise Lord Lansdowne. Amery went to the fashionable Kent resort of Westgate-on-Sea to get senior Conservative Austen Chamberlain. Lloyd himself went to Wargrave Hall, where he found Bonar Law and F. E. Smith insisting on finishing their game of tennis. He was accompanied by Admiral Beresford, who shouted at Law, purple-faced. Law and Smith were prised back to London, along with Sir Edward Carson, who had also been enjoying a summer weekend.

That evening in the capital there was a Conservative summit, in which General Sir Henry Wilson was happy to join. Winston Churchill's communications with the Conservative leadership on the Thursday evening had produced reassurances that the Conservatives were right behind British intervention, but the Tory leaders had not exhibited the zest for war which was so evident on their backbenches. Now there was urgency. Asquith would be leant on.[21]

What about the anti-war side? The Neutrality League and the Neutrality Committee were barely yet in formal existence. There were, however, peace organisations of longer standing, some of them internationally affiliated. The most obvious was the Peace Society. This had already wobbled over the Boer War. There was also the National Peace Council. Its President was Gordon Harvey, mill-owning Liberal MP for Rochdale.

Gordon Harvey was a progressive employer in the Quaker mode, well ahead of his time in worker provision (canteens, pension funds, educational facilities and employee houses). In the 1900 'Khaki Election' Harvey's opposition to the Boer War cost him defeat. He had to wait until the Liberal landslide year of 1906. He was a strong believer in the Concert of Europe and was a member of the Executive of the Anglo-German Friendship Society. He was heartened by the progress of the Social Democrats in Germany.[22]

The ideals of peace and conciliation had seemed to be doing well in recent years. Keir Hardie attended the International Arbitration and Peace Association; Arthur Ponsonby and Ramsay MacDonald were also among its supporters. There was the International Arbitration League, whose President was Thomas Burt, MP for Morpeth, Northumberland. Burt, who grew up as a boy collier worker, was first elected in 1874. Now seventy-seven, he was Father of the House. He was a Lib-Lab. He had refused to take the Labour whip with the miners' group of MPs, when in 1908 the Miners' Federation voted to move over from the Liberals to Labour. The Lib-Labs were seen as politically backward class collaborators by some in the Labour Party. The divisions between the politically old-fashioned Lib-Labs and the proudly ambitious Parliamentary Labour Party might snarl the cohesion of a campaign in the Commons of working class MPs against British war entry. But *would* the MPs representing the working classes be solid in their opposition to war? By this weekend certainties had gone.[23]

7

'The War Fever Beginning'

Sunday, 2 August 1914

ON SUNDAY IN LONDON there was a palpable sense of war closing in. Charles Trevelyan and his brother felt it:

> On Sunday, August 2nd, the suspense and anxiety increased. We began to see the first signs of war. We passed a lot of French people early in the morning waiting outside a paper shop near Leicester Square for the French papers. Elsewhere we saw a party of anxious Germans.[1]

War between Germany and France, though not yet declared, was on the way. Asquith's ministers, in near-continuous consultation, now had to make a decision. It had come on very suddenly. Asquith and Grey down the years had soothed worried backbenchers with their mantra that there was absolutely no military commitment to France and Russia. But now the alliances were about to fight the big war and France needed its partner Britain.

The first of two Sunday Cabinet meetings began at 11 a.m. It lasted nearly three hours. The Prime Minister and his allies now reached the conclusion that clear neutrality was no longer possible. This did not go down well. Asquith's Sunday letter to Venetia Stanley reported that there was 'a strong party who are against any kind of intervention in any event'. This included all the minor ministers, as well as Harcourt, Lord Morley (Lord President of the Council) and Lloyd George. The latter, having battled during the year to try to get the military and naval bill down, was the obvious leader of any anti-war party. Grey, Asquith and Churchill were for intervention. Grey threatened to resign if the Cabinet went for neutrality. It was, as Asquith put it, 'the brink of a split'. A compromise was reached with difficulty. The Foreign Secretary was authorised to tell the frantic French Ambassador that the Navy would not allow the German fleet to use the Channel for hostile operations. The anti-war majority of the Cabinet accepted this but on condition that the Expeditionary Force would be not sent abroad.[2]

So the consequences of the Anglo-French military planning had in the end caught up with the British Government. It was fleets and strategy. The British Admiralty had moved its warships from their Mediterranean bases to Gibraltar, leaving only a squadron at Malta. France meanwhile was responsible for securing the Mediterranean. It had moved some of its fleet from the Atlantic. An Anglo-French alliance was a practical fact.[3]

Some ministers were only now learning about the commitment to France. One relieved man on this Sunday was the French Ambassador. When Cambon heard about the move to deploy the British Fleet to secure the Channel against Germany and protect the northern French coast, he called it 'the decision I was waiting for ... A great country cannot half make war.' He believed that: 'it was inescapably fated to do so also on land'. The British Expeditionary Force would follow.[4]

Arguments were spun in the Cabinet to square the circle. The neutralists swallowed with a gulp the notion that some naval intervention was not war: Britain would be merely looking after its essential interests in the Channel. This held the Cabinet more or less together – for the moment. Walter Runciman, who was at the meeting, later said that this was 'the Cabinet [meeting] which decided that war with Germany was inevitable'. This was the truth behind the word games.[5]

During the meeting a letter arrived from Bonar Law and the Conservative leadership, stating that 'any hesitation in now supporting France and Russia would be fatal to the honour and future security of the United Kingdom'. The Lloyd/Amery group had done its work. The Conservative leaders were in a happier moral position than was the Liberal Government. The Tories wanted British entry into the war and their stance was quite straightforward. No conscience juggling was required. As for whether the Conservative representation had any effect on Cabinet thinking, it is difficult to say, but the party's position was known anyway, as was the implicit Conservative readiness to step in and fight the war.[6]

The Government had put more than a toe into the waters of the European war. Britain, with its detailed pre-arrangements, however tacit, to be an ally of France, had declined neutrality terms with Germany. The idea that the Navy, with Winston Churchill in charge, and his Conservative friends and *The Times* shouting for war, could patrol the French coast and warn off the German fleet, and yet manage to avoid triggering war, was in all honesty an unlikely one. And there was the Anglo-French contingency planning for a British Expeditionary Force. The Cabinet neutralists had their assurance that no Expeditionary Force would be sent. But now that the Anglo-French naval arrangements were swinging into place, how could the other half of the plan be set aside?

One Cabinet Minister refused to believe that half-in-half-out was possible. Trade Minister John Burns was the small boy who cried that the emperor had no clothes.

Burns was a veteran of independent Labour representation in Parliament and the first person of working-class origin to attain Cabinet rank. But he was Labour no more. Arthur Ponsonby recalled:

> He to all intents and purposes became a Tory. He was jealous of Lloyd George's early success. 'Lloyd George!' he exclaimed to me one day, in making a survey of his colleagues, ''e's got 'ousemaid's knee from cringing to the King'.[7]

Burns's behaviour could be eccentric. He once disguised himself as an Italian organ-grinder and toured his Battersea constituency to test out generosity. On another occasion he regaled the inmates of a Wandsworth workhouse on Christmas Day with a speech laden with Government statistics. He no longer cared about his old causes – except opposition to the Balance of Power and British involvement in the continental system. He now said that he could not be a party to the British Cabinet warning to the Germans regarding the Channel since it was a challenge to Germany which was tantamount to a declaration of war.[8]

Down on the Sussex coast there was domestic trouble. Hubert Parry had been making plans to take his factotum George with him on a cruise to Norway and Sweden. One of the servants, Gertie, was upset that George had not told her and had given in her notice. Parry's diary records her 'tears and fury'. It was a worrying time for Hubert, since as well as the prospect of war against a country of which he was dearly fond, there was the fact that George was a German.[9]

There were clear indications that the country was getting into war mode. Hubert Parry noted in his diary that his skipper was 'agitated by being told by the harbourmaster that in consequence of the war news the yacht would not be allowed to leave'. The entry also records that: 'Arthur went to confabulate with Harry Johnston about the situation.'[10]

Sir Harry was probably the most knowledgeable person locally to whom Arthur Ponsonby could talk. He lived at Poling, handily close. Johnston had led a wildly unlikely life for a middle-class grammar-school boy. He wrote of a weekend house party at Lord Salisbury's majestic Hatfield House where the then Prime Minister discussed with him the slicing up of the African cake – so much for the French, so much for the Germans, so much for the Portuguese. There were charades in which Salisbury's daughter sported a giant moustache and took the role of Lord Randolph Churchill trying to seduce the ladies of Harry's harem. Johnston, an explorer in his Africa days, had been initiated into 'a new and powerful tribe', as one historian has put it.[11]

Johnston was an admirer of the French nation (with provisos) but in his book he took a swipe at French foreign policy:

> ... she has not yet developed a national conscience, an ideal of abstract right and wrong to which philosophers may appeal with any hope that its influence will override material and commercial interests.[12]

He regarded France's alliance with Russia as damaging. It was, as Jonathan Schnell has noted, 'solely to win a war with Germany'. The treaty's provisions simply declared that if either power were attacked, whatever the reason, the other would come to its aid with all-out war. And recently the French President Raymond Poincaré had said, 'if Russia wages war, France will also wage war', meaning regardless of the cause or theatre. France, demoralised by defeat in the Franco-Prussian War of 1870–1, feared Germany and was as a result dependent on its alliance with Russia. There was a French blank cheque of support for Russia. With France, the Triple Entente engaged Great Britain, whatever assurances the Foreign Secretary might have given to backbenchers. It was this policy of support of one allied nation for another, regardless, which on this Sunday was pulling Britain into a great war. Britain was France's ally by reason of previous arrangements and understandings and it was as simple as that. Arthur Ponsonby's trust that his Government would keep Britain out of the war was bound to be misplaced.[13]

In the Welsh/English border country near Chester, a 29-year-old Liberal MP was visiting the Hawarden Flower Show near to his family estate. William Glynn Gladstone was the bearer of a famous name. A quarter of century before his Prime Minister grandfather William Ewart Gladstone had honoured this same event. For Will, who sat for Kilmarnock, an appearance on this Sunday was an opportunity to make a speech about the European crisis. He said:

> If all efforts for the preservation of peace fail, and if it comes to a general war between the powers on the continent, in my judgement there is only one thing for our Government to do – let them fight it out by themselves. The opposing combinations of powers are wonderfully well balanced. It is not a case of a big power oppressing a little country unaided and unsupported; but owing to the way in which the countries concerned have combined, I say there is no call of chivalry, no call of knight-errantry, no obligation of honour or wisdom or of humanity which would justify Great Britain taking part in it.[14]

Gladstone attacked the intervention campaign of *The Times* and issued a warning:

> To take part as a military power in the quarrels of the Continent is to ignore the facts that we are an island, that it is our sea power alone which makes us formidable, and that to supply a European army is a strain upon this country too great to be borne. I can tell you here and now the only way it can be done – by conscription . . .

Will Gladstone's words came true in January 1916 when the Government's first conscription bill passed through the House of Commons. By then the young MP was dead.

On this Sunday Gladstone concluded his speech, amid the blooms:

> Don't be misled by being told that France only expects us to help her to the tune of one hundred thousand men and more. Don't be deceived; if once we send a single regiment across the Channel we commit ourselves to send more if the first lot is not enough.

We cannot leave them unsupported in the event of defeat. We
shall be liable to send every man in the country to their support.
If this country goes in at all, it goes in to win, and once you send
a brigade across the Channel you have committed yourself to
send the whole British army after them in case of need.

This was the last speech that Will Gladstone delivered. Serving as a
lieutenant in the Royal Welch Fusiliers, he fell in France in April 1915,
to a rifle bullet to his forehead, the second of seventeen MPs to die on
active service.

The fact that war would be likely to bring conscription was no
problem to the Conservatives. For years many of their MPs had been
national service enthusiasts. How does it look a hundred years on?
Should Britain have had conscription (before the war)? *Should* Britain
have had a definite military alliance with France and Russia (before
the war)? Would these circumstances have deterred Germany in July/
August 1914? It is surely an empty speculation. A Britain as part of a
formal European military alliance, with conscription and maintaining
a vast land army like those of France and Germany, would have been
a different sort of Britain. Conscription would have been against the
temperament of the British nation as it was in 1914. The monster expense
of a continental-type land army on top of that of the Navy, would have
knocked the stuffing out of social reform. The uproar would have gone
far beyond the Ponsonby and Labour groups.

While Will Gladstone was warning his flower show audience about
the folly of continental military entanglement, Charles Trevelyan found
a few moments to scribble his thoughts for his wife:

> Everything is as bad as can be, except that our government are
> trying to keep out of the war if they can. They will certainly not
> fight to fulfil any obligation to France . . .[15]

Trevelyan thought that 'the majority of the Cabinet are strong
against war'. He considered that the danger was 'some quite accidental
thing to set our jingo matchwood ablaze'. Belgium was cause for worry:

> The great single point of danger is Belgium. Germany is almost
> certain to violate Belgian neutrality by passing through Belgium
> to attack France. She may do more and try to conquer Belgium.
> In the second case it would be a position of unfathomable

difficulty for a British Government however anxious to avoid a collision . . .

He managed to be positive:

> We are not going to war at once at any rate. It has been decided
> not to send an expeditionary force to the Continent in any case.

For this MP, it was on Sunday afternoon that 'the nightmare really began'. He noticed many indications that the Navy was being put on war readiness:

> I saw Reservists going off to the Fleet. Married sailors were
> parting from their wives and big daughters and brothers. I nearly
> went to them and said, 'Don't cry – there won't really be war'. So
> little did I still feel at bottom that we had really been betrayed.
> But I began to feel rage, and to say that I would work at any cost
> for peace. Little did I think there was no time at all; but that the
> cold man I had met last night [actually Friday night: the account
> was written sometime later] had already settled it, unknown to
> all but his clique and his unhappy muddled colleagues?[16]

In Westminster Abbey the Archbishop of Canterbury, Randall Davidson, preached at a service interrupted by suffragettes. He asked, 'who still goes forth conquering and to conquer?' He compared the present age with that of a hundred years ago, when he said 'no more than the barest handful of people could have been found in England or Germany or France who believed in any arbitrament except war'. He will have been thinking of advances in international conciliation and adjudication, like the Hague Conventions (one of which, in 1907, condemned Kitchener's Boer War concentration camp methods), the Permanent Court of Arbitration at The Hague (established in 1899), and the Peace Palace in The Hague, set up in the previous year (the forerunner of the International Court of Justice). The next international peace conference at The Hague was projected to be in the autumn of 1915. There was real hope that with globalisation and standard-setting, war between nations was becoming outdated.[17]

But this weekend, big power war looked set to make a comeback. In Germany Willoughby Dickinson and Allen Baker were in the midst of its unfolding. They had managed to get to their church conference, but security problems were interfering with the programme. There were frontier incidents nearby and the chief of police at Constance wanted to get the visitors safely on their way back. A very problematic return journey was in prospect.[18]

At Labour's Trafalgar Square rally, the Nelson memorial – a reminder that Britain was a naval power – was swept by showers of rain. The disparate organisations that made up the Labour movement sank their differences in the cause of opposing war. It was the biggest crowd seen there for years. With the Square's military and imperial imagery in stone, it was an incongruous venue for a peace demonstration. All the different brands of Labour were there: the ILP, the British Socialist Party, the big trade unions, and a galaxy of stars – Keir Hardie, Henry Hyndman leader of the BSP, the firebrand unionist Ben Tillett, and so on. Arthur Henderson moved the resolution, calling on the assembly to vote 'to unite the workers of the nations to prevent their Governments from entering upon war'. Bruce Glasier in his diary the following day picked out the contribution of Keir Hardie, who asked why Britain should not follow Italy in staying neutral?[19]

Not at the big event was Ramsay MacDonald. He was staying with Robert Donald, editor of the Liberal *Daily Chronicle*. He was telephoned on Saturday afternoon by the Liberal Chief Whip, Percy Illingworth and asked to come to London. A meeting with Illingworth at 12 Downing Street made it clear to him that 'war was inevitable'. His diary account (written a month and a half later) recalls: '[Illingworth] said that it would be unpopular. I laughed and told him no war was at first unpopular. Left with a sad heart.'[20]

Illingworth must have anticipated large difficulty in selling war to a party which for the most part did not want it. MacDonald's comment goes with the other indications that he thought that in time the war would lose popularity.

Meanwhile at the Trafalgar Square rally there were rousing cheers for neutrality but also severe heckling, and hostile renditions of 'Rule, Britannia' and the National Anthem. Reports depended on the politics of the newspaper. *The Times* presented a gathering of undesirables – 'the poorer section of the population . . . many foreigners the great majority of [whom] were Germans'. The report concentrated on disturbances and a counter-demonstration which it called a 'patriotic demonstration against socialists'.[21]

War noise was starting to register in public places. Asquith in his Sunday letter to Venetia Stanley mentioned 'crowds perambulating the streets and distant roaring'. He remarked that 'war or anything that seems likely to lead to war is always popular with the London mob'.[22]

But, despite the early signs of war fever, there is no evidence of any general will yet in Britain for going in. The defence of neutrality was getting itself organised. An example was in Carlisle. On Sunday evening Richard Denman received a telegram from the executive of Carlisle and Cumberland Liberals emphatically urging 'the maintenance of absolute neutrality' by Britain in the crisis. The Carlisle Journal reported that a large crowd assembled in Carlisle on the evening of 2 August and unanimously passed a resolution calling for the Government to keep Britain out of the war.[23]

Denman, thirty-seven years old, did not need any convincing. He had recently won a Private Member's Bill slot in the House of Commons lottery and was using his luck to pilot an Employment of Children Bill, to abolish the 'half-time' system, under which children below the age of fourteen alternated between the schoolroom and manual work – loom, colliery, farm or whatever. If Denman could get his bill through Parliament, it would kick factory drudgery out of the lives of children. The last thing this MP wanted was war.[24]

In London the Neutrality League and the Neutrality Committee were taking shape.

For the League there was to be mass publicity – leaflets, big advertisements in newspapers and sandwich-board men walking the streets.

The Committee's plans were more Parliament-orientated. Members Arnold Rowntree and Noel Buxton (the first Chairman of the Liberal Foreign Affairs Committee) made use of the experience of House of Lords elder statesman Leonard Courtney, a former professor of economics and Financial Secretary to the Treasury. Courtney, a Quaker, had been in the forefront of opposition to the Boer War. Through this weekend he was in consultation with Liberal MPs and peers.[25]

Meetings and campaigns to keep Britain out were in full swing. The previous day Lord Courtney's wife, Kate, had written in her diary that the Liberal rank and file were organising to 'put pressure on the Government'. Kate Courtney, also a Quaker, was in the thick of the peace fray with her husband. But the two neutrality organisations stayed in different compartments. Overtures by Norman Angell's League to the Wallas/Courtney Committee came to nothing.[26]

The League got to work on the Russian angle. Russia as ally had barely been mentioned in the war noise. The League's newspaper advertisements made the prediction that if Britain joined Russia and France in war: 'It would make the military Russian Empire of 160,000,000 the dominant Power of Europe. You know the kind of country Russia is.'[27]

Norman Angell recalled years later:

> The most astonishing thing about the public discussion, such as it was, which preceded the outbreak of war, was the all but complete disregard of the position of Russia.[28]

The Russian side of things would prove to be the start of a bloodsoaked conflict between Slav and Teuton, of which the coming war would be just the first phase. Angell quoted a military person who in 1914 predicted that, 'It will take us five years to get the Russians into Germany – and fifteen to get them out.' Angell added (he was writing in 1951), 'It will take us rather more than fifteen.' This was a considerable understatement.

The future power of Russia and the implications of Britain fighting alongside the reactionary Tsarist regime were among the many issues which were not debated at the weekend Cabinet meetings. Each country had its own perspective on the crisis. There was scarcely any discussion in Britain of Alsace and Lorraine, still rankling with the French. A war with Germany would afford France a chance to fight to get this territory back. But this was hardly likely to feature in any Government presentation to the House of Commons the next day.

Alexander MacCallum Scott's diary was page-a-day and he filled most of Saturday's and Sunday's pages with reasons for Britain not going into the war. He was clear: 'our material and moral interests forbid'. He put the argument thus:

> Germany probably wants to drag us in, in order to deprive us of the tremendous material advantages which would accrue to us by remaining out. Like the fox which lost its tail in a trap wanting all the other foxes to lose their tails . . .[29]

Here is the point missed in the regular argument, much paraded a hundred years on, that if Britain had stayed out of the war, it would have faced subservience to a victorious and supreme Germany, the consequence being supposedly self-evident. Actually, Britain would have kept its power and strength intact, while Germany was being battered and drained by fighting the vastness of Russia while needing to hold down France and Belgium. Whatever the terms of an eventual German victory against the Franco-Russian alliance, assuming such, German gains would have been offset by insecurity and the costs of managing, or trying to manage, its expanded zones of control: territory, colonies, protectorates, whatever. Germany was even now overstretched. It would surely have been a heavy burden to it, not the neat breaking of Franco-Russian encirclement envisaged by the German war-makers. An un-weakened Britain would have been well off in comparison.

But Scott's neutralism seemed on this weekend of decision to be wobbling. He ended with a hedge, saying that if Britain did mean to intervene, it should choose its own time and means and method, and distinguish clearly between 'our own direct and immediate interests and any supposed obligation to defend France because she is a friend'.

The prospective German violation of Belgium was the big worry for the neutralist cause now that it was drawing nearer. The mass circulation Liberal paper the *Daily News* reserved its position on Belgium, not calling for an immediate pledge of non-intervention. The *Manchester Guardian* remained untroubled in its neutralism.

The Cabinet assembled for its second meeting at 6.30. It was preceded by an informal meeting of some of the ministers, including Lloyd George. This seems to have been the critical hour. When Leo Amery went round to *The Times* later in the evening, where journalists were in the know, he was informed, as he recorded in his diary, 'that things had taken a much more favourable tone between 5.00 and 6.30, that the rotten element in the Cabinet had been largely talked round'.

Germany had occupied Luxembourg. Geography suggested that Belgium would be next. At the evening Cabinet meeting Sir Edward Grey was supported by most of his colleagues when he argued that a resisted invasion of Belgium by Germany must see Britain entering the war. If German troops passed through the south-east of Belgium and Belgium merely protested there could be no British declaration of war but if Germany interfered with Belgian independence this must mean Britain becoming a belligerent. For those ethically opposed to British war entry in support of the French ally, consciences would be squared by a *casus belli* on a point of moral principle, that is to say defence of Belgium against German aggression.[30]

Thus, violation of Belgium by Germany would be the reason given to Parliament for any declaration of war, and this, as well as accommodating anti-war consciences in the Cabinet, would rally ethical Liberals on the backbenches. Crucially, Lloyd George was now onside. The prospect of defence of Belgian neutrality, of which Britain was a guarantor, as the grounds for war, seems to have been decisive in swinging opponents of war round. Only Burns and Morley were not able to go along with the decision.

A declaration of war would be subject to approval by vote or acclamation of the House of Commons. Constitutionally it was not necessary since a declaration of war could be made simply on the Royal Prerogative, but in practice there would have to be a clear indication of Parliamentary support. Sir Edward Grey himself, speaking to the Commons several years earlier, had set out plainly the realities:

> It is absolutely impossible for any government to contemplate war unless it feels certain that when the moment comes the House of Commons would be prepared to endorse the policy of the Government, by voting the supplies which are necessary and without which it would be absolutely out of the power of the Government to go to war at all.[31]

The *casus belli* would be Belgium but what if, contrary to expectations there were *no* German violation of Belgium, or no wholesale violation? It would make things difficult for the Government, but entry into the war in support of France, with Asquith, Grey and Churchill leading the way, was going to happen anyway – Belgium or not – though perhaps with a Cabinet changed from Liberal to coalition and a rumpus in the House. But provided that Germany invaded Belgium in a major way, there would be no big Cabinet split.

Some neutralists were getting in rebuttals of the case for Belgium as grounds for British war entry. One was Joseph King. A regular of Arthur Ponsonby's committee, Joe was a near neighbour of Arthur, at Haslemere. He was a parliamentary gadfly. *Punch* cartoons represented him with a row of numbers stuck in his top hat like the price tag in that of the Mad Hatter in *Alice in Wonderland* (whom he slightly resembled).

The joke was that King asked so many parliamentary questions that he needed to have their Order Paper numbers on his person.[32]

King had already written to the *Manchester Guardian*. The letter, which appeared on Monday, analysed the international treaties of 1839 and 1870 guaranteeing Belgian neutrality. The MP concluded:

> If Belgium is invaded by German or French armies, we must protest but we need not fight. Our protest might go to the length of notifying the Power at fault that on the conclusion of the war we shall stand firm for the fullest reparation for any violation done to Belgian neutrality. It will be a terrible provocation if either France or Germany to get at each other does so by invading Belgium, but it does not necessarily drag Britain into the fight.[33]

What did 'Belgian neutrality', the phrase so often heard, mean? Why was it so often 'neutrality' rather than 'independence'? The reason was that the great powers were primarily concerned about making sure that Belgium was not taken into an alliance, hence keeping Belgium 'neutral'. But a war of the alliances was likely to pull in Belgium, given its geographical position. A German invasion of Belgium was the likely first event of such a war. In this crisis, while one Belgian division was positioned to keep an eye on the Germans, two divisions were guarding against attack by the French, and two were stationed on the coast in case of hostile action from a British Expeditionary Force. What would the British Government have done if France had moved first? The conclusion of David Fromkin's study of the origins of the war is that had Belgian neutrality been violated by France rather than by Germany, Asquith and Grey would have 'looked the other way'.[34]

On Sunday afternoon Freddie Whyte met up with Winston Churchill on Horse Guards Parade. Whyte's notes record:

> Winston stopped, jabbed his gold-headed cane into the ground, and, with his jaw thrust forward in the well known gesture said, 'How many of our people will follow Asquith if we go to war tonight?' . . .[35]

Whyte's reply was that it depended on whether reports of German troops having invaded Belgium were true. (In fact they were untrue.)

Churchill's PPS then had another encounter:

I went home to Barton Street; and on my way down Great College Street I met Charlie Trevelyan. We fought for two hours about the rights and wrongs, walking up and down College Street and Barton Street, and then parted.

Over in Sussex, as Dolly later told Arthur, two friends who went to Shulbrede on this Sunday: '. . . found it bombarded by people clamouring to see you – one man had motored all the way down from London'.[36] Ponsonby was evidently missed, but it is difficult to see what he could have done in London. He returned on Sunday evening. His first port of call was the National Liberal Club, the neo-Gothic landmark on the Thames Embankment. Here he found that the German invasion of Luxembourg was the big talking point. He wrote to Dolly next morning:

> The streets were crowded when I arrived and evening papers were being sold at every corner. I found over a dozen members at the Club, some already wavering because of Germany's entry into Luxemburg. I got some dinner and we sat talking till 11. I then went to see Lulu Harcourt. He said the Cabinet had not split yet but it might and then there would be a coalition . . .[37]

Harcourt seems to have told Arthur Ponsonby almost nothing about the day's Cabinet events.

Arthur Ponsonby's letter to Dolly continued:

> The financial position is very desperate – no cheques or fivers can be changed. I have got two fivers which are apparently useless. I borrowed 5/- [5 shillings] from Philip. He is in a wild state and our meeting at 2 o'clock is likely to be a job to manage. The streets last night at midnight as I walked from Berkeley Square (I had no money for a taxi) made me sick. Bands of half drunken men shouting, mafficking, waving flags: bands of French waiters shouting Vive la France, the war fever beginning. The situation changes every hour. If Germany really means to provoke us all is up. There is a danger that Winston will provoke an incident. I really feel almost as if the world were coming to an end.

It is easy to understand see why Philip Morrell would be so disturbed. He was an idealistic social reformer who now saw his hopes being sunk by war. Philip had been MP for Burnley since the last election. He and Ottoline were popular in the town. They had thrown themselves into Burnley life on their constituency visits. When Burnley Football Club won the FA Cup of 1914 before 70,000 at London's Crystal Palace, Ottoline was their mascot. The King presented the Cup and later Philip turned Westminster tour guide, as he and Ottoline took the victorious Clarets round the House of Commons.[38]

There was speculation everywhere. Better informed than most was Ramsay MacDonald, who was close to Government ministers. MacDonald's diary mentions Sir John Simon, Attorney-General, as announcing that he intended to join those set to quit the Cabinet. But by the evening, when MacDonald dined at the house of newspaper proprietor Sir George Riddell with Simon, Lloyd George and Charles Masterman, he found that the neutralist cause in the Cabinet had collapsed. Simon was 'broken'; Lloyd George, who had been expected to be a mainstay for keeping out of the war, was 'ruffled'; Masterman, once a beacon for social reform, had gone 'jingo'. The diary continues:

> [Lloyd] George harped on exposed French coasts and Belgium but I gathered that excuses were being searched for. Walked home through the Park feeling that a great break had come.[39]

Perhaps the Chancellor would have come round to war even without Belgium. His political principles were flexible enough. It has been suggested that, had there been no invasion of Belgium, Lloyd George might have led an anti-war Liberal Government, supported by Labour and the Irish Nationalists. This seems unlikely. Would the King really have summoned a Radical to form a Government to keep Britain out of a war into which the establishment was shouting for entry? One may imagine the King calling on Bonar Law to try to form a coalition if Asquith resigned – and Law succeeding. The solidity of neutralism on the Liberal backbenches would have been crumbling, as the press clamour for war mounted. (The King's aide Fritz Ponsonby would have approved.) But the most probable outcome of British war entry without the Belgium moral cause must surely have been the continuation of Asquith in power, with, however, the loss of a significant part of his Cabinet and dependence on the Conservatives.

The Government would have to take its intention to intervene in the European war before the House of Commons. A speech to be made by the Foreign Secretary to Parliament next day was discussed at the evening Cabinet meeting. Also being prepared was a Moratorium Bill to avert the looming financial meltdown. The bill included extension of the Monday bank-holiday closure and postponement of payments due on bills of exchange.

During the evening Charles Trevelyan went into Charing Cross station to meet up with his brother. He found signs of war much in evidence:

> A huge crowd blocked the station. It was largely French, seeing off their compatriots. They were not hilarious. They sang the Marseillaise. It was not a song of victory, more like a wail. I came away and went to bed sore and apprehensive.[40]

Among the departing French, it turned out, were the House of Commons chefs.

At his apartment Arthur Ponsonby retired to bed. 'Thank goodness I slept like a top,' he wrote after the events of the next day.[41]

8

'Hideous and Terrible'

Monday Morning, 3 August 1914

NEWS OF THE CABINET SUNDAY DECISIONS does not seem to have seeped out before early arrivals trickled into Westminster on Monday morning. Backbench Liberal Francis Neilson (a Radical) was one. On his way he had seen companies of soldiers in full uniform marching towards Victoria. He found not many MPs yet at the House. Those to whom he spoke still seemed to be in the Liberal mode of confidence that, whatever was happening on the continent, it would not come to Britain. The usual remark in his circle on this Monday morning, he recalled, was, 'There'll be no war.' He went along to the Commons library and read the French newspapers to try to get some idea of what was going on.[1]

Arthur Ponsonby wrote to his wife before he went to Westminster, 'It is all very hideous and terrible but there is still hope.' A later letter, describing the events in Parliament on Monday, states that he arrived early at the Commons and found 'alarming rumours' circulating.[2]

Charles Trevelyan certainly feared the worst. He wrote to his wife:

> It looks very bad this morning. Unless the Prime Minister gives a satisfactory account of what they are doing, I shall have to resign. But I am unable to tell at all yet, and there is no use discussing it. Everything just now is the decision of the hour.[3]

Around Parliament milling crowds were on the lookout for the famous. Public figures were readily recognisable from the newspaper and magazine pictures and caricatures and from the silent cinema news-reels. No doubt some people had been to Madam Tussaud's in Baker Street, now advertising: 'The European Crisis: Lifelike Portrait Models' (focussing on Austria and Serbia). A similar service was provided for

'The Home Rule Crisis', with Carson and Redmond in wax, but this was now yesterday's news.[4]

There were cheers as Ministers were spotted. On this bank holiday the Strand and Whitehall were thronged with holiday-makers dressed for the beach who had taken a diversion to try to get a sight of the political action. The newspapers had special editions in rapid succession. They were advertised by posters in bold scrawl and there was a brisk kerbside trade. The *Pall Mall Gazette* had a headline 'NOW' It declared:

> The news of this morning is decisive. The neutrality of Belgium
> has been invaded. This is the end of all doubt and hesitation.[5]

The *Pall Mall* was jumping the gun. Belgium had not yet been invaded. But the paper was already thinking about the Expeditionary Force. It had no doubt: 'For many and various reasons, it ought to be placed upon the soil of France'.

On the streets miniature Union Jacks and tricolours were being sold; here and there shouts of war excitement were heard. There was also scattered 'mob' behaviour, to use Asquith's word. However, the crowds were generally holiday-makers, well behaved, caught up with the excitement and tension, and rather anxious too.

There were plenty of arrivals to keep the watchers interested. Among the plentiful top hats – still the MP's trademark – were a few wider-brimmed soft hats, chiefly on the heads of Labour Members. Keir Hardie with his familiar tam o' shanter was one MP easily picked out.

The Times on this Monday, under the heading 'The Travelling Season', detailed the usual arrangements at this time of year for subscribers to have their copies sent on to the continent. Map sellers were doing well but not this year for holiday travel. An advertisement for the City Map Shop in Old Broad Street announced that it would be open on the bank holiday for the sale of 'WAR MAPS'.[6]

The lead headline in *The Times* was 'FIVE NATIONS AT WAR'. Readers will have been intrigued by a report headed 'LORD KITCHENER', under which it was stated that the famous man had postponed his return to Egypt because a journey across France was 'no longer practicable'. The paper added that a different route would be taken later in the week 'unless', as the writer put it, suggestively, 'Lord Kitchener's services should be required in the meantime for purposes other than those originally intended'.

Eyes will have been caught by a prominent report in the paper in bold type, with a strong hint of insider information:

> The Cabinet held two long sittings yesterday, both of them attended by unusual manifestations of popular interest outside.
>
> It is understood that divisions of opinion, which still existed in the morning, were closed by the news from the Continent which reached London before the afternoon sitting. If they now take shape in any resignation from the Cabinet, it will be of a small and unimportant character.

For those who knew how to read these things, it unmistakeably meant that the Government had decided for war. But what about Parliament? The Foreign Secretary had often said that the Commons had the last word on great questions.

News which had not arrived in time for the previous evening's Cabinet meeting was that at 7 p.m. on Sunday a German ultimatum was given to the Belgian Government. This offered friendly relations with Germany in return for the passage of German troops through Belgium. But it was an ultimatum: German troops must enter Belgian territory, to anticipate French attack. Twelve hours was given for reply. Mid-morning on Monday the information reached the British Foreign Office along with the news that the Belgian Government had rejected it. This was shortly before the Cabinet gathered again at Downing Street.

At this meeting, following the earlier announcements of intended resignation by John Burns, Sir John Simon and Lord Morley, a statement was made by the First Commissioner of Works, Earl Beauchamp that he too must go. But the ministers (except Burns) agreed to sit on the Government front benches during the Foreign Secretary's statement. 'Until the H. of C. had indicated its opinion', Charles Hobhouse put it in his diary, calling this 'not very brave conduct'. He presumably meant that if Grey's call for war went down badly there would be no war and the ministers would not have to resign but should there be enthusiastic assent they could find themselves persuaded to stay.[7]

The Foreign Secretary's speech was scheduled to follow Questions, shortly after 3.00.

An MP who, as Churchill's PPS, probably had some idea of what to expect in Sir Edward's speech was Freddie Whyte, whose account of the crisis days continues into Monday:

Even as late as noon on Monday, August 3rd, there were still
many Liberal MPs who were shaking their heads over Grey's
policy and were still inclined to press for a neutral attitude
by HMG.[8]

It must be said that there was no unanimity on the Conservative
benches for war. Leo Amery's diary for 1 August states that 'except
Hugh Cecil, and in a milder degree Robert Cecil', there was no section
of the Conservative Party in favour of neutrality, 'though of course the
Jewish influence generally, in so far as it affected the *Daily Telegraph*
and some other circles in the party, looked with great aversion on the
idea of war'. But it is likely that there were Conservative neutralists who
were keeping their heads down.[9]

Philip Morrell lunched at his Bedford Square Georgian house near
the British Museum, where he and Ottoline were joined by Bertrand
Russell, philosopher and political writer, who was Ottoline's former
lover in the open marriage. The war occupied the conversation. Philip
said that he was determined to make a speech in Parliament against
British entry. He was told by Ottoline that he must not fail to do so.[10]

The Parliamentary Labour Party and the Ponsonby committee held
their meetings before Commons proceedings began.

Ramsay MacDonald had no problem with his MPs. His diary states
that he 'communicated to party meeting what I proposed to say and
received their approval without dissent'. After the weekend's rallies and
demonstrations anything other than a Labour call for Britain to keep
out of the war would have been extraordinary.[11]

Arthur Ponsonby's meeting was attended by twenty-five. They will
have wondered how their colleagues Allen Baker and Willoughby
Dickinson were faring in Germany on their peace mission. They will
have imagined a nightmare; and it was. The Conference broke up
prematurely on Monday morning. The returning delegates from twelve
countries left by the last through train out of Germany, standing for
most of the journey, without food as their luncheons were stolen by
troops, and making a common pool of their gold, since this was now
the only currency.[12]

Little detail has survived of Arthur Ponsonby's meeting. The
chairman's papers have not much more than time and place and the
attendance record. But an Arthur to Dolly letter speaks of the meeting

as 'very difficult to handle', with 'marked differences of opinion showing themselves'. Something had altered things since Friday.[13]

It was certainly Belgium. A German invasion of Belgium, as the opening phase of a war between the two big alliances, had long been a likely prediction. Now that it was actually going to happen, it was causing shock in the Liberal Party. The idea of a British role in maintaining international good behaviour had been part of Gladstone's philosophy. Liberalism was committed to peace but there was its occasional crusading strand favouring war to impose justice. Germany was set to make an unprovoked attack on a smaller nation. If some members of the Ponsonby committee wondered whether this was a case for British intervention to assert international justice, this was to be expected.[14]

The Ponsonby meeting pulled in two of the most combative back-bench Liberals, Josiah Wedgwood and Leonard Outhwaite. Both sat for Staffordshire Potteries constituencies and both were ardent proponents of the campaign for taxation of land values.

Tall, balding and moustached, Leonard Outhwaite, forty-five, originated from Tasmania where he had been a farmer before becoming a journalist and migrating with his family to Britain. A spell in South Africa as the correspondent of five British Liberal papers had been a formative experience. Outhwaite's passion was to find a means of enabling the population to enjoy fair shares in the benefits of the land, not just in rural areas but in the industrial cities too. In 1912 he contested a by-election for the Liberals in Hanley, near Stoke on Trent. He proclaimed the land tax cause. Three meetings went on non-stop in the town centre, while a gramophone blared out 'The Land Song'. Labour, which had previously held the seat, sent in big-hitters Keir Hardie and George Lansbury. The two stormed around Hanley preaching socialist revolution. It backfired. The conservative-minded local potters and miners opted for the Liberals as being more moderate, a quirky outcome given that Outhwaite was a Radical on the left of his party. When the poll was declared, Outhwaite had beaten the Conservative, with Labour back in a poor third place.[15]

Outhwaite and his land-taxers felt in the summer of 1914 that their cause was taking off. But all social reform risked being buried by war if Britain got into a European military adventure. Outhwaite detested war. He had seen the graveyards of the Boer War fallen.[16]

His colleague Josiah Wedgwood had a very different history. He had once worked in naval construction and in the Boer War he had commanded a field artillery battery supplied by his firm. He was another reformer from within the social establishment. He was a prominent supporter of women's suffrage and had been at the forefront of the protest against forced feeding of hunger-striking suffragettes. His family is listed in the 1911 Census as having a governess and five servants, including a lady's maid – fairly usual for the upper middle class. But he proudly gave his occupation to the enumerators as 'Radical Member of Parliament'. Philip Morrell once pondered on Wedgwood's contradictions: 'radical and revolutionary as he likes to think himself, he is at heart one of the most traditional of men'.[17]

The Ponsonby committee men completed their meeting and made their way downstairs. Noise from the streets was filtering in, adding to the buzz of the corridors and foyers. Around the Palace of Westminster many were hoping to get into the public galleries to hear Sir Edward Grey's speech. Most were unlucky. Bertrand Russell was one of those excluded by the crush.

Ottoline Morrell fared better. As an MP's wife she was in the Ladies' Gallery. Today the viewing areas were heaving. Squashed in among the reporters in the small press gallery were the Archbishop of Canterbury and Lord Chief Justice. Everyone wanted to be there. Arthur Ponsonby was as usual among the Radicals below the gangway. If the Foreign Secretary showed signs of going for British entry into the European war he could expect trouble from here. It was an area that the reporters would be watching closely.[18]

The debating chamber had nothing like the capacity to take 670 Members comfortably if all turned up. It was thought that overcrowding was good for charging the atmosphere on big occasions. On this day extra chairs had to be shoehorned into the aisle and the gangways, for the first time since Gladstone's Home Rule Bill of 1886. The chamber was a jam of solid seating with not a space anywhere.

Asquith and Lloyd George had needed the police to clear a way through the crowds for them to get to the House. Now they were here on the Government front bench, Asquith sitting by his Foreign Secretary. Among the junior ministers behind the Government front bench was Charles Trevelyan.

Trevelyan had lunched with his brother George at Victoria Station.

With them was Edmond Dene Morel, prospective Liberal candidate for Birkenhead, famous for his Congo Reform Association campaigns against the brutal fiefdom of the Belgian King Leopold II in the Congo. The death toll of forced labour in the collection of rubber amounted to millions. The Morel group's protests were instrumental in having the Congo territory transferred to the jurisdiction of the Belgian government on Leopold's death in 1909. With the Congo campaign completed, Morel switched his publicity machine to exposure of the secret arrangements of the Anglo-French Entente.[19]

Charles Trevelyan put his brother and E. D. Morel in his office below the 'No' Lobby. Then he then went up to the chamber, and took his place. He was prepared for bad news.[20]

Presiding was Mr Speaker, James Lowther. He was a Conservative of the landed classes. The office which he held embodied ancient traditions of liberty and respect for dissent. The Radicals and socialists on the backbenches who were opposed to war entry had to hope that Lowther would remember the history of his great office and allow them to be heard.

Proceedings began as usual at 2.45 p.m. As always, even today, it was Questions first. Two were in the name of Joseph King about Belgium. It was not expected that the answers would provide much illumination. Most people just wanted Questions out of the way so that Sir Edward could put everyone out of their agony of suspense.

Grey's Under-Secretary, Francis Acland, answering King, declined to furnish the details of three Treaties of London (1831, 1839 and 1870) and other documents of relevance to Belgium's status as a neutral state. He said that a statement was going to be made, a fact of which no Member could be unaware.

In this period most questions were put orally but there were some written ones. On this day one stands out. It was from Charles Bathurst, Conservative Member for South Wiltshire:

> MR C. BATHURST: Asked the Prime Minister whether, in view of the present European crisis and the desirability of absolute solidarity among the classes and political parties in this country, he will consider the advantage of adjourning, for the present, this Session of Parliament, and so rendering impossible the continuance or development of acute party controversy with

a consequent suggestion of internal discord to the minds of the subjects of Foreign Powers?

THE PRIME MINISTER: The matter referred to is receiving full consideration.[21]

The questioner evidently thought that politics, and therefore democracy, should be put into abeyance when the country was facing possible war. This shows why MPs like Edmund Harvey were so perturbed about Conservative backbench conversations. Britain was not even in the war yet, but here was an MP calling for Parliament to be shut down while the Government got on with hostilities. The question foreshadowed a four-year fight to keep democracy open in wartime.

Question Time was shortened. Lloyd George then presented the Moratorium Bill. It was through its Commons stages in minutes. The decks were cleared for the Foreign Secretary. The Commons would now learn whether or not the Government wanted to take the country to war.

Just after 3 p.m. Grey stood up. Arthur Ponsonby, who was scheduled to chair a second meeting of his committee afterwards, hoped that he would be expressing his satisfaction and relief that Britain would be staying out of the war. It was not a confident hope.

9

'The Fatal Afternoon'

Monday Afternoon, 3 August 1914

SIR EDWARD GREY stepped to the table. The memoirs of Labour's J. R. Clynes capture the moment. Before the Foreign Secretary could get a word out, 'the silence was broken with cheering and yelling, while a flutter of handkerchiefs waved from Liberal and Opposition benches alike'. Handkerchief flapping meant approval in this nasally innocent age. Cheering and handkerchiefs indicated that here was a minister widely respected. And perhaps it relaxed the pent-up tensions.[1]

The geography of the House of Commons means that a Government minister, while addressing his words to the Speaker at the top of the chamber, is facing the Opposition benches, while swinging round in various directions. Arthur Ponsonby and his friends, below the gangway on the Government side several benches back, had a sideways rear view of Sir Edward as he made his speech from the Despatch Box above the gangway. Ponsonby was distantly related to Grey, both being descendants of Earl Grey of the Reform Bill.

Sir Edward was anything but a natural politician. He was happiest on his estate of Fallodon in Northumberland, where his pursuits included ornithology. He suffered from deteriorating eyesight, hence the habit of peering closely at his notes. Until this crisis he had been intending to visit Germany – which would have been his first visit there – to see an eye specialist (while perhaps quietly furthering his attempts to improve Anglo-German relations). He saw himself as stoically soldiering on. He cared little for public opinion and he was rarely disposed to take Parliament into his confidence. Today he had to.

He began with news. He was not able to go further than to state that Russia and Germany had declared war on each other. War between Germany and France was close and near-certain but Sir Edward was not able to announce it yet. It would be a fact by the end of the day. The Foreign Secretary recalled that 'the cooperation of the Great Powers of Europe was successful in working for peace in the Balkan crisis'. But this time, he told the House, 'it has not been possible to secure the peace of Europe'.

All eyes and ears were on Grey. Francis Neilson recalled that, 'the silence was intense', as everyone waited for the moment when he 'would cast the die'. Would it be war? Neilson remembered the Foreign Secretary's hands trembling and, when he raised a glass of water to his lips, drops trickling down on to his hand. He knew, he said, as soon as Grey rose that negotiations were over and that there was no hope: 'Something in his demeanour communicated to me the notion that he was conscious that he had lost control of the situation.'[2]

Neilson had had a premonition before he went to the House of Commons of what was going to happen:

> Always in times of crisis in my life, in some clairvoyant way, I have tried to project myself into a situation which I knew was imminent or that I had to face. It was not difficult for me to picture the scene in the House, for I had gathered the material for such a visualisation over a period of long years. I had seen Leicester Square and Piccadilly Circus the night before. I had seen troops and troop trains on the move for two days.[3]

As Grey continued his speech, Arthur Ponsonby and his friends no doubt kept an eye on the Tory benches opposite. They will have seen approval here when the Foreign Secretary went on to make his first comment. It was vocabulary that the Conservatives wanted to hear:

> I would like the House to approach this crisis in which we are now, from the point of view of British interests, British honour, and British obligations, free from all passion, as to why peace has not been preserved.[4]

War and honour went back to Shakespeare's 'soldier jealous in honour'. The Liberal backbenches were glum.

Grey continued: 'In the present crisis up till yesterday we have given no promise of anything more than diplomatic support.' Now there were cheers from the Liberal benches below the gangway and from the two Labour benches. From here many an anxious question had been addressed to ministers about military commitment to France. Grey was repeating the old denial. But *was* he? But what did he mean by 'up till yesterday'?

Then the Foreign Secretary came to the Anglo-French naval 'conversations', which had previously been kept from the Commons. He took the House back to the Moroccan crises of 1906 and 1911 which he said had necessitated the working out of general principles of possible mutual armed support between France and Britain. He said that he had told France that he 'could promise nothing to any foreign power unless it was subsequently to receive the whole-hearted support of public opinion here if the occasion arose'.

Did that mean that Grey was preparing the way for a bid for 'the whole-hearted support' of MPs for war? The House listened intently.

The Foreign Secretary said that without the military preparations the British Government could not give France the armed support which they would like to give if popular opinion backed it: hence the liaison. He mentioned a letter of 22 November 1912 which he had given to the French ambassador asserting the freedom of both nations to decide whether to use armed force, but saying that 'an unprovoked attack by a third power' would justify Britain and France deciding 'what measures they would be prepared to take in common'.

Grey was giving hope to both the neutralists and the interventionists. It was difficult for the reporters in the press gallery as they scribbled their material for the special editions.

Now he gave 'honour' another airing:

> The present crisis ... has not originated as regards anything with which we had a special agreement with France; it has not originated with anything which primarily concerned France. It has originated in a dispute between Austria and Servia. I can say this with the most absolute confidence – no government and no country has less desire to be involved in war over a dispute with Austria and Servia than the Government and country of France. They are involved in it because of their obligation of honour under a definite alliance with Russia. Well it is only fair to say to the House that that obligation of honour cannot apply in the same way to us. We are not parties to the Franco-Russian alliance.

This was what neutralists wanted to hear. It produced cheers from below the Government gangway. The shorthand-writers now had something for their first 'stop press' pieces which would soon be hitting the streets of London, the 1914 equivalent of the 'breaking news' banners on twenty-four-hour news screens. One went to the bedside of Arthur Lee, Conservative military spokesman, who was recovering from an appendix operation. Lee's autobiography tells that the quotes from the Foreign Secretary's speech 'plunged me into the depths of gloom, as he seemed to be vacillating on the brink and irresolute on the point of honour'.[5]

But Lee was gloomy too soon. Grey was feeling his way.

The audience, despite occasional cheers, was listening intently. The Foreign Secretary employed what was widely reported as an 'almost conversational' style. Asquith while enthusing about the speech to Venetia Stanley, mentioned Grey's 'usual ragged ends' and there were other comments about the apparent lack of preparation. The speech was certainly not polished. Grey was not an accomplished orator; nor was histrionics in his usual repertoire. But a conversational manner could be taken to mean sincerity rather than artifice.[6]

Now came the vital passage. Grey went on to say (with an interruption recorded in Hansard):

> I now come to what we think the situation requires of us. For many years we have had a long-standing friendship with France. [AN HONOURABLE MEMBER: And with Germany!] ... But how far that friendship entails an obligation let every man look into his own heart, and his own feelings, and construe the extent of the obligation for himself. The House, individually and collectively, may judge for itself. I speak my personal view ...

The MP who interrupted was Josiah Wedgwood, from below the gangway. He was identified by the *Daily News*, whose Parliamentary correspondent was a former Liberal MP.[7]

The Foreign Secretary was not deflected at this crucial part of his argument. His subject was fleets. The French fleet, he said, was in the Mediterranean. The north and west coasts of France were 'absolutely undefended'. France was relying on the confidence which it placed in its friendship with Britain. The Foreign Secretary went on:

> My own feeling is that if a foreign fleet engaged in a war which
> France had not sought, and in which she had not been the
> aggressor, came down the English Channel and battered the
> undefended coasts of France, we could not stand aside and see
> this going on practically within sight of our eyes, with our arms
> folded, looking on dispassionately, doing nothing!

On the word 'nothing' Grey brought down his clenched fist
crashing down on the Despatch Box. The *Westminster Gazette* called it
'passionate eloquence'. The Foreign Secretary was giving the Commons
the Cabinet's primary case for intervention. The Channel was the
funnel down which ships bound for London and other ports passed. If
Germany gained control of the continental side of it, while being hostile
to Britain, British military security would be jeopardised.[8]

There was a roar from the Conservative benches. Feet stamped. And
the frenzy was not confined to the Conservatives. Among the Irish
Nationalists there was wild excitement. This was utterly unexpected.
Willie Redmond, brother of the Irish Nationalist leader and another
Nationalist, Arthur Lynch, jumped on to their benches and stood
waving their Order Papers. This, the *Westminster Gazette* told its
readers, 'was when the cheers reached climax'.[9] The Speaker's memoirs
spoke of 'the most thrilling occasion I ever witnessed in the House'.[10]

Here was Parliament's thunderous acceptance of Sir Edward's
invitation to enter the war. Or was it? Certainly Grey's fireside chat with
emotional bursts was producing rapturous assent. And yet the reaction
was mixed. On the Liberal benches below the gangway there was stony
silence. The reporter of the *Westminster Gazette* noted, 'The speech
made a painful impression on the Liberal Party, which above all has
sought to avoid a war with Germany.'[11]

What British military action was the Foreign Secretary envisaging?
Grey's war bid was along the lines of what had been worked out in
Cabinet. He was not yet calling for a British land campaign. What he
wanted was British naval intervention.

Now came some further spelling out of the rationale of the Anglo-
French naval cooperation in the war, which the Foreign Secretary
wished Parliament to approve:

> If we say nothing at this moment what is France to do with her
> fleet in the Mediterranean? . . . Let us assume that out of some

consequences unforeseen, which make it necessary at a sudden moment that, in defence of vital British interests, we should go to war and let us assume – which is quite possible – that Italy who is now neutral [HON. MEMBERS: Hear, hear!] – because, as I understand, she considers that this war is an aggressive war and that the Triple Alliance being a defensive alliance her obligation did not arise – let us assume that consequences which are not yet foreseen ... make Italy depart from her attitude of neutrality at a time when we are forced in defence of vital British interests ourselves to fight, what then will be the position in the Mediterranean?

The Italy argument looks strained: that Britain should enter a war of the alliances *in case* a country staying out and declaring neutrality should change her mind and enter. The shouts of 'Hear, here!' when Grey said that Italy was staying out of the war (despite being in the Triple Alliance) indicated the feeling of Radicals and Labour below the gangway that the British Government should be following Italy's example.

The Foreign Secretary now told MPs that he had given the French ambassador a statement that:

> If the German fleet comes into the Channel or through the North Sea to undertake hostile operations against the French coasts or shipping, the British Fleet will give all the protection in its power. This assurance is of course subject to the policy of His Majesty's Government receiving the support of Parliament.

Here in effect was confirmation that Britain was on the way to war – provided that Parliament approved. It apparently did. Grey's announcement produced what the *Westminster Gazette* reporter called 'a loud burst of cheering' with 'several of the Irish Members waving their handkerchiefs in their enthusiasm'. The paper commented that 'it was remarkable that the Nationalists seemed no less enthusiastic than the Unionist [Conservative] Party'.

Thoughts of an alternative way of dealing with the situation must have been occurring to some. Could there not be some agreement with the German government regarding the seas, instead of hostilities? There had been the rumour that swept the Commons on Friday morning. For a moment neutralist hopes rose as Grey went on to say:

> Things move very hurriedly from hour to hour. Fresh news
> comes in, and I cannot give this in any very formal way; but I
> understand that the German Government would be prepared,
> if we would pledge ourselves to neutrality, to agree that its fleet
> would not attack the northern coast of France.

This was a further German offer to Britain following the one which
had been withheld by the Government from Parliament. There were
different reactions from different parts of the House. From below the
gangway cries of 'Hear, hear!' indicated to the Foreign Secretary that
he should use the German offer as a basis for negotiation. Shouts of
'Oh!' from the Conservatives and war supporters elsewhere warned
the Foreign Secretary of trouble if that avenue were entered. But it
soon became clear that Grey was not seriously thinking of it. He was
mentioning the German proposal only to make clear why it had been
rejected. He said:

> I have only heard that shortly before I came to the House, but it
> is far too narrow an engagement for us.

The Foreign Secretary had to get his own party behind him or the
Liberal Government might have to be diluted with Conservatives. The
speech now took a new direction. Grey said, properly addressing Mr
Speaker Lowther:

> And, Sir, there is the more serious consideration – becoming
> more serious every hour – there is the question of the neutrality
> of Belgium.

Sir Edward admitted that the multi-power treaties did not mean
that Britain was under any obligation to intervene over Belgium. But he
set out a moral case. He quoted the French and German Government
communications in reply to his question about Belgium: while France
was respecting Belgian neutrality, Germany equivocated.
He went on:

> It now appears from the news I have received today . . . that an
> ultimatum has been given to Belgium by Germany, the object
> of which was to offer Belgium friendly relations with Germany
> on condition that she would facilitate the passage of German
> troops through Belgium . . . We were sounded in the course of

last week as to whether if a guarantee were given that, after the war, Belgium integrity would be preserved that would content us. We replied that we could not bargain away whatever interests or obligations we had in Belgian neutrality.

Belgian integrity after the war, Grey said, would be meaningless if it were invaded. Its independence would be gone, as would that of Holland. He invoked Gladstone as an upholder of international law. He again used the key phrase 'honour and interests'.

As the clocks clicked on to 4 p.m., Grey went on:

> For us, with a powerful Fleet, which we believe able to protect our commerce, to protect our shores, and to protect our interests, if we are engaged in war, we shall suffer but little more than we shall suffer if we stand aside. We are going to suffer, I am afraid, terribly in this war whether we are in it or whether we stand aside.

The Times report picked up a shout of 'No!' from an unnamed MP.

Charles Trevelyan now knew that he would be resigning from the Government. The letter which he later wrote to his West Yorkshire constituents in Elland included a reply to the Foreign Secretary's prosperity calculations:

> However overwhelming the victory of our navy, our commerce will suffer terribly. In war too, the first productive energies of the whole people have to be devoted to armaments. Cannon are a poor industrial exchange for cotton. We shall suffer a steady impoverishment.[12]

Grey continued:

> I do not believe for a moment, that at the end of this war, even if we stood aside and remained aside, we should be in a position to use our force decisively to undo what had happened in the course of the war, to prevent the whole of the West of Europe opposite to us – if that had been the result of the war – falling under the domination of a single Power, and I am quite sure that our moral position would be such as to have lost us all respect.

Arthur Ponsonby was appalled. The next day he wrote to his wife:

> The horrible raucous cheers which greeted the strongest anti-German passages in Grey's speech gave me a despairing feeling of utter hopelessness. We are accustomed to cool well balanced moderate speeches from him and to see him carried away by passion and presenting such an obviously biased view was most alarming.[13]

Sir Edward was working the House. J. R. Clynes recalled 'a magnificent piece of emotional oratory, in which vital facts were suppressed, and patriotism was inflamed almost to a degree of agony'. He added (with the sexist imagery of the times) that Grey:

> ... was cheered after almost every sentence, and the atmosphere soon resembled that of an hysterical meeting of excited ladies, rather than that of a Parliamentary debate on which the lives and happiness of millions depended.[14]

There was certainly plenty of noise, but had Grey carried the House?

He had the Conservatives cheering. That was to be expected. Quite astonishingly he had with him the bulk of the eighty-strong Irish Nationalists. There was no protest from their benches. On the contrary there was some frantic enthusiasm.

The Irish reaction did not take Sir Edward completely by surprise. His speech called Ireland 'the one bright spot'. Something was happening.

Now came mention of the Expeditionary Force. Were Britain and Germany really about to fight each other in battle, as in the novels? Grey's words were guarded:

> We must take very carefully into consideration the use which we make of sending an Expeditionary Force out of the country until we know how we stand.

He cautioned that the mobile force might be needed in the Empire.

The presumption had to be that, whether the Expeditionary Force went or not, Britain's chief role would be naval – use of the Fleet to safeguard Britain and France and, if the war were an extended one, to blockade Germany, while France and Russia bore the brunt of the land war.[15]

Grey moved towards his peroration:

If we [said] . . . 'We will have nothing whatever to do with this matter' under no conditions – the Belgian Treaty obligations, the possible position in the Mediterranean, with damage to British interests, and what may happen to France from our failure to support France – if we were to say that all these things mattered nothing, were as nothing, and to say we would stand aside, we should, I believe, sacrifice our respect and good name and reputation before the world, and we should not escape the most serious and grave economic consequences.

Then came clear indication that British involvement in this war would be likely to involve more than merely the Fleet patrolling the Channel:

We know, if the facts be all as I have stated them, though I have announced no intending aggressive action on our part, no final decision to resort to force at a moment's notice, until we know the whole of the case, that the use of it may be forced upon us.

The reporter of the *Westminster Gazette* recorded that 'at this the enthusiasm of the Unionist [Conservative] Party knew no bounds'.

Behind Grey, Charles Trevelyan was listening with increasing dismay. In his Personal Record he wrote:

I was prepared for bad news but not for the bare-faced appeal to passion. He gave not a single argument why we should support France. But he showed us he had all along been leading her to expect our support and appealed to us as bound in honour. However I want to record here that the Liberals, very few of them, cheered at all, whatever they did later, while the Tories shouted with delight.[16]

Another Liberal reaction came from Arnold Rowntree, who scribbled a pencil note for his wife Mary. He described developments as 'as grave as they could be' and predicted that the country would be at war in 'a very few hours'. He admitted that the speech of the Foreign Secretary had had a big effect, but said that, 'it is really a daunting indictment of the Balance of Power'. This, he called 'Grey's pet policy'.[17]

As the Foreign Secretary sat down, 'the pro-war storm broke', as Francis Neilson put it:

> The great demonstration that was made by the Opposition
> infected loyal supporters of the Cabinet and, perhaps three
> parts of the House were in the mood for Mafeking.[18]

'Mafeking' refers to the wild crowd demonstrations (sometimes
called 'maffiking') in London in 1900 which greeted news of the relief of
the Boer War siege. Parliamentary rules were swept aside. There was loud
applause in the public galleries, which was normally strictly forbidden,
as presumably was foot stamping in the chamber and jumping on the
benches. Commons etiquette was suspended on this afternoon. Francis
Neilson's worked-out premonition was confirmed.[19]

But what about the quarter of the House, which was *not* 'in the
mood for Mafeking'? The Parliamentary reporter of the *Northampton
Daily Echo* was watching MPs' reactions carefully:

> The Labour Party and the majority of the Government's
> supporters only indulged in faint cheers when some gleam
> of hope of England's neutrality seemed to brighten the dark
> horizon, but the Tories and – very significant this – most of the
> Irish Party hailed with delight and frantic cheers every sentence
> which seemed to point to the ultimate resort to arms.[20]

The private secretary of Sir Arthur Nicolson, Lord Onslow, was at
the Commons. On his return to the Foreign Office his report to his
superior was emphatic: 'He has had a tremendous success, sir. The whole
House was with him.' The reception was of critical importance: if the
speech had not caught the ear of the House, that would have been the
end of the Government's intention for war entry since there would not
have been the necessary confidence that the House would vote supplies.
But how could Onslow make the statement that the *whole* House was
with Grey? The reason is that there *were* some Liberals who cheered
the Foreign Secretary, not many, but enough for claims of cross-party
support for war. The pro-war Liberals were sitting above the gangway
behind the ministers. There was a reference to them in an exchange in
the chamber during the evening between two Liberals, Annan Bryce, a
neutralist, who was MP for Inverness, and Sir Charles Henry, a pro-war
Shropshire Member. Bryce had been standing at the Bar of the House
(the edge of the chamber) and assessing how much support the Foreign
Secretary had. His view was:

Arthur Ponsonby, aged about eight.

Arthur Ponsonby, *c.* 1900.

Arthur Ponsonby's home, Shulbrede Priory, Sussex, from his own drawing, 1919.

Top left: Arthur Ponsonby as prospective Liberal candidate at Taunton, 1904.

Left: Arthur Ponsonby (right) as Private Secretary to Prime Minister Sir Henry Campbell-Bannerman, *c.* 1907.

Labour MPs on the Terrace of the House of Commons, 1909.
Front row, third right is Keir Hardie; second row, far right is Philip Snowden;
second row, third right is Ramsay Macdonald. Dolly Ponsonby has entitled this picture:
'Labour Members & A. P'. (Arthur Ponsonby must be one of the background
figures to the right.)

Engagement photograph of Charles and Molly Trevelyan, 1903.

Charles and Molly Trevelyan and their children, 1910.

Arthur Ponsonby, *c.* 1908, at the start of his parliamentary career.

IN THE ALMOST CERTAIN PROSPECT OF A STORMY SESSION, WHY NOT ADOPT THE "TERRACE" SYSTEM AS NOW USED AT THE ZOO?

Above: A *Punch* view of the House of Commons as a zoo (4 March 1914). If one discounts the zoo 'terrace' joke, one may see the layout of the chamber, with the be-wigged and bearded Speaker James Lowther presiding; above the gangway, on the left of the drawing Prime Minister H. H. Asquith is on his feet on the Government front bench; headgear is top hats except for on the front two benches below the gangway on the left of the picture, where the varied hats of Labour Members may be seen.

WASTED LAVA.

Mr. Ramsay Macdona'd in full eruption, tearing passion to tatters with his accustomed transpontine vehemence, was bl'ssfully unconscious of the effect of his oratory on Mr. Joseph King, of North Somerset.

Right: Punch's view of Joseph King dozing in the House of Commons behind an orating Ramsay MacDonald (16 March 1910).

Thomas Edmund Harvey.

Arnold Rowntree.

Richard Denman, as an artillery officer, 1917.

Sir Hubert Parry on his boat *The Wanderer*.

Keir Hardie speaking at the 2 August 1914 Labour peace rally in Trafalgar Square.

Philip Morrell, 1910.

Robert Leonard Outhwaite, *c.* 1912.

Above: Artist's impression of Sir Edward Grey speaking in the House of Commons on 3 August 1914.

NO THOROUGHFARE

BRAVO, BELGIUM!

Right: Punch cartoon of 12 August 1914.

Those who sit in the high places cast the people into the pit

1915

Above: Leonard Outhwaite's view of the war in his 1915 *Ghosts of the Slain.*

Top left: Crowds outside the Houses of Parliament awaiting news on 4 August 1914.

Left: Crowds in Trafalgar Square greeting the declaration of war on 4 August 1914.

Above: Dolly Ponsonby.

Top left: Ramsay MacDonald at Shulbrede Priory, 1915.

Left: Shulbrede Priory, July 1915. (Left to right: Sir Hubert Parry, Arthur Ponsonby, Lady Maud Parry, Matthew Ponsonby.)

A FIRM CHIN IN ANNIE'S DEFENCE.
COMMANDER WEDGWOOD.

Left: Punch depiction of Josiah Wedgwood speaking in the House of Commons in support of Indian Home Rule campaigner Annie Besant, 4 July 1917.

Right: Stoke-on-Trent area newspaper advertisement for Government candidates in the 1918 General Election.

Below right: The Trevelyan family, 1919: Charles and Molly are back row, right; George middle back row; George Otto middle left.

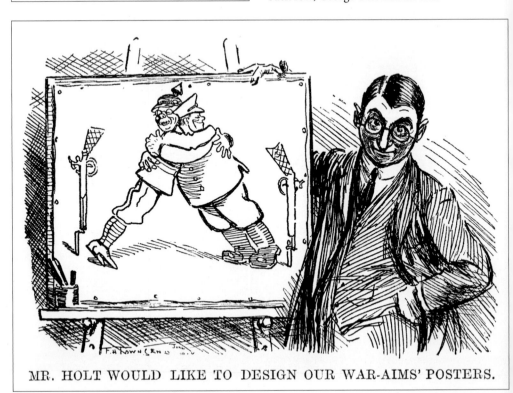

MR. HOLT WOULD LIKE TO DESIGN OUR WAR-AIMS' POSTERS.

Punch's view of Richard Holt's request for an exhibition in the House of Commons Tea-Room of Government war aims posters so that Members might see their 'disgraceful character' (12 June 1918).

Why YOU should Vote for the Lloyd George Candidates

Because they will Vote to
HANG THE KAISER,
Keep out the Germans, and
Prevent any more Dumping.

To Support Mr. LLOYD GEORGE.
BURSLEM Electors should Vote as under:—

ESSEX	...	...	...	...
FINNEY	...	...	...	...
WALKER				**X**

Your decision NOW affects the future of the whole British Empire in years to come. There never was a greater responsibility placed on voters to select the RIGHT Representatives. By giving YOUR vote to the Official Coalition Candidates you are supporting no particular party — but ONE GREAT UNIFIED GOVERNMENT, who have sunk Party Politics in the interest of the Nation.

To Support Mr. LLOYD GEORGE.
HANLEY Electors should Vote as under:—

GRIMWADE	...	...	...	...
OUTHWAITE	...	...	...	...
PARKER	...	...	...	...
SEDDON				**X**

To Elect **WALKER** for **BURSLEM**,   To Elect **SEDDON** for **HANLEY**,

Put YOUR Cross opposite the BOTTOM Name on the Card.

1919.

Bob   Rossie G.O.T. Kitty   George Marjorie Humphry   Janet Florence Julian   C.T.   Molly   Charles

Mary   George   Pauline

Arthur Ponsonby at his Foreign Office desk, 1924.

1930s sketch by Arthur Ponsonby of his left-wing politician old self saying to his royal page of honour young self (centre): 'Pause, child! Reflect!'

I believe the great body of opinion in this country is for maintaining our neutrality in this war, and the striking evidence of that was that during the whole course of the speech of the Foreign Minister this afternoon there was not one single cheer from this side of the House. The whole of the cheering came from the other side.

This produced a retort from Henry:

I hope no such statement as that will be made. I sat in that part of the House and the Foreign Secretary was cheered time after time. Honourable Members above the gangway were in complete sympathy with him.[21]

This drew Liberal shouts of 'Withdraw!'

The fact the there was *some* Liberal support for Grey is indicated in the diary of Leo Amery, who comments that, '[Grey] was received by his own party very much better than apparently the Government expected . . .' There had probably been fears in the Government that the revelation of the military understanding with France, and Grey's bid for British participation in the European war based on this, would cause uproar on the Liberal backbenches. It did not, thanks to the Foreign Secretary's skill in presentation, which kept the lid on the Radical quarter of the House, but this did not mean that rank and file Liberals liked it. This would be made clear later in the day.[22]

Among those unimpressed with the Foreign Secretary's statement was John Burns. Writing his diary, he predicted 'misery and depression when excitement dies'. He said that he had been 'in no way influenced' by what happened.[23]

What about the Labour MPs? The *Northampton Daily Echo* commentary puts the two Labour benches with the Liberals in the category of the unhappy. But there were some signs of a shift. Herbert Samuel, the Local Government Minster, writing to his wife Beatrice, considered the Labour Party to be 'about equally divided'.

Samuel's comment on the speech is revealing: 'Grey has made his able statement. But too much France and not enough Belgium and Channel in it to please me.'[24]

Samuel was one of those whose conscience was eased by the fact that defence of Belgium, a chivalrous and principled cause, was going to be a part of the Government's *casus belli*. But Grey's speech was mostly about the understanding with France and Britain's national interests. A. J. P. Taylor's *The Troublemakers* also picks up that Grey's speech had 'little about Belgium compared with the general argument in regard to France'. He thought that the speech caused the Radicals to respond to 'the old call of the liberal alliance', that is to say with France. But this is to assume that the 'troublemakers' were among those cheering Grey. They were not. Most of the Radicals, as would be shown later in the day, remained unconverted. Taylor's analysis is that it was a stroke of luck for Grey that no imperialist issue was involved – no mention of Morocco or Persia. But in fact the Commons would hear anti-war protests invoking Persia from the Radical quarter of the House before the end of the day.[25]

The Foreign Secretary's speech had confirmed the worst fears on the backbenches of his own party and in the Labour Party about secret military understandings with France. Backbenchers were not able to reply to Grey. All that was scheduled was a response from each of the party leaders.

War was not yet declared. Sir Edward had stressed that 'no final decision' had been taken. Whether Britain would go in would presumably depend on events. And it also depended on the support of the chief parties in Parliament. Grey was assumed to speak for his own Liberal Party. In reality he was much more the voice of the Opposition Conservatives. There was no such thing as a Leader of the Radical Liberals: there would be no speech by Arthur Ponsonby or anyone else on behalf of that part of the House. There would just be the statements by the Conservative, Irish Nationalist and Labour leaders.

With the leader statements about to start Charles Trevelyan made a quick dash out of the chamber to get the news out to his waiting companions: 'I went down to poor George and Morel, taking with me my notes of Grey's speech. I said something to the effect that I thought it was war.'[26]

Trevelyan missed Andrew Bonar Law's speech. The reason was that Law was on his feet for less than five minutes. The Conservative leadership wanted Britain in the war and it was going to happen. Probably some of the Conservatives who cheered Grey were cheering the decision to go to war rather than the line of the Foreign Secretary's speech. Leo Amery wrote in his diary:

As an effort at persuading his own party to move along, it was very adroit. As a statement of British policy on the eve of a great war, it seemed to me narrow and uninspiring . . .[27]

Bonar Law's speech is not mentioned by Amery. It was measured, but there was a chilling note when he spoke of the 'contingencies which [Grey] has not put into words but which are all in our minds as possible'. MPs could picture fleets, armies and bloodshed. Law promised Conservative support for whatever steps were necessary 'for the honour and security of this country'. He spoke 'amid an unceasing uproar of cheering', J. R. Clynes's memoirs recall. The cheers were not coming from the Government backbenches.[28]

Trevelyan was back in time for John Redmond's speech on behalf of the Irish Nationalists. Drama was anticipated. There was some expectation that politics was about to be turned on its head.

The Irish Nationalists were not known as enthusiasts for Britain's wars. During the Boer War their sympathies had been with the Boers. The settlers were seen as a small nation like Ireland striving for independent statehood. The present Member for West Clare, Arthur Lynch, had raised 'The Second Irish Brigade' for the Boers and was given the rank of colonel. After the war he had been convicted of treason and sentenced to death. He was reprieved and later pardoned. Irish Nationalist support for a British war might seem improbable in the extreme. But the reactions on the Irish benches, including from Lynch, while Grey was speaking suggested that this was what was going to happen. What would John Redmond say? There was more suspense.

The image of Redmond, as he rose at the top of the gangway, was indelible for Irish Nationalist MP Stephen Gwynn: 'the erect, solid figure with the massive hawk-visaged head thrown back, standing squarely'.[29]

The House gazed up. Redmond spoke with his accustomed emphasis:

I say to the Government that they may tomorrow withdraw every one of their troops from Ireland. I say that the coast of Ireland will be defended by her armed sons, and for this purpose armed Nationalist Catholics in the South will be only too glad to join arms with the armed Protestant Ulstermen in the North. Is it too much to hope that out of this situation there may spring a result which will be good not merely for the Empire, but good for the future welfare and integrity of the Irish nation?[30]

The reception was a sensation. Gwynn recalled Conservative MPs sitting around him uttering 'ejaculations of bewilderment, approval and delight', while the Conservatives behind the Opposition Front Benches were waving their Order Papers. When Redmond sat down many of the Tories stood up to cheer him.

Among the Liberals below the gangway on the other side of the chamber there was no rapture. Llewelyn Williams, a lawyer who sat for Carmarthen, wrote in his diary a week later:

> John Redmond on Monday delivered himself of some transparent flapdoodle. He told the Government they could take every British soldier from Ireland, and the Irish would themselves guard their own coasts. The Tories cheered themselves hoarse, and some of them had tears in their eyes.[31]

The Irish Nationalist turnaround was jaw-dropping. How had the Irish Party, implacable opponents of the British establishment, suddenly become supporters of it in the interests of war? It came about because there was a new narrative. According to this, Ireland was in the same boat with Belgium: two countries each trying to assert their nationhood. The rescue of Belgium from Prussian tyranny by a grand alliance including Ireland would give a boost to Ireland's own claims. There is also the fact that Belgium was one of the most Catholic countries in Europe. *Whitaker's Almanack* for 1914 states that 'nearly all the inhabitants are at least nominally Catholics'. Belgium and Ireland could be viewed as comrade nations. At the end of the war, the 'integrity', to use Redmond's word, of Ireland would be secure – that could mean Home Rule with no Ulster opt-out.[32]

Charles Trevelyan did not blame Redmond's opportunism. He wrote: 'Why indeed should he not use his splendid political opportunity? Let Ireland live while our best hopes die for other causes.'[33]

The Irish Nationalists and Conservatives who cheered together had very different visions. Both did indeed see war as a requirement of the nation, but it was not the same nation. John Redmond's party saw war against Germany as a just cause but secondary to the establishment of Ireland's nation status. Ireland's support for Belgium would give it a place in its own right at the peace conference and clinch Home Rule on the terms which the Nationalists wanted. But for the Conservatives who cheered Redmond, while the Irish Nationalist leader's speech was certainly welcome, very much so – and those who cheered were genuinely moved – the Irish would be kept in their place. There was no visualisation of Ireland and Belgium as two small nations equally deserving of independence. Backbench Liberal scepticism of the new Irish/Conservative alliance had ample justification.

Eyes now swung down to the Labour benches as the last of the scheduled quartet of speakers rose.

The ordeal facing Ramsay MacDonald as Labour spokesman on this day was formidable indeed. His seat was at the end of the front Labour bench below the gangway, which put him close to the focal point of the packed House. MacDonald was a consummate orator who beguiled Labour audiences, but he was always afflicted by nerves when he was due to speak in the Commons. In his diary on another occasion he mentions the 'usual tortures at the prospect of speaking'. Today it was worse than just daunting. And now as he stood up there was an ostentatious march to the exits by a number of Members.[34]

He opened on safe ground. He disavowed wanting to speak at all. He promised to be brief. He praised the Foreign Secretary's speech:

> The right honourable gentleman, to a House which in a great majority is with him, has delivered a speech the echoes of which will go down in history . . . The speech has been impressive, but however much we may resist the conclusion to which he has come, we have not been able to resist the moving character of his appeal.[35]

'We' must refer to the Labour Party sitting alongside him. But was the Labour Chairman still able to speak for his party after Grey's speech?

MacDonald had not risen to join in with the cheers for Grey. He went on:

> I think he is wrong. I think the Government which he represents and for which he speaks is wrong. I think the verdict of history will be that they are wrong. We shall see . . .

This was emphatic, but there was a qualification:

I want to say to this House, and to say it without equivocation, if the right honourable Gentleman had come here today and told us that our country is in danger, I do not care what party he appealed to, or to what class he appealed, we would be with him and behind him. If this is so, we will vote him what money he wants. Yes and we will go further. We will offer him ourselves if the country is in danger.

MacDonald continued:

He has not persuaded me that it is [in danger]. He has not persuaded my honourable Friends who cooperate with me that it is, and I am perfectly certain, when his speech gets into cold print tomorrow, he will not persuade a large section of the country.

'My honourable friends who cooperate with me' is a rather curious phrase, if it is MacDonald's own party. It looks like a reference to Liberal backbenchers, especially in view of what was to follow. The 'when it gets into cold print' rebuke about the emotional effusions in Grey's speech was pointed.

Then MacDonald turned to the Foreign Secretary's appeal to honour:

There has been no crime committed by statesmen without appealing to their nation's honour. We fought the Crimean War because of our honour. We rushed to South Africa because of our honour . . .

He moved on to Belgium:

What is the use of coming to the aid of Belgium, when, as a matter of fact, you are engaging in a whole European War which is not going to leave the map of Europe in the position it is now?

MacDonald was here exposing a key flaw in the Belgium justification for the war. It was all very well talking about justice for Belgium but that country was part of a much wider canvas of war. The prediction here about changes in the map was understated. The war and its consequences would spread far beyond Europe.

The Labour Leader next raised the issue of Russia:

The right honourable gentleman said nothing about Russia. We want to try to find out what is going to happen, when it is all over, to the power of Russia in Europe.

Surprisingly MacDonald did not exploit the huge fallacy in the just war argument of having as an ally Tsarist Russia, which as well as its internal repressions had scant regard for the integrity of other nations. He did not spend long on Russia. Instead he turned to the question of France:

Finally, so far as France is concerned, we say solemnly and definitely that no such friendship as the right honourable gentleman describes between one nation and another could ever justify one of those nations entering into war on behalf of the other. If France is really in danger, if, as the result of this, we are going to have the power, civilisation, and genius of France removed from European history, then let him so say. But it is an absolutely impossible conception.

MacDonald conceded that the feeling of the House was against those who wanted Britain to keep out of the war. He foresaw Labour coming under attack for its opposition, as in the days of the Boer War:

I have been through this before, and 1906 came as part recompense. It will come again. We will go through it all. So far as we are concerned, whatever may happen, whatever may be said about us, whatever attacks may be made upon us, we will take the action that we will take of saying that this country ought to have remained neutral, because in the deepest parts of our hearts we believe that that was right and that that alone was consistent with the honour of the country and the traditions of the party that are now in office.

The 1906 reference chimes with MacDonald's remark the previous day to Percy Illingworth. He was anticipating that the war would be popular at first, like the Boer War, but would be followed in due course by disillusion. This happened when British military successes in 1900 were followed not by an early victorious conclusion but by the guerrilla tactics of the Boers which prolonged the war until 1902. There had been electoral success for the Conservatives in the 1900 'Khaki Election', held on the crest of a military wave, but in the next General Election in 1906 things turned round: there was a Liberal landslide, in which Labour also did well.

The mention of 'the traditions of the party that are now in office' looks like a bid for the support of dissident Liberals in an anti-war coalition. MacDonald was reminding Liberals that Sir Edward Grey was inviting them to discard their party's basic principles. For the Labour Leader, personal unpopularity as a result of opposition to a national crusade would be anything but welcome but the calculation was that this would only be temporary. Politically there would be dividends in the longer term.[36]

And so the statements ended. The shock and indignation felt by some MPs had no outlet. Or so it seemed. But one MP was going to try. Philip Morrell, sitting below the gangway, rose to try to catch the Speaker's eye. At 6 foot 3 he was not inconspicuous.

Hansard records it:

> MR MORRELL: I listened to the speech of the right honourable gentleman – [Interruption.]
>
> MR STANLEY WILSON [Conservative]: On a point of Order. Is there any Motion before the House?
>
> MR SPEAKER: There is no motion before the House. If the House shows any disposition to discuss the situation as it has been developed this afternoon – HON. MEMBERS: NO! No! – the House will remember that we have to meet again in order to receive the Royal Assent to the [Moratorium] Bill that has just passed. I think I shall meet the general convenience of the House if I left the Chair until the Royal Commission is received.
>
> MR WEDGWOOD: Something more behind our backs!
>
> MR SPEAKER: Perhaps the best course will be for me to leave the Chair now.
>
> MR MORRELL: ... We on these Benches ... wish to have an opportunity – an early opportunity – of expressing ourselves with regard to the proposed intervention of this country in the European war. I therefore wish to ask you –

THE PRIME MINISTER: Certainly, Sir, the House will have an early opportunity.

HON. MEMBERS: Today?

THE PRIME MINISTER: No.[37]

So there was to be no accountability to Parliament at large on the Government's decision for war. The country might be in the war by the time Parliament debated it. Philip Morrell would not sit down. The exchange went on, with angry shouts raining on the Burnley MP.

Philip was watched intently by his wife in the Ladies' Gallery. Ottoline recorded in her memoirs her husband protesting 'splendidly and courageously'. To the disgust of many, Morrell's persistence brought success. The Speaker granted an adjournment debate to allow backbenchers to make their comments. This was to follow several hours later. It was Ottoline's view that without Philip's intervention, 'there would have been no debate on the question of England joining in the war'. Where did he find the courage from to get up on such a day? Was this one of his 'wild' moments? Certainly no one with any normal sense of self-preservation would have dared to take on the House of Commons when it was worked up in this state. Wherever it came from, Morrell performed a memorable service by repairing what would have been a gaping democratic gap. The arguments against British entry into the war would now be heard by the House of Commons.[38]

Charles Trevelyan found time to scribble a note to Molly to say, 'I am going to resign as soon as I can get at the Prime Minister.' He added that his brother and E. D. Morel approved of his decision.[39]

So ended this part of the day of decision. A year later Leonard Outhwaite, speaking in the House of Commons, would describe it as 'the fatal afternoon'.[40]

10

'The House that Jack Built'

Monday Evening, 3 August 1914

───────────

FRANCIS NEILSON HAD BEEN TOLD by someone that a meeting of MPs opposed to the policy of the Foreign Secretary was to be held in a committee room. This was the second meeting of the day of Arthur Ponsonby's committee. Neilson doubted whether it would attract more than about half a dozen, since it was too late for opposition to be effective. To his surprise, when he went into the room he found that fifteen or twenty MPs had already arrived. More came in, just ones and twos at first; then the arrivals increased. Evidently this room had become the focus of opposition to British war entry.[1]

But there were no Labour MPs. Leonard Outhwaite remarked, 'Not a single Labour Member!' and someone else added sarcastically, 'Where are our great representatives of the working classes who believe in peace?' But they spoke too soon. Into the room walked the Labour Leader. Neilson recalled Outhwaite's reaction: he 'stammered in amazement, 'Ramsay MacDonald!'[2]

MacDonald was later joined by Labour's Secretary, Arthur Henderson.

The committee decided to issue a statement. After the events downstairs in the chamber, it was not going to be easy to get one decided and supported. The effect of the Foreign Secretary's speech on some of the Members was evident. Arthur Ponsonby told his wife that, 'I had great trouble in getting a resolution passed: it took more than an hour.'

What was said? The lack of minutes leaves us largely guessing. However, among Ponsonby's papers are the resolution and the voting figures:

> After hearing Sir Edward Grey's statement this meeting is of the opinion no sufficient reason exists in the present circumstances

for Great Britain intervening in the war and most strongly urges His Majesty's Government to continue negotiations with Germany with a view to maintaining our neutrality. This was passed by nineteen votes to five, with three abstentions.[3]

The *Daily News* has the detail that an amendment making the violation of Belgium grounds for war was defeated only by sixteen votes to thirteen.[4]

At the meeting was Christopher Addison. He voted against Arthur Ponsonby's motion. Addison's account, written up a month later, is confused. He thought that the vote on the war was on the previous Friday and that the Monday meeting was about relief of home distress and 'crushing of Kaiserism'. The avalanche of events which followed (including Addison joining the Government) will have had something to do with the considerable garbling of memory. But Addison's account does have pieces of information which help to reconstruct this meeting. It mentions that it was large and that most of those present did not vote. Taking those who did vote, therefore, as a minority of the attendance we have over sixty, perhaps well over sixty, as the eventual attendance. There were clearly plenty who did not yet see British war entry as a done deal. There were also the Labour's MPs, mostly not here but whose leader had spoken against Grey's proposal.[5]

The presence of Ramsay MacDonald and Arthur Henderson confirmed the hints which MacDonald had been dropping about a new political alliance. This meeting would prove to contain the first seed of the movement which became the Union of Democratic Control.

Arthur Ponsonby's letter to his wife continues his account of the day: 'I was then torn to pieces by people who wanted to see me and finally had a few moments on the terrace with Massingham and a few others.'[6] The terrace, a strolling and sitting area for MPs and their guests, overlooked the river. Then there was just time to eat: '. . . a very hurried early dinner which I could not pay for as I only have 1/6 [one shilling and sixpence] left'.

By the time MPs gathered for the evening debate the British Army had received mobilisation orders. Arthur Ponsonby reported to Dolly that the reassembled House was again 'crowded to the full and excited'.

The Prime Minister moved the formal motion for the adjournment debate and the Foreign Secretary gave an update on events. He had further news about the ultimatum given by Germany to Belgium at 7 p.m. the previous evening, with a twelve-hour limit, threatening in the case of refusal to treat Belgium as an enemy. Belgium, said Sir Edward, 'is firmly resolved to repel aggression by all possible means'.

Asquith and Grey soon disappeared. Apart from a brief appearance by Lloyd George, Cabinet ministers were nowhere to be seen. The debate was downgraded by the virtual boycott. The Government did not want off-message speeches getting publicity.

With the Conservatives watching closely but not making speeches, the floor was largely left to Liberal backbenchers. A viewer in the galleries, panning across the chamber, would have observed that from three-quarters of the assembly most of the time there was hardly anyone getting up to speak. But they would have seen in the Radical and Labour quarter a succession of MPs rising to make points about the Foreign Secretary's speech. Nearly all of these either rejected Grey's proposal for British intervention in the European war or called for further attempts at conciliation. It was not that the House had turned anti-war since the afternoon. War supporters wanted to get on with fighting Germany rather than making speeches to justify British participation, which seemed to have been secured. But it did mean that there was a significant minority opposed to Grey's call.

Just one MP in the Radical and Labour part of the House spoke in favour of British intervention in the war. William Pringle invoked Gladstone on the rights of small nations such as Belgium and argued that British entry into the war was required in order to uphold international law. The *Westminster Gazette*, leading its Liberal readers away from neutralism, noted that Pringle was speaking from below the gangway, which meant a breaking in the previously solid anti-war ranks of the Radicals.[7]

Pringle's speech influenced his friend Alexander MacCallum Scott. The Glasgow MP had not been convinced by Grey's speech. He was unmoved, as he wrote in his diary, by the argument of an obligation of honour to assist France and he thought that the Foreign Secretary's appeal to each man 'to look into his own heart' was 'sharp practice'. However, he said:

> I am impressed by Pringle's contention that the issue is which policy is to prevail in Europe, the policy of blood and iron alone

or the policy of enforcing international obligations. May we not
use this calamity to set up an international court of arbitration
in Europe. Will they try?[8]

Here was the start of rationalisation of the war as 'the war to end
wars', whereby nations with right on their side would employ their
might to defeat wrong and then use their triumph to install a civilised
way of ordering relations between nations in the future. The Pringle/
Scott view saw the war as international policing, bringing to book a
lawless rogue state.

Others below the gangway did not think much of Pringle's con-
version to war. They shouted 'Persia! Persia!' reminding the MP that
Britain's prospective ally in the war had broken international law by
its plundering of Persia. Russia was an unlikely Concert of Europe
policeman.

Several speeches on various issues implied support for war but only
two set out a case for it – Pringle's, and that of a Nottinghamshire Liberal
above the gangway. Sir Arthur Markham, who employed 25,000 people
in coal mines and iron foundries, conceded that he had always opposed
the Triple Entente, and predicted that the war would be unpopular, but
urged that Belgium must not be allowed to be overrun by Germany. He
compared the situation of the Belgians with that of the Boers.

The case against going to war was led by Philip Morrell. He looked
at the two reasons presented for intervention – protection of the
northern coasts of France and prevention of the passage of German
troops through Belgium. He argued that neither required Britain to go
in. On northern French coast defence Morrell reminded the House of
the German offer:

> With regard to the coast of France, he made it perfectly clear
> that the German Government had offered to this country, that
> if we would pledge ourselves to neutrality, Germany would
> undertake not to attack the northern coast of France. That was
> an undertaking which was cheered from this side of the House
> and which found a good deal of sympathy.[9]

He looked at the matter of German troops in Belgium:

> We are asked now to involve this country in all the perils of
> this great adventure because Germany is going to insist on

her right to march some troops – [Interruption] – because
Germany insists on her point of view. I am quite prepared
to admit that if Germany threatened to annex Belgium, or if
she disregarded the rights of nationality, we might be bound
under our treaty obligation to go to war to protect Belgium.
But what after all is the actual fact? What is it we are asked
to do? We are asked to go to war because there may be a few
German regiments in a corner of Belgian territory. I am not
prepared to support a Government which goes to war under
those circumstances.

The speech was interrupted by furious yells. Indeed the estimate that
German troops would be in just a corner of Belgian territory would
be very wide of the mark: the invasion would be wholesale. However,
Morrell was correct in saying that the international treaties were meant
to protect against any state attacking Belgium in order to subvert its
independence and that the treaties did not say that if a general European
war began with a particular country invading Belgium in order to get at
its enemy that should mean other countries joining in.

The Burnley MP was one of those who invoked John Bright:

I ask myself whether we have not in times past suffered enough,
paid enough treasure, and paid enough of the blood of the
subjects of this country in order to preserve what John Bright
once called that 'foul fetish – the balance of power in Europe'.

Bright, Liberal Member for Manchester, famous for his opposition
to the Crimean War, was quoted by a number of MPs in this debate.
The Speaker James Lowther, in his memoir account of this day, called
to mind Bright's speech on the eve of that war: 'when he spoke of the
Angel of Death and the fluttering of his wings – almost audible in the
House itself'.[10]

A succession of neutralist speeches followed Morrell. Richard
Denman challenged the argument of moral crusade for Belgium:

Does anyone really think that it is in the best interests of Belgium
to make it the cockpit of this Armageddon? To make Belgium
the scene of a vast European war is not in the best interests of
the country whose neutrality we wish to guarantee.

Denman then addressed his appeal personally to the Speaker, as a fellow Cumbrian MP. He invoked the history of the wars between the Scots and the English which plagued the border country in medieval times and suggested that, had the Speaker been living in those days, he would not have wanted his backyard to be a battlefield. Lowther was not moved: his autobiography describes the debate as 'discursive, desultory and deplorable'.[11]

Discursive it certainly was. But that was scarcely the fault of the MPs participating. This was an adjournment debate in which odds and ends like future Commons business arrangements were allowed to butt in, breaking the flow of arguments about the war.

But at least there was a chance for those who disagreed with the plunge to war to register their indignation. The war fervour came under examination from Sir William Byles:

> We saw here a remarkable scene. The House crowded at every corner, the galleries crowded and great eagerness on the part of Members. If one goes outside the House one sees the same excitement, because Europe is plunging into war, which I am afraid will far too soon become popular. We heard the shouts of exultation which came from the other side. It is not more than a dozen men in Europe that have brought this thing about, yet tens or hundreds of thousands of people in these four or five nations will be reduced to terrible misery. That is what men shout about with glee! It is not a war to defend our hearths and homes. It is to defend our honour. It is for honour that a German duellist fights his fellow officer. Whether he kills his opponent or is killed by him, honour is revenged. So it is to be now. We are to hire a number of men, a number of soldiers, to go and blow out the brains of another number of men – to vindicate our honour.[12]

The kind of 'honour' which was being invoked in Europe, as Avner Offer's study has shown, was based on the continental military code, especially the German one, inspired by the conventions of duelling. British honour evoked the rules of public school sport or proper business behaviour. Continental honour was about the throwing down and acceptance of challenges, and about prestige. It was to the European version of honour that MPs were being asked to subscribe. The French requirement for British war support was nothing to do with any moral cause. It was simply a matter of allies supporting each other on a point of honour, just as France was supporting Russia.[13]

The Salford MP was interrupted by a call of: 'Why do you not serve yourself?' Sir William had been the butt of Tory bloods before. He asked whether Britain would go to war if it were French troops violating the sovereignty of Belgium, continuing through interruptions:

> In my judgement it is the duty of the Government to defend its own people and look after their happiness and develop the arts of peace, and it is violating that duty to plunge the nation into war. There is no declaration and the House of Commons can stop it. There is still time. I am an old man and have been fighting for peace all my life. I implore [the Government] now not to lead the nation into disaster.

The likely effects of war were examined in a number of speeches. Leonard Outhwaite wondered how his Potteries constituency would fare: 'I go to my constituency tomorrow; there the factories are already closing down – for they do not make war with earthenware.'[14] Unemployment would indeed soar during the early months of the war. It was one of the reasons why so many men volunteered to join the Army.[15]

The Hanley MP examined the Foreign Secretary's speech. He saw demonization of Germany:

> All through his speech he seemed to be actuated by a veiled hostility to Germany. Germany was the enemy . . . Germany terrorising the world and eating up smaller states in military aggrandisement.

He went on:

> The right hon. Gentleman suppressed one great main factor. I do not think that during the whole of that speech he mentioned Russia . . . I do not see an all-conquering Germany as a result of this. I see a Germany crushed, and an all-conquering Russia. Power in the end in such a war as this rests with that nation which can bring its last hundreds of thousands to the slaughter, and it is Russia which can bring her peasantry last into the field.

Outhwaite then turned to the question of Belgium:

[Grey] talked of the neutrality of Belgium. While I can undoubtedly see a technical violation of the neutrality of Belgium
in the marching of troops through Belgium, that is very different
to the conquest of Belgium by force and the holding of Belgium
by force.

Outhwaite was one of those who pointed out the selective nature of
the argument that violation of Belgium by Germany required Britain to
enter the war. There had been no call for Britain to take on Russia when
Russia 'suppressed the integrity of Finland' or when Northern Persia
was 'overrun by Russian troops'. The Hanley MP described Russia as
'this semi-civilised, barbaric and brutal race'. A number of speeches
of war opponents had more than a tinge of Russophobia, but there was
real concern about the regime of Britain's prospective ally. The majority
of Russia's 164 million peasants had been in serfdom until only a
generation earlier. Russia was now industrialising. The Tsars, fearing
that this would lead to demands for further political reform, suppressed
dissent with some brutality. Russia had a degree of absolutism which
was alien to Western Europe.[16]

Outhwaite challenged the moral grounds for war:

I honestly hoped for a justification of the war from the Foreign
Secretary but I did not find it. I looked for some justification
from him for the shedding of blood, and for the casting on one
side of the moral obligations that I always thought greater than
any treaty obligations, but I did not get it. I recall the words of
John Bright: . . . 'I cannot believe that civilisation in its journey
towards the sun will enter endless night to gratify the ambition
of those men who seek to wade through slaughter to a throne
and shut the gates of mercy on mankind.'

The longest speech came from Joseph King. He was greeted by
hostile yells. He was perplexed about the lack of speeches in support of
British intervention in the war:

Although we have evidence of great numbers of supporters
of the Government backing them up – although we have the
whole of the official Opposition supporting the Government –
we have heard during the course of this debate, I think, only
one whole-hearted speech supporting the policy outlined by the

Foreign Secretary this afternoon. Why is it that the supporters of this policy have lost their voice? Are they afraid, or are they ashamed? Why is it that the Leader of the Opposition is not here now?[17]

He had a rough reception. There were shouts of 'Divide! Divide!' (that is, have a vote to end the debate). The MP taunted the Ulster Unionists with being desirous of fighting 'the most Protestant power on the continent of Europe', causing according to the *Westminster Gazette*, 'a slight sensation'.

The Somerset MP was another anti-war MP who examined the ally about whom the Foreign Secretary had been silent: 'If we are fighting for Russia at the present time, we are fighting for an amount of tyranny and injustice and cruelty which it is quite impossible to think of without the deepest indignation . . .' King pointed out that 100,000 people were in prison in Russia without trial and that executions in Russia under martial law were currently running at a thousand a year.

The speech brought an intervention from a Conservative, Sir John Rees:

> Is the hon. Member in order in accusing a friendly Power of atrocious tyrannical government? I believe it has been ruled that an hon. Member is not in order in using such language in regard to this particular Power.

For some MPs, Russia was a friendly power and that was that. Ethics did not come into it.

A regular critic of the Government's foreign policy, Josiah Wedgwood, delivered a warning about the Foreign Secretary's 'wonderful Jingo speech':

> Members must realise that this is not going to be one of the dear old-fashioned wars of the eighteenth century over again. This is going to be a war in which it is not going to be a question of feeding your armies, but of feeding the people left behind . . . Starvation is coming in this country and the people are not the docile serfs they were a hundred years ago. They are not going to put up with starvation. When it comes you will see something far more important than a European War – you will see a revolution.[18]

This followed the theory of Norman Angell that war between the nations of Europe would bring unemployment, starvation and economic ruin. Government committees had been deliberating for years about feeding the people in the event of war and the management of unemployment. Blockade had always been a part of war between maritime powers and in the case of industrialised societies starvation was a risk. The British Government later had a Ministry of Blockade, effective in creating food shortages in Germany, with a substantial number of German deaths by starvation at the end of the war attributed to it. And the German U-boat campaign brought critically serious food worries to Britain in 1917. Josiah Wedgwood was correct to link war with the risk of starvation.[19]

Arthur Ponsonby felt that Josiah Wedgwood's speech was 'too wild'. However, though revolution did not happen in Britain, it did come to Russia in 1917 and to parts of Germany and (briefly) to Hungary at the end of the war. As for Britain, had the German U-boat campaign succeeded in bringing starvation, who knows?[20]

Wedgwood reported in a family letter that he received 'oceans of letters' in support of his speech.[21]

Arthur Ponsonby was not going to make a speech. He had not had time to prepare. However, he was persuaded to speak by Philip Morrell. He told the Commons what he had witnessed on the streets:

> I cannot remain seated at what I feel to be the most tragic moment I have yet seen. We are on the eve of a great war, and I hate to see people embarking on it with a light heart. The war fever has already begun. I saw it last night when I walked through the streets. I saw bands of half-drunken youths waving flags, and I saw a group outside a great club in St James Street being encouraged by members of the club from the balcony. The war fever has begun, and that is what is called patriotism. I think we have plunged too quickly . . .[22]

He turned to the balance of power system:

> I think the Foreign Secretary's speech shows that what has been rankling all these years is a deep animosity against German ambitions. The balance of power is responsible for this – the mad desire to keep up an impossibility in Europe, to try to divide

the two sections of Europe into an armed camp, glaring at one
another with suspicion and hostility and hatred, and arming
all the time, and bleeding the people to pay for the armaments.

How fair was this? It could be said that 'the balance of terror' after
the Second World War between NATO and the Warsaw Pact in the
end did not result in a clash of nuclear weapons. But it nearly did, in
the Cuban Missile crisis of 1962. As Margaret MacMillan interestingly
mentions, US President John F. Kennedy, who resisted pressure from
his military to take action and instead started talks with the Soviet
Union, had just read Barbara Tuchman's *The Guns of August*, about
1914. In 1914, as events were showing, the balance of power in Europe
had demonstrably failed to prevent general war.

Ponsonby went on:

> I believe there is still a ray of hope. I regret the tone of the
> Foreign Secretary's speech. I felt it was in keeping with the
> scenes I had seen last night. But still he declared that not yet has
> the fatal step been taken. It is by this House of Commons that
> the decision must be taken, and however small a minority we
> may be who consider that we have abandoned our attitude of
> neutrality too soon . . . I think that in the country we have a very
> large body of opinion with us. I trust that, even though it may be
> late, the Foreign Secretary will use every endeavour to the very
> last moment, looking to the great central interests of humanity
> and civilisation, to keep this country in a state of peace.

The *Westminster Gazette* reported a hostile reaction to the speech
from MPs:

> Mr Ponsonby angered the House by attacking the tone of Sir
> Edward Grey's speech as bellicose and his appeal to the great
> central interests of humanity and civilisation rather lost their
> [*sic*] effect after this.[23]

Writing to his wife, Ponsonby described his reception:

> I had as I always do for some reason or other dead silence and
> rapt attention. I shot out half a dozen sentences amid protests
> and a few feeble cheers. My reference to Grey's speech was much
> resented but I genuinely felt it at the time.[24]

A stinging denunciation of the Government came from Liberal Percy Molteno, who represented Dumfriesshire. Molteno, a ship-owner and barrister of South African birth, was the son of Cape Colony's first Prime Minister. He was a supporter of African nationalism in South Africa and had been shocked by the white racist laws which were introduced in the Union of South Africa. He was one of the friends in the British Parliament of the new African National Congress. (But he was one of those for whom democracy stopped short of women's suffrage.) Molteno declared:

> No part of this country has been invaded at present; no vital interest in this country has been attacked. Yet we are asked to assent to war with all its terrible consequences ... This is a continuation of that old and disastrous system where a few men in charge of the state, wielding the whole force of the state, make secret engagements and secret arrangements, carefully veiled from the knowledge of the people who are as dumb driven cattle without a voice.[25]

The fact that the Government wanted to take the country into a great European war with all its perils when Britain was not under attack or threat of attack was an affront to some on the Liberal backbenches.

Molteno was one of the MPs who had suspected the now confirmed collusion between French and British military and diplomatic personnel and ministers about continental war. The fury expressed in this debate by Molteno and others about the subversion of democracy did not fade. More would be heard in the coming years about the abuse of executive power that had stitched Britain into what amounted to a war alliance.

There was one speech which resonated especially strongly. It came from Edmund Harvey. The Leeds MP called for a positive response to Germany's offer to keep its fleet out of the Channel if Britain stayed neutral. He protested that this war was not wanted by the people:

> I am convinced that this war, for the great masses of the countries of Europe, and not for our own country alone, is no people's war. It is a war that has been made – I am not referring to our leaders here – by men in high places, by diplomatists working in secret, by bureaucrats who are out of touch with the peoples of the world ... I want to make an appeal on behalf of

the people, who are voiceless except in this House, that there
should be a supreme effort made to save this terrible wreckage
of human life, that we may not make this further sacrifice upon
the altar of the terrible, blood-stained idol of the balance of
power, but should be willing to make great sacrifices of patience
in the sacred cause of peace.[26]

The MP called on Asquith and Grey to take the role of 'great mediators'.

Sitting nearby was Harvey's brother-in-law. Arnold Rowntree
scribbled a note to his wife on her brother's speech, calling it 'quite the
best speech made against the Government and excellently received'.
Rowntree in his own speech asked whether Britain should be fighting
against German civilisation:

> Do not let us forget that when we go to war against Germany
> we go to war against a people who hold largely the ideals which
> we hold. I do not mean the military element, but the German
> civilisation is in many ways near the British civilisation. We
> think of their literature, we think of what they have done for
> progressive religious thought, we think of what they have done
> for philosophy, and we say these are not the men we want to
> fight. I, as a very humble Member want, at any rate, to take this
> opportunity of saying that I for one will have nothing to do with
> this war.[27]

The affinities between British and Germans were deep. Sir Harry
Johnston's 1913 *Common Sense in Foreign Policy* goes as far as to say
that: 'England and the south east of Scotland constitute the oldest, the
most successful, and the most complete of German colonies beyond the
limit of Germany.'[28]

The historical ties-ups between the nations which Johnston lists
in considerable detail include the monarchy, use of German troops
by Britain and so on. One could add the kinship of the English and
German languages. In recent times there had been the attempted move
in the direction of a German alliance between 1898 and 1901 by the
Conservative Colonial Secretary Sir Joseph Chamberlain. There were a
hundred thousand Germans currently in Britain. Germans could enter
without a passport. The publicity for the Anglo-German exhibition at
the Crystal Palace in 1913 urged, 'Cousins should not be allowed to drift

apart.' The relationship went much deeper than the cousin monarchs heading the two nations. Efforts in the years before 1914 to try to forge an alliance or an understanding between Britain and Germany are strange only in the retrospect of a later history which could not be predicted.[29]

Any positive words about Germany, it might be thought, are refuted by the twentieth-century history of German aggression. It has been argued that Germany's move in 1914 was the culmination of a long-prepared bid for domination of Europe. The real history was much messier. German aggressive military planning was certainly there. It related to fear that the balance of power would turn against it as Russia's strength grew in alliance with France, leaving Germany hemmed in and weakened. General Helmuth von Moltke was of the view that war against the Triple Entente was sure to break out not much later than 1916 or 1917 and that Germany would be beaten unless it launched an immediate preventative attack. It was military theory, but in 1914 a chain of events ran out of control.[30]

What about the Kaiser? Wilhelm II was an unbalanced ruler, notorious for his ranting call to German soldiers setting off to put down the Boxer Rebellion in China in 1900, to be like the Huns of history: 'anyone who falls into your hands falls to your sword'. Some German troops did behave very badly, but the Russian and the French allies of the Germans were also very bloodthirsty. It was an ugly patch of history which threw into question the civilised values of Europeans generally. There was of course Kitchener at Omdurman and in South Africa. The anti-war MPs in this debate hated European aggression and shared common cause with like-minded people in Germany and elsewhere who had been trying to promote a more humane approach.[31]

Then there is the special argument that the genocide committed by Germany in South-West Africa in its colonial war of 1904–8 was a precursor of Nazi history. This is misconceived. Genocide in various forms featured shockingly in the colonial expansion across the world of the European races, who considered themselves superior to others. In recent years there had been the genocide and slavery perpetrated by the agents of Belgium's King Leopold in the Congo. Atrocities were not some sort of racial or national speciality of Germans, though Germans were certainly among the Europeans who committed them. Naziism was a product of the First World War. Had the arguments of Arnold Rowntree and his allies been accepted and had Britain not expanded the war by joining it in 1914, the poison of Naziism would probably never have happened. Arnold Rowntree's defence of the better aspects of German culture as a reason for not going to war is not invalidated either by previous or subsequent history.[32]

Germany was actually a complicated mix. The Reichstag had been elected by universal male suffrage since 1912, a more democratic electorate than that of Britain. German science, scholarship and thought were admired in Britain and there was British progressive approval, Lloyd George included, of German advances in state welfare. There was, it is true, the German love of regimentation, exemplified in everything from pedantry in classification to an exaggerated respect for military rank. And there was the aggressiveness of the German military, and the great fuss which German society made of its army. Arnold Rowntree and his friends loathed this aspect. But it was just one side of German culture. There was plenty of Anglo-German cross-fertilisation. In 1913–14 the thirty-four German students, some of them Rhodes Scholars, who matriculated at Oxford made up the largest group of foreign students at the university. A letter from a group of British intellectuals published in *The Times* at the start of August 1914 praised Germany as 'a nation leading the way in Arts and Sciences'. Had the conflict of 1914 not become a prolonged world war, the twentieth-century history of Germany might been very different and Germany's progressive elements, rather than the unlovely ones which the First World War fostered, might have led that nation.[33]

Wails of woe from the Liberal backbenches were not going to quench the war steam on the Conservative and Irish Nationalist benches. The only chance would be an indication that the Labour movement was not going to deliver the manpower and the goods required for war. But where were the Labour speakers? Labour MPs seemed to have been struck by reticence, unless of course they were unluckily failing to catch the Speaker's eye. There was one exception. It was Keir Hardie.

The Merthyr MP took a class line on the war:

> Both Houses of Parliament have passed, with absolute unanimity, a bill for the relief of the Stock Exchange. We Members, from these benches, offered no objection, but we now demand to be informed what is going to be done for relief of the inevitable destitution which is bound to prevail among the poor? . . . We

are far more interested in the sufferings of the poor than we are in the inconvenience to members of the Stock Exchange. Most of the Members of this House have a more direct interest in the Stock Exchange than they have in the sufferings of the poor.

HON. MEMBERS: No! No! Shame! and Name! [calling on the Speaker to suspend the MP].

Arthur Ponsonby commented in his letter to Dolly that Hardie 'dwelt on a bad point'. It was not the best time for vintage class venom.
Hardie continued:

We belong to a party which is international. In Germany, in France, in Belgium, and in Austria, the party corresponding to our own is taking all manner of risks to promote and preserve peace... Some of us will do all we can to rouse the working classes of the country in opposition to this proposal of the Government.

The Merthyr MP voiced the complaint heard many times during this evening – the lack of democratic consultation:

The decision of the Government has been come to without consulting the country. It remains to be seen whether the Government and the House of Commons represent the country on this question. So far as some of us are concerned – here I do not speak for the party with which I am connected for the present moment but for myself personally – I shall endeavour to ascertain what is the real feeling of the country, in regard to the decision of the Government.[34]

The differentiation by Hardie of himself and his party suggests that already Labour's previously solid opposition to the war was falling away.
Mythology dies hard. One stubborn nugget of these days is that Labour MP Will Crooks led the Commons in singing the National Anthem. There was no such scene. It was on 18 September at the prorogation when Crooks got the Commons to their feet. That was a month and a half into the war.[35]
It was left to the Liberal backbenches to sustain the flow of the arguments for staying out. Sir John Jardine, Member for Roxburghshire, had observed the mixing of crisis-viewing and holiday recreation among the crowds: 'We are entering on this venture in somewhat the same

spirit as we might take part in a gorgeous parade or in a magnificent picnic at somebody else's expense.'[36]

Jardine had been acting Chief Justice in the Imperial government of India and Vice-Chancellor of Bombay University. His comment here is echoed by Keith Robbins, who describes popular reactions on streets across Europe in 1914 as like 'a fete involving a temporary suspension of social behaviour and an indulgence in unproductive expenditure'. Some of the aspects of military culture are listed by Douglas Newton: children's imperialist adventure stories, school textbooks, military-orientated youth movements, invasion novels and plays, military and imperial leagues, military pageants and 'the all-pervasive military and imperial themes in everyday advertising and public memorials'. This culture was resonating now. While Sir Edward Grey was making his speech, big columns of troops were marching by the Palace of Westminster and crowds cheering them could be heard in the House.[37]

Jardine remarked on the suddenness of what had been sprung on the Commons:

> It is only a few days since I returned from Scotland, and I can tell the House that there was not the least suspicion there that anything like this was going to be debated. Speeches in profusion on Irish Home Rule but not a single word said about the balance of power in Europe or about the fact that we were likely to be involved in war on that account.

Another Liberal Llewelyn Williams demanded to know:

> What is going to become of our social reform if we embark on this hideous carnage? I urge the Government in the name of common sense as well as humanity to stay their hand and to avert this terrible danger from our country.[38]

Annan Bryce saw the network of honour leading to carnage on a huge scale:

> We have the French joining the Russians on a point of honour and we are joining the French on a point of honour – a regular house that Jack built! We are being asked to undertake an enterprise which is going to lead to the loss of perhaps hundreds of thousands of lives.[39]

The prediction would prove to be an understatement. Over 700,000 British lives were lost.

The neutralists would have expected a speech from a Government minister replying to the debate and dealing with their points. But there was no one on the Government front bench to perform this role. Instead there was a remarkable occurrence which looks like a prefiguring of the history of the following years. From the Conservative front bench Arthur Balfour rose to wind up for the Government. At least that is what it amounted to.

Balfour presented no arguments on the war, but described the anti-war speakers as 'the dregs and lees of the debate'. His attitude was with Leo Amery, who recorded in his diary that, 'a string of the radical crank section aired their protests'.[40]

Was the Unionist (Conservative) Party guiding the destinies of the Empire as Balfour had once said that it always did? The ex-Prime Minister, nephew of Lord Salisbury, had taken over this debate and his blessing was on British participation in the war and his contempt was for those who spoke against it. The aristocracy, which had lost ground in the political struggle of recent years, was apparently back in charge tonight. Balfour, Conservative grandee par excellence, was the spokesman in this debate of the new emerging war establishment. The emotions of Britain's war would be Conservative ones. They would dominate the British twentieth century. They were, in Gerard DeGroot's analysis, 'nationalism, traditionalism and an enduring sense of cultural superiority'. On this night, as Britain prepared for entry into the European war, Peers versus People, and its Unionism versus Home Rule proxy, was set aside as the nation rallied behind its traditional rulers in the name of war. It was the same in Germany, where the challenge of the Social Democrats to the dominant classes now yielded to a military agenda.[41]

Arthur Balfour's call for the close of the debate was accepted by the Speaker. Balfour assured those who still wanted to speak that there would be 'a full opportunity for a debate upon a Vote of Credit'. This would be when the Government applied to borrow from Parliament the money which would be required in order to fight the war. But by then the issue would be determined. The democratic process such as it was, was over. It had been over before the start of this bits and pieces adjournment debate.

Arthur Ponsonby was not giving up. He was preparing for further debate. A declaration of war on Germany would require grounds for entry. Grey's remarks about Belgium suggested that it would be German violation of Belgian neutrality. Ponsonby now made some notes, putting together a detailed case against war entry with the Belgium *casus belli*.

He set out the perils which Britain would incur by entering such a war:

> Great Britain is to go to war if Germany does not withdraw from Belgian territory. That is the only Government decision as declared by Sir Edward Grey. It is plainly the only *casus belli* that any Government could find for joining in a quarrel in which England has no interest and no concern. But is it a *casus belli* for the sake of which the people of England are justified in risking the existence of the Empire and in increasing the magnitude of the greatest catastrophe in history? The answer is and must be an emphatic 'No'.[42]

Ponsonby was not an imperialist but he did not want to see Britain's empire lost to the Germans in a military adventure.

What about the treaties?

> The war cliques say that we are bound by Treaty and in honour to declare war on any Power that sends its troops into Belgian territory. It is a wild distortion of the truth. Britain has no obligation, legal or moral, to enter on a European war for such a course.

Ponsonby set out what it would mean. Britain would somehow have to put troops into Belgium to repel invading forces, 'either French or German'. Britain, while protecting Belgium, would need to keep out of the European war. Clearly this was impossible:

> No state is bound to attempt the impossible, and to incur the intolerable risks that attempt may involve ... Britain cannot by taking part in the war save Belgium from becoming the theatre of operations. She will indeed merely precipitate and incalculably magnify misfortunes, which there is a hope that Belgium may otherwise avoid.

Britain, argued Ponsonby, could keep out of the war and by so doing help Belgium:

> Britain can best save the independence of Belgium today, not by plunging into a general European war which she has no obligation to undertake, but by accepting the guarantee of Belgian integrity which Germany has offered. If Britain remains neutral, she will be strong enough at the conclusion of the war to insist that Germany lives up to her promise.

He concluded:

> If [Britain] enters on a General European war she will be risking her existence to achieve a doubtful result. She will in all probability only be completing the wreckage of that state system, to render stable a part of which was the main object of the guarantee to which the war party is now so unscrupulously appealing.

He was ready to argue the case but his hopes were not good. Sir Edward Grey's speech that afternoon had attached Britain firmly to the Armageddon train, which a week earlier Asquith had thought that Britain would observe as a spectator.

11

'More Like a Book by Conan Doyle'

Tuesday, 4 August 1914

TUESDAY DAWNED. Britain hung between peace and war. But there was a sense now that the decision was taken. An ultimatum from the British Government to Germany was expected.

The scrambled-together peace campaign was working hard as hopes dwindled. The Neutrality League attempted to address the British people directly. Newspaper readers blinked at advertisements of enormous size. The *Manchester Guardian* that morning was one of a number of papers which carried Neutrality League Announcement Number 2:

BRITONS DO YOUR DUTY
and keep your country out of
A WICKED AND STUPID WAR.
Small but powerful cliques are trying to rush you into it;
you must
DESTROY THE PLOT OR IT WILL BE TOO LATE . . .[1]

The argument looked at the consequences of a war in which Britain, France and Russia fought together: 'It would make the military Russian Empire of 160,000,000 the dominant Power of Europe. You know the kind of country Russia is.' The League also printed half a million leaflets entitled 'Shall We fight for a Russian Europe?'[2]

The advertisements addressed the issue of Belgium: 'Our treaties expressly stipulate that our obligations under them shall not compel us to take part in a general European war to fulfil them.'

The writers of the neutrality appeal called for branches of the trade unions, the ILP and the BSP to pass strong resolutions in favour of Britain keeping out of the war.

The Neutrality League and the Neutrality Committee continued to be disjointedly separate. The Neutrality Committee was working on a newspaper appeal of its own. This was drafted by Lord Courtney. He put his name to it at 10 a.m. It picked up the German offer for British neutrality. The Committee accepted the rejection of it by the Foreign Secretary as it stood but argued that there was room for negotiation: 'The neutrality of Belgium has up to the moment of writing not been infringed; the French coast has not been attacked.' The appeal urged:

> Press the Government, press the Foreign Secretary to exhaust the resources of diplomacy in developing the proposition of Germany, so that an agreement may be reached . . . and British neutrality preserved inviolate.[3]

To Sir Edward Grey, the development of Germany's proposition would have been shameful since it would have let down France. That was not how the neutralists saw it. Parliament and the public had not been a party to the military understanding with France to which the Foreign Secretary found himself morally committed.

Arthur Ponsonby meanwhile wrote to his wife:

> The fact remains there *is still no need for our going in.* Belgium neutrality and independence can be preserved without our fighting Germany. The news is no worse this morning. But the uproar and excitement makes one feel we shall be forced further. Some of us are conferring with the labour party today.[4]

The British news would not stay 'no worse' for long. Reports arrived that Germany had formally declared war on Belgium. But the peace campaign was not finished. The collaboration between Radicals and Labour had potential. It was essential that Labour versus Liberal rivalry should be set aside.

The International Arbitration League's Thomas Burt presided over a meeting. Its statement was a rebuttal of the Belgium as *casus belli* argument. While declaring that 'the only international interest worth defending is the neutrality of Belgium', it drew a sharp distinction between this cause and the Government's call for war:

> We may at any hour be at war simply because we belong to a
> certain group of Powers. In such a situation we are compelled to
> adhere to our declaration of absolute neutrality. Out of this welter
> of anarchy we must be kept. We therefore urge the Government
> to confine its efforts to the preservation of neutrality rights and
> to the use of the machinery of Hague Conventions or other like
> means for bringing about peace.[5]

'Welter of anarchy' would prove to be prophetic. 'Hague Conventions'
pointed to alternatives to war as means of redress. At The Hague, the
Permanent Court of Arbitration had settled a dozen cases. Could it
now settle the dispute between Austria and Serbia? For the states of
Europe now to ignore the international procedures of conciliation and
arbitration in favour of old-fashioned, brute force was to set the world
back a long way. The problem was that the Arbitration Court depended
on the willingness of nations to bring cases before it. The Kaiser, while
not opposing it, had jeeringly declared, 'I shall appeal only to God
and my sharp sword.' The Hague Peace Palace was built of materials
from all over the world. Germany provided the wrought-iron gates. In
this crisis Serbia, with Russia's support, had offered to take the points
of dispute to The Hague, but the offer had been refused by Austria.
The machinery was there but the necessary will on both sides to use it
was not.[6]

Sir Edward Grey had asked so far only for naval involvement in the
war, leaving the question of the Expeditionary Force hanging. Thomas
Burt in his statement predicted that the plan of naval aid to France was
'unlikely to stop there'.

Arnold Rowntree was at the Neutrality Committee in the morning,
breaking for the *Nation* lunch and then on to the House. He wrote to
his wife that he felt 'almost powerless' against the forces which were at
work and 'unutterably sad'. The problem, he said, was that 'the action
of Germany makes it much more difficult to keep even men of goodwill
straight'.[7]

At the *Nation* lunch, Rowntree will have found H. W. Massingham
back. Here was the place to check the Liberal pulse. When Bertrand
Russell approached Massingham with an offer of an article strongly
opposing British intervention, he found it accepted with alacrity. There
was no sign of the *Nation* weakening its neutralist stance.[8]

During the day Fritz Ponsonby was writing to his mother from Buckingham Palace:

> Really it is more like a book by Conan Doyle than real life, the whirl we live in now. The newspapers full of preparations for war and the crowds cheering and singing in the streets.[9]

Fritz was in a quandary as to whether to stay with the King or volunteer to go to the front, if possible on the staff, where his fluency with French and German would be helpful. The letter went on:

> I saw Johnny today. He appears quite ready for Battle. I thought Arthur's speech very feeble. He appears to have struck a jarring note when he said we were embarking on war with a light heart. Many Liberal Members objected to this and his remarks about the crowd and jingoism were hardly to the point.

Dolly Ponsonby was still with her parents at Rustington. Arthur's Monday letter had not yet reached her. During the morning she wrote:

> Darlingest. As I have not heard from you I wired – as I wanted so to hear how you were, and especially as I see you spoke and I am afraid you will be quite done up. It gets more and more awful – and now Sir E. Grey says we are to go in – I feel quite desperate. This being hampered by treaties at every turn seems to be the deuce, and we are to fight and bring our own country to perdition because of some lifeless and academic code of honour. Is it true about John Burns? If so how splendid of him – I shall write and congratulate him.[10]

The following day Molly Trevelyan wrote to her husband from Northumberland: 'I am so proud of what you have done, Charles, and so convinced you were right.'[11] She reported on their eight-year-old daughter who had recovered from a recent illness:

> She is rosy and her eyes bright and she is fully of pretty new ways. At the moment she is sitting up at the dining room table eating bread and butter: 'I think Daddy's quite right', and added, I'll be sending him a postcard to tell him so.'

Another daughter, who was six, had herself dictated a telegram. With the world closing in against dissent, family support was precious.

The *Manchester Guardian*'s headline today was 'Sir Edward Grey's Strange Blunder'. The paper's leader picked up Grey's comment about Britain suffering 'but little more' by going into the war than if it stood aside. The writer remarked on 'a strange ignorance of the working of trade' and that the Foreign Office was 'not remarkable for its commercial knowledge'.[12]

The *Daily News* was also still for Britain staying out. The paper had an *in memoriam* notice for Jean Jaurès:

> While all most sacred things and sweet
> Are trodden under jingo feet –
> He, being dead, yet lives and cries
> Against the bloodshed and the lies.[13]

The *Daily News* was not ready to join the jingo roar. But it was expecting the worst: 'if we are not yet at war with Germany, war is a matter of hours'.

The majority of the papers, including the Liberal *Daily Chronicle* and the Liberal *Westminster Gazette*, backed Grey. *The Times* was already writing up what would be the mythology of general support for Sir Edward Grey's call for war, its report informing readers that: 'The one weak voice of dissent which was heard served but as a foil to the general unanimity.'[14]

German troops crossed the Belgian frontier in the morning. News reached London about midday. In London the National Peace Council was setting out its position: The *Westminster Gazette* reported:

> The National Peace Council met under the chairmanship of Mr Gordon Harvey MP and placed on record its utter detestation of the renewed resort by the Powers of Europe to the barbarous arbitrament of war. It protests most strongly against the failure to reveal to the House of Commons and to the country the fact of the existence of conferences and conversations between the military and naval experts of England and France, which, in spite of the denial of engagements and obligations, has led the Government of this country into a definite undertaking to protect by armed force the northern and western coasts of France.[15]

The Council urged:

. . . that unceasing effort be made by the British Government to
limit the field of war, and to find opportunity for the restoration
of peace.

For Gordon Harvey, special difficulties lay ahead. If Britain did enter
the war, his textile works would be likely to have orders for khaki. It
would not be an easy time for a cloth manufacturing MP who detested
war. Harvey wrote to his agent in Rochdale, assessing that things were
'black indeed but not absolutely lost'. He wanted demonstrations and
petitions to limit Britain's involvement. He spoke hopefully of 'a great
movement which may become international'.[16]

The coming war was rearranging politics. The Government was
moving towards a political truce with the Conservatives. Meanwhile
the coming together of Labour and anti-war Liberals was taking serious
shape. A conference did take place. Arthur informed Dolly, in a letter
written the following day, that a joint meeting of anti-war Liberals and
Labour was held on this day and that it was presided over by Ramsay
MacDonald. This vastly intriguing event has left almost no record. It
probably took place between the *Nation* lunch and the mid-afternoon
start of parliamentary business, as intense expectation hung over
Westminster about whether the Government was about to declare war
on Germany.[17]

Ramsay MacDonald makes no mention of the meeting in his time-
delayed diary summary. Presumably it looked at possible arrangements
whereby Labour and anti-war Liberals could work together. This would
be the new politics presaged a week or so earlier by C. P. Scott. At any
other time it would have been a political sensation but it was barely
noticed. Currently most minds were on one thing: when was the British
declaration of war coming?

The Neutrality Committee was collecting names. About twenty Liberal
MPs signed its appeal during Tuesday. These included some who were
neither members of Arthur Ponsonby's committee nor among the MPs
who had spoken against British intervention on the previous evening.
With Labour, there could be the nucleus of an anti-war parliamentary
alliance which could make its voice heard. But the ground was shifting.
With the names there was a letter from Thomas Burt:

I could safely with confidence give my name to any suggestion
of yours bearing upon peace. As regards the enclosed appeal

> I am entirely in sympathy with you. But it seems that Germany has already invaded Belgium, and from day to day if not from hour to hour the situation is changing.[18]

From the President of the International Arbitration League this wavering was very bad news for the neutrality cause. The Belgium effect is well illustrated by Richard Holt's diary retrospective of the following Saturday. For the Hexham MP, the German violation of Belgian neutrality, which Britain had guaranteed, meant that, 'it seemed impossible for us to stand by'.[19]

Why was the Belgium issue so potent in the Liberal Party? The key factor was the way it was presented. It engaged irresistibly the emotions of fair play. And there was the Pringle/Scott view of entry into the war as imposing principled international control on lawless Germany. Richard Holt was one who took this line, though later he became disillusioned and campaigned for peace by negotiation. Of similar view was Charles Trevelyan's brother. Charles and George had always been close. Their differences on the war hurt both.

There were parallels for liberals across the belligerent zones of Europe, as liberals on the two sides of the great clash of the alliances found idealistic grounds for war. Support for war on the two sides was solidifying. The rapidly shrinking British remnant of those sticking to their anti-war principles was facing a tide of Canute proportions. But still British war was not yet declared and while there was peace there was hope.[20]

MPs assembled in mid-afternoon. If things went to plan soon there would be close cooperation between the Labour MPs and their below-the-gangway Radical Liberal neighbours, with Ramsay MacDonald and Arthur Ponsonby as the respective chief organisers. But would MacDonald's men follow him when British entry into the war was declared? There were reasons to doubt. Will Crooks, who represented Woolwich, had addressed a meeting in his constituency the previous evening. The *Westminster Gazette* (which came out at midday) reported it:

> Will Crooks was loudly cheered in addressing a meeting of his supporters at Woolwich (last night) when he begged them to support the Government at all costs and to see the old country through.[21]

Bearded, well-built, affable, Crooks was a fierce champion of pro-gressive reform but he was not averse to patriotic populism. The Union Jack went down well in a constituency whose Woolwich Arsenal provided employment.

Today the seating of the Commons chamber was slightly more comfortable. About a hundred MPs, most of them Conservative but including some twenty Liberals, had joined their units of the Territorial Force.[22]

There was tense expectation. Still every seat was occupied, *The Times* correspondent noted. The mood in the chamber, according to the reporter, was 'a grim and all but unanimous determination'. According to the paper, the ranks had been closed in the manner of its call the previous week. The diaries and letters of the parliamentary dissenters tell another story.[23]

At Question Time those Members aching for confirmation that war was on the way had to sit through some prosaic business: the length of the shifts of motor omnibus conductors; the lifting of foot and mouth cattle restrictions in Tipperary. And there were more questions about force-feeding of suffragette prisoners.

At about 4 p.m. the announcement came. The Prime Minister confirmed the German invasion of Belgium. It was, he said, 'a flagrant violation of the law of nations'. He informed the House that the Government had sent a message to the German government asking it to respect the neutrality of Belgium and stating that a satisfactory reply must be received by midnight (11 p.m. British time). War against Germany was on the way. It is interesting that Asquith on this day wrote about the German entry into Belgium to Venetia Stanley that, 'This simplifies matters.' Indeed it did. There would now be no need of any major restructuring of the Government.[24]

The last word on Belgium as *not* the British Government's reason for entering the war must go to Arthur Ponsonby, in his 1928 book *Falsehood in Wartime*. Among Ponsonby's evidence is a statement by Lloyd George Coalition Cabinet Minister Austen Chamberlain, in the House of Commons on 8 February 1922, referring to the events of 1914 and the British commitment to France:

> Had it been France [invaded] only, we could not have stayed out
> after the conversations which had taken place. It would not have

been in our interests to have stayed out, and we could not have stayed out without loss of security and honour.[25]

It is a neat summary: 'the conversations' with France and British interests were the motivation. Ponsonby summed up on Belgium in the book:

> The invasion of Belgium was *not* the cause of the war; the invasion of Belgium was *not* unexpected; the invasion of Belgium did *not* shock the moral susceptibilities of either the British or French Governments . . . To excite popular indignation was imperative, and it was done with complete success.[26]

Ottoline Morrell was in the outer lobby of the House of Commons. In her memoirs she described 'excitement and war elation gaining ground', as news was awaited, a few looking unhappy but 'the majority flushed and excited'. Then Lord Ridley came out and told his brother that it was 'all right'. Ottoline asked what that meant. Ridley explained, 'Why of course, Sir E. Grey has sent his ultimatum.' He was 'flushed and happy'.[27]

Soon newspaper boys were running down the Strand, shouting 'British ultimatum to Germany! England at war by midnight!' Those MPs who were still working against intervention continued to hold meetings, with each other, with journalists, at the neutrality organisations, wherever there seemed to be any chance of halting the charge to war. But hope was plummeting.[28]

MPs were no doubt wondering how it was going down in their constituencies. The electorate in these times, as Martin Pugh has noted, was 'already a fairly democratic one', for men. (Of the four and a half million men not on the register only one and a half million were not qualified as a result of the law.)[29] Leonard Outhwaite was on his way to the Potteries to see what the feeling of his electorate was. He and Josiah Wedgwood had arranged for a public meeting of electors, to pass, they hoped, a resolution in favour of British neutrality. Posters and notices advertised the event, in the Square at Burslem.

After the announcement of the ultimatum, Outhwaite headed northwards, battling with the disruption of trains being commandeered for troops. He went alone. Josh Wedgwood sent his apologies. As the final hours of peace ticked away, he listened to the crowds in his London road, telling his daughter in a letter the next day:

I listened all last night and the night before, to vast crowds who sang under my bedroom window all about, 'The boys of the bulldog breed', varied by the information that 'they', the singers, 'never would be slaves' and certainly would 'save old England's name'.[30]

Outhwaite was half an hour late for the meeting. The crowd, numbering about 1,500, was, as the reporter of the *Staffordshire Sentinel* put it, 'worked up to a considerable pitch of feeling by discussing the position among themselves'. It is evident from the report what that feeling was. The paper commented:

When Mr Outhwaite did arrive he found the majority of the audience unmistakeably out of sympathy with him. There was no misunderstanding or misinterpreting the trend of opinion.[31]

Outhwaite needed to call on all his public meeting skills. He insisted on speaking first, overriding the convention that the first speech is that of the chairman. There was good reason. The chairman was strongly pro-war. The resolution in favour of neutrality was tacitly abandoned.

In the crowd were some youths who were looking to stir things up. The MP challenged the interrupters: 'Instead of howling down one who is trying to present the duty as it seems to him, go to the nearest recruiting station and enlist and fight for your country.'

Cheers silenced the disruptors. Outhwaite analysed what had led up to the war and promised that he would speak up in Parliament for the constituency's needs. He forecast the consequences of war:

Unhappily it will not fall upon those who make wars, on the Czar, or King, or Kaiser, or Emperor: the tragedy of war will fall upon the humble homes; the tragedy of war will fall upon the brave lads – I do not care whether they be Englishmen or Germans or Russians – none has enmity in his heart today, but by some unseen power they are being sent out to the slaughter-house, to the field of battle. My sympathy goes out to them because upon them falls the tragedy and the horror of war, not upon the great men who make wars for their own interests. And it will fall upon the worker at the loom and the worker in the mine. I say let us consecrate ourselves tonight. Let us get rid of feelings of exultation because there is war. Be as patriotic as you may, but let your patriotism concern itself also with the home that is made desolate because of war, the home in which starvation enters because of the war. And I say to you no longer am I just a politician. I care not if you never return me again for this constituency, but I say I come here tonight to tell you the truth, as it appears to me, and ask you to help me mitigate as far as can be, the sorrows and the widespread miseries that will fall upon the people of this country.

The *Sentinel* called it 'a brilliant peroration'.

At about the same time a women's peace meeting was taking place at London's Kingsway Hall. There were speakers from five European countries, including Germany. A resolution called on the governments to support every effort to restore peace and urged those not yet involved 'to work unceasingly towards a settlement, not by force but by reason'. Not represented was the militant wing of the women's suffrage movement. The suffragettes' violent anger was being re-directed towards the Germans.[32]

As war approached, Allen Baker and Willoughby Dickinson arrived at Victoria Station, exhausted after a day and a half of travel across a Europe in the chaos of transition into war. A few days had destroyed the hopes of their movement.

At the Bedford Square home of the Morrells those dining included Ramsay MacDonald and Arthur Ponsonby. There was excitement in the street outside. Ponsonby described it in his letter to his wife: 'As we talked the yells of the crowds kept on coming through the windows as an accompaniment to our conversation.'[33]

War enthusiasm in these days, or the lack of it, has been the subject of controversy. Adrian Gregory in his analysis correctly rejects the notion of the war 'as an inevitable outcome of mass jingoism and anti-German antagonism'. There was no general mass reaction to the European crisis. Men were more favourable to British war intervention than were women, middle class more than working class, young more than old; and so on. But it was the governing circle which decided war entry, exciting popular mood in favour of the decision which it took, not being led by it. When Arthur Ponsonby, in the House of Commons debate, deplored the 'war fever', which he had witnessed on the previous day, he was certainly not saying that it was popular clamour which was taking

Britain into the war. There always had been, since far back in British and English history, excited demonstrations when war was in the offing. Ponsonby found these repellent. They were, however, product not cause. The significant point which Ponsonby made in his speech (causing some offence) was that Sir Edward Grey was whipping up the same sort of war fever in the House of Commons that he (Ponsonby) had witnessed on a London street. The scenes in parts of the House of Commons were indeed not unlike those which were occurring in the London hotspots. The war demonstrations in Parliament were democracy degraded.[34]

Ordinary people, it may be said, were discussing the international crisis much more calmly than their representatives in the House of Commons who whooped at the Foreign Secretary's call for war. The *Dunfermline Express* had an account of the atmosphere in Arthur Ponsonby's constituency on 3 August:

> The European situation, as is natural, is having its reflex in Dunfermline. Yesterday it was practically the sole topic of conversation in the city. There was a great rush on provisions during the day, and some merchants were reported to be practically sold out. Ladies were seen hurrying home with parcels of groceries, which were only procured at enhanced prices. On the principal street last night groups of men stood around, newspaper in hand, discussing the situation, which was generally admitted to be very grave.[35]

Charles Trevelyan recorded his impression on the same day: 'That night the streets were crowded with quiet, unexcited, anxious folk, it being a Bank Holiday.'[36] Here was contrast with the mafficking in the House of Commons.

Now, on this Tuesday, the war noise was getting louder in some public places, but this was an inevitable consequence of what was happening at Government level.

Arthur Ponsonby in his letter gave Dolly his impressions of the behaviour of ministers in the crisis:

> I had a talk with Burns at the club. He has resigned and nothing will induce him to reconsider his decision. Morley goes too and Charles Trevelyan. It is splendid of them. Lulu of course has not gone and I hear Ch Masterman's attitude has been contemptible,

also Lloyd George's. I thought the Liberal League was dead. It has triumphed after all. Grey while declaring we were free had committed us to France after all.

As Arthur Ponsonby made his way home on this day which ended the peace, assemblies were in place ready for the declaration of war at 11 p.m. Union Jacks and tricolours waved colourfully, to the accompaniment of 'Rule, Britannia' and the Marseillaise. Trafalgar Square was the focal point. At Buckingham Palace King George held a Privy Council, attended by one minister (Lord Beauchamp) and two court officials. This sanctioned the proclamation of a state of war with Germany from 11 p.m. The Cabinet had played no part in the sending of the ultimatum and was not involved in the declaration of war. After the ceremony of assent to war, the King and Queen Mary appeared on the balcony for the crowds. Arthur Ponsonby avoided the excitement. He arrived home at his flat and slept badly as peace ended.[37]

12

'Protest is Futile'

Wednesday, 5 August 1914

BRITAIN WOKE ON WEDNESDAY, 5 August to a state of war with Germany. Arthur Ponsonby wrote to Dolly: 'It's all over. War is declared. Chaos reigns. Protest is futile.'[1]

The *Daily News* signed off its neutrality campaign with a testament for posterity: 'We place on record our conviction that it was possible and that it would have been just and prudent and statesmanlike for England to have remained neutral.'[2]

The neutrality campaign had been sunk by the British commitment to France behind the back of Britain's supposed democracy. Britain, it turned out, was part of the balance of power system. With or without Belgium, Britain would have gone to war with its partner-in-honour. 'For Friendship and Honour', declared *Punch*'s caption to a full-page helmeted Britannia, sword in one hand, flag in the other, going into battle. It was for France. Chivalry for Belgium was an add-on.[3]

Arthur Ponsonby and his friends had to address the world as it now was. Righteous nationalism had won the day. The scenes in the House of Commons on Monday were already re-written as the House's dignified, considered and noble decision to do what had to be done for civilisation and the national interest. The mythology would prevail. MPs now had to choose their public words very carefully. This was not going to be a Boer War, fought far away on another continent. It was going to be waged against a formidable European power, capable of invading Britain. Britain's independence could be at risk.

Among those numbed by the news was Bruce Glasier. His diary records that he was 'stupefied'. The Labour peace movement had been overwhelmed by the speed of events.[4]

Much was happening. Arthur Ponsonby told Dolly: 'Johnnie is

ordered to Belgium.' The Expeditionary Force was to be sent to the continent. Johnnie Ponsonby commanded a battalion of the Coldstream Guards. The crossing over of the BEF would begin on Saturday, 8 August. Johnnie evidently expected to go to Belgium, but the initial destination of the BEF was France, not Belgium. Britain was supposedly entering the war to defend Belgium but the military operations had to be according to the previous plans. Arthur Ponsonby had been entirely correct in his prediction that the arrival of a British army in Belgium to fulfil the treaty role of keeping out invaders would be impossible. Britain actually was France's ally in the European war. As such, the British force would be positioned on the French left. The BEF was not heading to Antwerp or anywhere else in Belgium to commence its campaign, but to Maubeuge, close to the Belgian border but in France.[5]

Arthur Ponsonby's organisation was not folding its tents. The MP's letter to his wife continues:

> Those few of us still, about 20–30, who believe the war is un-necessary and our action has been precipitate are combining with Labour. When our combination with Labour is announced today it will cause a certain sensation as we have never openly cooperated before. But those who think alike must stand together and watch.

Ponsonby mentioned that there would be a meeting during the day. Labour plus Liberal dissenters would make an alliance of MPs in Parliament. For Ramsay MacDonald, here was an opportunity for his Labour Party to advance. It would be strengthened by an influx of unhappy middle-class Liberals. Labour, with new blood and a broader social base, could perhaps supplant the Liberal Party as the progressive opposition to the Conservatives. Such seems to have been the MacDonald thinking. His aim would be to absorb the Liberal dissidents. Earlier in the year he had rejected a personal appeal to take Labour into alliance with the Liberals, with a Cabinet place as his reward. His political ambitions went beyond his party being an adjunct of the Liberals. Now, opposition to the war, if the war became unpopular, could offer the Labour Party a route to power.[6]

Arthur Henderson had written to members of the Labour Party's National Executive Committee convening a meeting for 10 a.m. today, 'to consider what action should be taken in the very serious crisis in

Europe'. He had also launched arrangements for a conference of Labour delegates at the House of Commons at 2 p.m. to form a National Peace Emergency Committee, to be a large body drawn from right across the labour movement. There was a list of objects for the new organisation, which included, 'To urge the strictest neutrality possible in the present crisis'.[7]

That was yesterday when Britain was still at peace. Now, with the country at war, the NEC assembled at the party's Victoria Street offices for its meeting. A sub-committee was set up to draft resolutions in accordance with the party's position. It was a meeting apparently without controversy.[8]

At 11 a.m. a melancholy company assembled. The British Neutrality Committee was meeting to dissolve itself. The Committee's campaign had barely got off the ground. Graham Wallas took the chair, with Arnold Rowntree among those present. Two visitors were recorded: Allen Baker and Willoughby Dickinson, recovering from their journey ordeal.[9] The British Neutrality League which had started to make its case to millions, through its newspaper advertisements, also disbanded itself. There had been no time to develop the arguments in the country.

It was clearly Belgium which had pulled the Liberals onside. Kate Courtney, in a 9 August diary retrospective, wrote that Belgium was 'the rock on which all the anti-war feeling shipwrecked'.[10] Belgium as the justification of British entry into the war has played strongly in the re-examination a century on. The case has been presented as clinched by the outrages by the Germans in Dinant and Louvain in Belgium in late August, when hundreds of civilians were butchered and much of Louvain, including its medieval university library, was burnt. The Belgian events were certainly a terrible episode of war. But British forces were not able to do anything to save the Belgian victims. Arthur Ponsonby's argument, before Britain went in, that Britain could best help Belgium by staying out of the war makes some sense. Had Britain been neutral, its Government could have used its influence to try to halt the bloodshed, as the Ponsonby group wanted. The slaughter of civilians in Belgium was the first of innumerable horrors perpetrated on many sides in many places in the succession of twentieth-century European wars which began in 1914. They were 'the crimes of war', to use the Ponsonby family circle's phrase on the eve of the Great War.

On this first day of Britain's war, Arthur Ponsonby wrote to Dolly:

> The horror and misery before us is immeasurable. If only in all
> countries it could result in the overthrow of monarchies and
> aristocratic governments there might be some hope for the
> world for it is they that make wars. If Germany had attacked us
> I should be in the street waving a flag but to plunge us into a war
> because of the technical interpretation of a treaty made in 1839
> is criminal folly.[11]

Here is a reminder that Arthur Ponsonby was *not* 'a pacifist', the label
which certain modern historians have attached to him.

At 2 p.m. Labour's NEC reconvened at the House of Commons.
The sub-committee's resolutions repeated the line taken by Ramsay
MacDonald in his House of Commons speech. They blamed the war on
Sir Edward Grey's policy of secret diplomacy and entanglements with
France and Russia. They pledged that the party leadership would work 'to
secure peace at the earliest possible moment on such conditions as will
provide the best opportunities for the re-establishment of the amicable
feelings between the workers of Europe'. There was an acceptance of
the fact that since Britain was now in the war, the call for neutrality no
longer applied. There was no declaration of discouragement of Labour
people from joining up to fight. It was a moderate anti-war position.
The resolutions were confirmed by eight votes to four.[12]

The assembly which gathered at the House of Commons to set
up the new Labour organisation had over a hundred delegates, from
socialist, cooperative, trade union and women's organisations. Arthur
Henderson took the chair. It was at this point, on day one of the war,
that the first cracks appeared in organised labour's qualified anti-war
position.

The meeting described itself as a 'War Emergency Conference',
not a Peace Emergency Committee. One of the delegates was Bruce
Glasier. He made diary notes, reporting that it was 'ominous' that
Henry Hyndman, leader of the British Socialist Party quickly endorsed
the suggestion that the first matter for consideration should be relief
measures. The meeting was on the point of breaking up without the
politics of the war being raised. Glasier and two others intervened but
were blocked by a vote being taken. This produced a majority, including
Hyndman, for adjournment. Dissent was pushed aside.[13]

Hyndman, it should be said, was not completely successful in putting his British Socialist Party into a position of war support. Already before the war there had been a serious split occasioned by his increasing nationalism and this would now deepen. Later when the BSP moved into opposition to the war, Hyndman left the party and founded the National Socialist Party, not the only party with a proto-fascist whiff which the war produced in Britain.

The leaderships of the two great parties, Liberal and Conservative, were united on war. It had been presaged when in 1910 Lloyd George proposed a great Liberal–Conservative coalition to break the log jams. One of the concessions to the Conservatives would have been compulsory military training. Now, if Liberal values were ruffled, this would not concern Lloyd George too much.

After lunch Arnold Rowntree had a talk with Education Minister Jack Pease. Unsurprisingly the conversation turned on Pease's decision not to resign from the Cabinet. He gave Rowntree two grounds of justification: 'to urge settlement at the earliest opportunity and to help to feed 9 million children if this is necessary'.[14]

On this day Lewis Harcourt wrote to a friend to explain why he was now in line with the war. Key considerations were that the German fleet should not occupy the North Sea and the English Channel, or seize north-western France, and that Germany 'should not violate the ultimate independence of Belgium and hereafter occupy Antwerp as a standing menace to us'. These arguments had been in the Conservative papers for some time. Harcourt, previously not persuaded by them, suddenly was. It was the regular Liberal story.[15]

The House assembled at its usual mid-afternoon time. There was a statement by the Prime Minister that a state of war with Germany had existed since 11.00 the previous evening. Asquith reported a request from Belgium for Great Britain, France and Russia, as guarantors of Belgium's territory, to cooperate in defence of it; and that: 'Belgium is happy to be able to declare that she will assume defence of her fortified places.'[16]

The European war was happening.

There was also from Asquith an announcement that the following day: 'I shall move a Vote of Credit of £100,000,000.' This was the equivalent of twice the country's 1914 naval bill in one go, and it would be just the first of however many requests were needed, unless the war was very brief.

The battle to preserve civil liberty was starting. The Home Secretary, Reginald McKenna, asked for new power to impose restrictions on foreigners. Members of Arthur Ponsonby's group expressed their anxieties. It could be a crime simply to be the wrong nationality. Joseph King reported 'a great deal of apprehension among German subjects resident in Britain for many years and more British in sentiment than German'. King was followed by Sir William Byles (who was greeted with a shout of 'Sit down!'):

> I rise to ask whether there is any duration mentioned in the Bill and whether the power which is given under it endures until the House of Commons takes it away again [AN HON. MEMBER: 'During the war']. I think we ought to know this in giving such exceptional powers to a single Minister, because we may not always have the present Minister dealing with it, and therefore we ought to safeguard the duration of this power in some way.[17]

Ronald McNeill, a Conservative barrister, was concerned about whether the Government was up to the traditional despatch of spies: 'I want to know whether there is any power taken to shoot spies, and if not, why not?'

The spectre of German soldiers pouring off the beaches, their progress assisted by secret agents in the British towns and countryside, had been the stuff of the invasion serials in the Northcliffe Press. The first year of the war would see spy mania.

It was just a week since the Commons had been debating Britain's colonies. Now, as A. J. P. Taylor put it: 'Some 50 million Africans and 250 million Indians were involved, without consultation, in a war of which they understood nothing against an enemy who was also unknown to them.'[18]

In the early evening the dissident Liberals gathered – 'a meeting re cooperation with Labour', Arnold Rowntree, writing to his wife, called it. It was chaired by Arthur Ponsonby. Though probably most of those who attended were members of the Liberal Foreign Affairs Committee, this was the start of a new organisation, the aim of which was to join with the Labour Party in setting a new direction in British politics. No record has been left but some inference may be made from notes made by Edmund Harvey (and preserved in the papers of Richard Denman) of a meeting two days later. The plan was apparently for a joint committee representing an alliance of the Labour Party and anti-war Liberals.[19]

No single line would be possible on the request which the Government would be making to Parliament for the grant of war credits. Ramsay MacDonald's intention was that the Labour Party should abstain. Arthur Ponsonby said that he would support the credits, as did Josiah Wedgwood. The Prime Minister had promised a full debate on the war and the credit debate would be the Government's chosen occasion. British participation in the war could not be sustained unless Parliament voted the money. How many MPs would vote against? The lobby correspondent of the *Manchester Guardian*, filing his copy for the next day's paper, predicted fewer than ten.[20]

The big moment of the meeting of Liberal dissenters was the arrival of Charles Trevelyan. The MP recalled in his Personal Account what happened when he entered Committee Room 16:

> I went down to a meeting of the group at the House of the members who oppose the war policy. They are just about 30. When I came into the room there were loud cheers. Poor fellows, they have been deserted by almost everyone.[21]

Trevelyan's presence was inspiring and the anti-war group was desperately in need of some boost.

All depended on the Labour Party. In another committee room the party's MPs were preparing the line for the following day's credit debate.

The Labour meeting confirmed what had been emerging during the day, the collapse of the party's stance against the war. Ramsay MacDonald proposed abstention on the war credits vote and a declaration of the Labour Party's position as formulated in the resolutions. It now became clear that MacDonald was no longer carrying his party. The majority voted to back the request for war credits and furthermore refused the Chairman permission to quote from the party's resolutions. Labour's position was to be unequivocal support for the war. Since he could not acquiesce with silence on the war, MacDonald relinquished the leadership.[22]

Parliamentary Labour split between the ILP minority, who opposed the war, and the trade union mainstream, which now backed British participation uncritically. Even the ILP group did not all stay anti-war. The British Labour Party would not be alone in its division over the war. Across the belligerent zones of Europe socialist parties would split into pro-war majorities and anti-war minorities. The German Social Democratic Party had voted on Monday by 78–14 to support war credits and on this day, while the British Labour Party was deciding to back war credits, it supported without opposition a vote in the Reichstag of 5 million marks. Keir Hardie's dream of a mass blocking of war by the workers of Europe was blown away.

Where now was the projected joint movement of Liberal dissidents and Labour? Ponsonby reported to his wife 'difficulties' and 'incessant talks and consultations'. The talks have left no record, which is not surprising given the onrush of events. But the enterprise now looked impossible. Arthur Ponsonby and Ramsay MacDonald had wanted to coordinate a Radical/Labour front which would call for the war to be settled and protest about how British entry had come about, while still giving patriotic support to the British forces. The project now looked hopeless.[23]

13

'I do not Want my Country to be Beaten'

Thursday, 6 August 1914

ON THURSDAY ARTHUR WROTE TO DOLLY, now back at Shulbrede:

> Everything seems dislocated. It is just as if one had got a high temperature and saw all familiar things rather changed. Absurd rumours and frantic shouting of newsboys go on all day long.[1]

Those who had campaigned for neutrality were taking stock of the world of war now into its second day. Gordon Harvey was writing to his Rochdale constituents:

> I have long held that to avoid a European conflict, the only way was, not to arm the nations to the teeth, but to bring them closer together in a free and mutual understanding. We have, for the moment, failed, and those who believe in force and whose business it is to use force are now in possession of the field. When their work is done I shall hope to lay once more before those who will listen to me the view of a common humanity, and it may be the events through which we are about to pass will . . . make them readier hearers.[2]

No one knew what the 'events' would be.

The revamped foreign affairs group met at 2 p.m. Arthur Ponsonby deferred to Charles Trevelyan's political seniority by stepping down to be his deputy. Edmund Harvey was secretary. Thirty names are attached to the minutes. They were the old faithful plus Trevelyan and a few others, but the big coming change, it was hoped, would be when Labour MPs joined.[3]

The meeting began with a report by Ponsonby. The outcome of the negotiations which he and Trevelyan had held with MacDonald and Henderson, he told his colleagues, was discouraging. A large joint committee was 'not practicable at present', though a smaller committee of representatives from the two sides might be possible. (It turned out not to be.) After the Labour Party meeting MacDonald was in no position to deliver Parliamentary Labour into an anti-war alliance.

The new organisation decided on a press statement:

> That this meeting agrees that a group of Liberal Parliamentary Members should be organised for the purpose of watching the progress of the European crisis and for taking such steps in Parliament and in the country as shall relieve the distress resulting from the war and expedite a speedy settlement . . .

All that the group could do for the moment was to watch. 'A speedy settlement' would only happen if one side won quickly. The war would certainly cause distress: to say that steps for relief should be taken in Parliament was merely a statement of the obvious.

The next day Charles Trevelyan reported that in view of the resignation of Ramsay MacDonald as Labour Leader, 'any question of further arrangements for joint action with Labour Members must be left in abeyance for the present'. The beleaguered Liberal dissidents would have to make their own arrangements.

Today the big build-up was to the debate on the Government's request for £100 million war credit. One Labour Member who would not be present was Keir Hardie. Following his vow in the 3 August debate, Keir Hardie was at Aberdare in his Merthyr Tydfil constituency.

Hardie's meeting was chaired by the local miners' leader. It became clear when the MP stood up that something was going on at the back of the hall. There was an eruption of shouting, bells and singing. His speech was drowned by barracking and by choruses of 'Rule, Britannia', 'Sospan Fach' and the National Anthem. It was evidently organised. Hardie tried to present his arguments, that the real enemies were the Kaiser and the Tsar, not the German people, and that he was opposing the war in the interests of civilisation and the class to which he belonged, but he could not make himself heard. The meeting had to be abandoned. The MP was badly shaken.[4]

Behind the wrecking was Charles Stanton, miners' agent and Hardie's own local organiser. Stanton was formerly a syndicalist militant, who (to Hardie's disapproval) had urged violence in the miners' industrial struggle.

At Commons Question Time Charles Trevelyan, now a free agent on the backbenches, asked:

> May I ask the Prime Minister whether he can undertake that, so long as the war continues, no Adjournment or Prorogation of this House should extend for a period of longer than six weeks; and that should circumstances arise calling for any suspension of civil rights or curtailment of civil liberty, Parliament will meet immediately?[5]

For democracy, this was vital. It was essential that MPs should meet frequently in order to hold the executive to some sort of accountability. The likely threats in wartime to civil liberty were obvious. The next day the Government would introduce the first instalment of the Defence of the Realm Act, to which there would be many subsequent additions. This gave the Government the power to 'authorise the trial by courts-martial' of anyone whose actions were considered to 'jeopardise the success of the operations of His Majesty's forces or to assist the enemy'. Asquith brushed away without comment his former junior minister's plea for Parliament not to disappear at this critical time.

Another of the Trevelyan committee had a question. Aneurin Williams, Member for North West Durham, had just got out the words 'President of the United States' when the Speaker cut him short. Williams had a special interest in international conciliation. A lawyer and social reformer (and leading light of the Garden City movement), Williams would later be prominent in the League of Nations campaign.

There was plenty about the war. Joseph King wanted to know about a county lunatic asylum left without adequate staff as a result of the call-up of reservists. Two MPs were anxious that alien naval pilots whose countries of origin were not friendly should have their licences cancelled, one hoping that these pilots would be detained.

Military dress was now starting to appear in the chamber. *Punch*'s correspondent remarked that, 'Captain Lord Dalrymple of the Scots Guards lends opportune gleam of martial splendour to bench where he sits arrayed in khaki uniform that has seen service in the Boer War.' This went down well in *Punch*: the aristocracy leading the soldiers into battle in age-old tradition.[6]

The War Credit debate was opened by the Prime Minister, with the Commons sitting as a Committee of the Whole House, with Deputy Speaker J. H. Whitley – a Liberal – in the chair. A Government Blue Book had been laid on the table of the House, detailing the correspondence with other governments in the run-up to the war.[7]

Asquith presented the Government's 'utmost reluctance' in declaring war against Germany 'for generations past a friendly Power'. On the German offer for British neutrality, he said that Germany had not been able to give a guarantee that no French colonial territory would be taken if it were victorious in the war. On Belgium, the Prime Minister stated that Germany had offered respect of the country's integrity but only after the end of the war. If the offer had been accepted, he said, 'we should have covered ourselves with dishonour'.

Asquith knew that, with dissent still evident among some of his backbenchers, he needed to get a firmer grip on his own party, and he now made a grandiloquent moral pitch:

> I do not believe any nation ever entered into a great controversy with a clearer conscience and a stronger conviction that it is fighting, not for aggression, not for the maintenance even of its own selfish interest, but that it is fighting in defence of principles the maintenance of which is vital to the civilisation of the world.

But otherwise the Prime Minister avoided purple patches. He said that he did not want to 'inflame passion' and generally his speech was calm. But he did have some news. The new War Minister was Lord Kitchener of Khartoum.

Lord Kitchener, Asquith reminded the House, was not a politician: he had 'responded to a great public call'. But Kitchener had his views and purposes. What these were started to be evident when the Prime Minister asked for Parliament's approval for the expansion of the Army by 'no less than 500,000'. He did not say what was going to be done with the extra men or what the eventual size of the Army might be. He did not tell MPs that the new War Minister had predicted to the Cabinet a war lasting at least three years and that far more than one million troops would be needed.[8]

One word which did not pass the lips of the Prime Minister was conscription. But it did not need much imagination to foresee its eventual arrival if sufficient soldiers did not volunteer for Kitchener's Army.

Another word not heard from the Prime Minister was coalition. But the appointment of Kitchener to the Cabinet was a large move in this direction. Whatever the old soldier's politics were, they were not Liberal and his would be a powerful voice in a Government which had lost several of its most strongly anti-militarist members.

Asquith's speech was well received by most. Francis Neilson recalled that, 'most of the members burst into a noisy demonstration and tore their White Papers into shreds'. (He actually thought that he remembered the White Paper [Blue Book] shredding following Asquith's announcement of the ultimatum on the Tuesday, but this was a day before publication.) Neilson took his copy home. He found that 'the correspondence was not complete and there were many errors in it'. He called the confetti episode 'typical of the time'. Of course ripping up of paper in the House of Commons in joyous anticipation of war does not feature in the account of grave and noble assent to war.[9]

For the Conservatives, Andrew Bonar Law was warmly supportive of the Prime Minister. The unity of the two front benches was firmly in place. Law made unexpected reference to the *Manchester Guardian*:

> I should like to say that I read yesterday with real pleasure an article in a paper which does not generally commend itself to me, the 'Manchester Guardian'. In that article it still held that the war ought not to have been entered into, but it took this view that that was a question for history, and that now we were in it, there was only one question for us, and that was to bring it to a successful issue.[10]

A hundred years on, history's question remains open. The *Manchester Guardian* and the *Daily News*, the biggest left of centre newspapers of their day, have left statements on the record that they entered into the role of war cheerleaders under protest and out of necessity given the fact of war. The article quoted by Bonar Law highlights the problem facing the backbench dissenters. Now that war against another major power was in progress, with all the perils that that entailed, protests were going to look unpatriotic (or worse).

There was no Labour Leader's speech this time since Labour's decision was for silence, though on this day Labour's National Executive went ahead with issuing its statement condemning Britain's part in the balance of power politics which had led to war.

John Redmond did not speak this time. Irish Nationalist support for the war credits was taken as read. The debate was thrown open to the floor. The first MP called was Arthur Ponsonby.

Ponsonby rose to shouts of 'Agreed!' from MPs who wanted the credit agreed to without debate. He gave his 'heartiest support' to the Government's credit request and said that the case for war on the basis of the recent correspondence with Germany which the Government set out in its White Paper was 'overwhelming'. But he went on to say that the real roots of the war went back much further:

> I profoundly disagree with the policy that has been pursued and that has culminated in this war. I profoundly disagree with the policy of high expenditure on armaments, which has meant the continuance of the policy of the balance of power, which has been carried on by secret diplomacy. This is a diplomatists' war and not a peoples' war, and I feel that we are only confronted today with the disastrous and complete failure of that policy.[11]

He protested about MPs being deceived over the commitment to France, which was made despite 'declarations to the contrary'. He said: 'The time will come when the whole of the policy which has led up to this calamity will have to be reviewed very carefully, and to be analysed very closely.'

The speech was met with a storm of noise, with shouts of 'Sit down!' and jeering laughter. Arthur Ponsonby quickly concluded with a reiteration that he was supporting the Government's requests.

As ever, Ponsonby was his own sternest critic regarding his performance. He wrote to Dolly:

> I have just been making a complete fool of myself and felt pretty wretched in consequence. I spoke again and the House, both sides, howled at me. I said very little, it was quite ineffective and it would have been far better if I had been silent. However it is done now and I said nothing that I regret.[12]

When Willoughby Dickinson was called, he attempted to talk about the growth in friendship between British and German people in recent years. Such was the barrage of yelling that he needed the Speaker to restore order. He insisted that it was the dominant military caste in Germany which was making the war, not the German people, even though inevitably ordinary people were enthusiastic in their support for their armies as in Britain. He looked forward to victory over the German military caste and the overthrowing of its supremacy, but to restricting the war as far as possible, and to preparing for a constructive settlement which would not cause further problems. He spoke of German fear of 'the possibility of Slav domination'. The heavy interruptions drove him to a cry of despair: 'I do not know why they do not listen.'[13]

He was followed by Josiah Wedgwood. The Potteries MP, like Ponsonby and Dickinson, supported the Government's request for war credit. He said, 'I do not want my country to be beaten.' He got this in at the start of his speech. But he was not in favour of giving the executive £100 million all at once, since that meant loss of democratic control. He supported Dickinson's argument about the different Germanys – the people and those responsible for the war. He predicted a long struggle and called on the Government not to carry it out, 'as in the case of the Boer War, in a boastful spirit'. He said of war:

> It is murder. It is contrary to Christianity, and there is nothing
> to be proud of and nothing to boast of. It is a thing to bring
> an end to at the earliest possible opportunity, and I hope with
> honourable Members opposite that the war spirit will cease, and
> that we shall regard this war as something to be gone through
> doggedly, but looking upon it as a curse instead of a blessing.[14]

The presence of khaki in the chamber was a sign of how Parliament was starting to change from a political forum to an assembly for prosecuting war. But still there was dissent. A Cumbrian Liberal rose.

Sir Wilfrid Lawson was Member for Cockermouth. He denounced his Government's abandonment of Liberal principles:

> We have heard in the last few days a great deal about honour;
> we have heard something about morality and something about
> self-interest. As to honour, I see nothing honourable whatever

in our present proceedings; surely the most supreme of British interests lies in peace, and not in war. As far as the morality is concerned, when we are engaged, as we are now, in organised murder, I think the less said about morality the better. I was sent to support – as I understood – a policy of peace, retrenchment and reform. Where are they all now? All swallowed up in the bloody abyss of war![15]

Lawson's representation of war would be echoed nearly a century later in the memoirs of Harry Patch, the last survivor of the trenches. Patch wrote, 'War is organised murder and nothing else.' In August 1914 he was a sixteen-year-old plumber in Somerset. He did not welcome war. He wanted to 'continue my apprenticeship, rather than pick up a gun'. His sentiments were shared by many.[16]

Sir Wilfrid Lawson was followed by Arnold Rowntree. The Quaker hopefully urged the avoidance of enmity towards the German people. He pressed for the maintenance of commerce as far as possible in order to enable employers to keep people in full employment.[17]

Then Aneurin Williams got in his plea for the Government to use the mediation services of the American President, in which no one was interested. He sat down and Allen Baker rose, to make a speech which he must have known would cause pandemonium.[18] Firstly Baker deplored the failure of the Government to promote friendship with Germany, arguing that there had been 'offers again and again' from Germany, adding:

> I believe heartily, from intimate knowledge of the people of Germany, that the mass of them, including many in high station and positions, have been entirely against this war.

Then he spoke of what he saw as the German perspective:

> They fear, not without reason, the great Slav population, who are double the number of the Germans, and who have been arming and preparing for this conflict for years. To Germany, with enemies right and left, east and west, it is a matter of life and death. They feel that they are in a desperate position, and if you could realise their position, I think you would see that there is very much to be said for the hasty action that they have taken. [HON. MEMBERS: 'No! no!']. I believe they are entering into this

war with deep regret, and certainly, on the part of the masses of the people, with great friendship towards us.

Baker was the only speaker in this debate who tried to excuse the German military strike. He condemned the enthusiasm in the chamber for war, saying that he had been 'most deeply pained to hear the almost laudatory cheers and to hear sentiments of gladness – almost of joy' on both sides of the House:

> Perhaps I may be permitted to put it in this way: In the enthusiasm of loyalty there are expressions often used, that make one almost weep with sadness to see with what alacrity we are ready to go and slay – [HON. MEMBERS: 'No, no' and 'Sit down!'] . . .

This was the first time that Baker was shouted down in the House of Commons. He insisted that he was not accusing any particular individual but he condemned the mood:

> I have just passed through the country where war is about to be waged, and then coming to this country I have found the same thing in our streets. Already almost we see the spirit of 'Mafficking' [HON. MEMBERS: 'No, no', 'Withdraw', 'Sit down!'] . . . We are entering on one of the most horrible acts in this and other countries of Europe, that will have effects and results that we can in no way estimate. War is of such a horrible character with the present weapons and with the machinery of slaughter to mow down men. I do not intend to vote against this Vote. In entering on this war it should be with the feelings of the deepest sadness, and with the prayer that it may soon come to an end, and with the desire that a generous and lasting peace may soon be agreed to.

The Government's requests were passed without a vote, amid cheers. The war was a fact and the Government had the money for it.

For those who still rejected the case for war, civilisation seemed to be crumbling. Even the National Liberal Club had the jingo bug. A Chancery Lane solicitor, Scott Duckers, who was living there in 1914, recalled that during the closing days of July and the early days of August the club 'became a sort of whirlpool of jingoism in which it became almost treason to speak a word of Liberalism or to remind members that they were supposed to belong to a political party whose watchwords were Peace, Retrenchment and Reform'.[19]

After the Credit Debate, Arnold Rowntree dined with John Burns and Edmund Harvey, a trio of politicians at variance with the sentiment of righteous war, combined with national interest, now carrying all before it. Rowntree found consolation. He wrote to his wife of 'a very strong spirit of comradeship growing up amongst those of us opposed to the war which cheers one'. This spirit had been manifested in the joy of the Ponsonby group when Charles Trevelyan made his first appearance in their room. The shaken minority of those sticking to their principles against the earthquake were showing the first signs of pulling together. It was the start of a process.[20]

A stand had been taken. The war promoters wanted unanimous, or near unanimous, support. Arthur Ponsonby and his allies denied them this, while still asserting their patriotism. Instead, alternative values were presented. As righteous war slid into imperial war, these would be offered in and out of Parliament. The stall was set out. The ideals of democratic debate, civil liberty and international cooperation would at least stay alive. The British neutrality campaign of 1914 was far from completely a story of defeat.

14

Afterwards

WAR SENT WHAT HAD BEEN the parliamentary neutralist campaign in an assortment of directions. Several of its MPs saw military service. Josiah Wedgwood, who had said in the credit debate, 'I do not want my country to be beaten,' after some agonising came to the decision that his place was in the fighting line. Josh's service was characteristic of the man. In 1915, at the Dardanelles, he was wounded in the groin by shrapnel while running between machine-gun emplacements, but rejoiced that 'my seat is safe'. The socialist *Herald* newspaper appealed to him to 'leave Armageddon for a worthier fight'. He kept the cutting.[1]

Another military service MP was Richard Denman. The Carlisle MP's war story is an unusual one. Denman wrote a pamphlet, called 'On the Road to Peace', which included castigation of Church of England bloodthirstiness. It was picked up by the German press, with dire consequences. The MP was jeered at as 'pro-German'. He was de-selected by his constituency Liberal committee. He was badly shaken. Soon afterwards he joined the Army with a commission as an artillery officer. While in training in January 1916 he was one of four MPs in khaki in the No lobby against conscription.

He served on the Western Front. Denman's memoirs give what must be a unique glimpse of an anti-war MP in the fighting line. He found 'frank expression of views unmentionable in England' such as 'were we really on the right side in fighting for Russian as against German civilisation?' This would not have been tolerated in a London club but could be freely discussed by officers at the front, he recalled. He wrote to his constituency press:

Your virulent armchair warrior would probably suffer some shocks if he overheard conversations of soldiers, or had to censor their letters. Today I saw in the London papers a paragraph telling how a sentimental lady, after listening to portions of *Parsival*, rose in the concert hall and shouted, 'I protest against German music being played while Englishmen are being slaughtered by the Germans'. I read this out to three fellow-officers. One of them laughed at the excellence of the joke. Another said impatiently, 'What a —— fool!' The third remarked, 'how —— silly'. The realities of war are a potent medicine to cure stupid sentimental hatred of that sort.[2]

An ineradicable memory was the 'sinister date' in August 1916 when a high-velocity shell without warning entered the shelter where he and five companions were lunching. They had just begun soup. It was he said, 'a marvel that only one was killed'. He held his head in his hands checking that it was intact and for a fortnight was subject to sudden outbreaks of tears without any apparent cause.[3]

Denman attempted to resign his commission to return to Westminster. This was refused. The MP then wrote to Arthur Ponsonby to ask whether he could table a resolution to summon back to Parliament the military service Members. Ponsonby consulted fellow Liberal MP Gilbert McMicking, the father of Denman's sister-in-law, a military man himself and a decorated Boer War veteran. The two MPs took a poor view of Denman's scheme. They agreed that soldier MPs should be on the same footing as any other soldiers. Here we see Ponsonby as a man of military family values. Denman had made his choice to take a commission. His parliamentary allies had disagreed with his decision but had wished him well. Now he had to see it through.[4]

In March 1917 Denman, while on leave, visited his Carlisle constituency and held a meeting. The *Cumberland Evening Mail* reported:

We scarcely knew Mr Denman when we met him on his flying visit to Carlisle. He was in his full regimental khaki. If he hadn't been thus, he might well have been locked up. He certainly looked well and, like all when they get into khaki and get straightened up with drill, appeared about several inches taller. But oh, isn't his hair turning grey! The trials and hardships and excitements of service at the front have told a tale.[5]

Denman applied again for release from his commission, this time successfully. He became Parliamentary Private Secretary to H. A. L. Fisher, the Education Minister.

Perhaps the most remarkable of the war stories of the Ponsonby people was that of Hastings Bertrand (Bertie) Lees-Smith. A young ex-professor of public administration, Lees-Smith, Member for Northampton, was quiet in Parliament during 1914's fateful days. He volunteered for the Army in 1915 (the sanitary division of the RAMC). Almost alone of the 200 or so service MPs, he did not have an officer's commission. He was another soldier in the No lobby on the conscription vote. Later in the year he returned from the Western Front, invalided out. Back at the House of Commons, he made a striking appeal to his Liberal Party to return to its former values. The occasion was a December 1916 debate on what was called the German Peace Note.

Lees-Smith, urging a constructive response, advised:

> Go back to the old Liberal tradition and trust yourselves boldly to those decent, kindly, humane forces which are to be found in every man and nation; see only terms of peace which will enable you to substitute the possibility of friendship for the continuance of hatred and on those terms of peace erect a league of nations.[6]

It was Lees-Smith who, in July 1917, using Parliamentary privilege, read out to the Commons the denunciation of the war by Western Front officer and poet Siegfried Sassoon.

The MP was one of the little 'peace by negotiation' group, led by Charles Trevelyan, Arthur Ponsonby and Philip Snowden. In February 1917, after one of the debates which the group instigated, the *Bradford Pioneer* newspaper made a prediction:

> We rejoice there is still left even a small group of members of the House of Commons prepared, in an atmosphere alien and hostile, to voice an outraged and suffering humanity. When these dreadful days are over their names will be honoured throughout the world as men who kept their heads and held to the faith when all seemed black as night and when their fellow politicians could only clamour for blood and conquest.[7]

A hundred years on the prediction remains unfulfilled. The story of the group is untold.

The group was not for peace at any price. Arthur Ponsonby and his peace by negotiation friends, though often called 'pacifists', were pacifists only in the broad sense of promoting peace – which was a regular use of the word in these days. Several of the Quaker MPs *were* perhaps pacifist in the fundamentalist sense of being opposed on principle to all war-making but even they did not argue in these terms in Parliament. MPs had constituents to represent, some of whom were in the forces. The peace by negotiation group did, however, challenge the notion that military means were the only way of achieving a settlement. It saw the war as doing great harm and wanted it settled as quickly as possible on decent terms. Negotiation was *one* of the possible ways and the group felt that it should be tried.

The group's members suffered social ostracism, abuse and even physical attack. In the face of this, the support provided by nearest and dearest was vital. Arthur Ponsonby described it in his diary:

> In such a time as this, Shulbrede and home and family have been a wonderful standby, a refuge from the storm, an atmosphere in which to reflect and see things in their true proportions. D[olly] encouraging, standing with me, fortifying me in my opinions ... uncompromising on the side of real right, rejecting with scorn the sham cries of newspapers, crowds and foolish ignorant people ... [The children's] spirits and laughter, their charm and companionship has day after day revived me and lifted me from morose dejection ... God knows I appreciate this wonderful Shulbredian home. Would to heaven I could help them and help my fellow men in proportion to the blessings that are heaped upon me.[8]

The friendship of Arthur Ponsonby and Charles Trevelyan grew as the war continued. In correspondence 'Dear Trevelyan' and 'Dear Ponsonby' were dropped in favour of first names. Dolly Ponsonby reflected on Charles Trevelyan in December 1914:

> He is a good honest creature but doesn't listen much. Still I do admire him; and somehow his simple, straightforward point of view carries conviction – more than very subtle reasoning does sometimes.[9]

And in June 1915, following a chance lunch encounter:

His sanguine, unmorbid point of view did cheer one and of course he is not sensitive and [he is] physically enormously strong – his nerves are strong too – so it enables him to take a more cheerful view than A[rthur], Ramsay [MacDonald] or [E. D.] Morel.[10]

The wartime successors to the anti-war campaign of July/August 1914 had some achievements. They worked to secure the best provision possible for conscientious objectors in the Government's conscription legislation. And during the war the project of a new political movement took real shape: working-class ILP came together with middle-class Liberals. The organisation was the Union of Democratic Control. The UDC aimed to make politics more democratic and to find a better way of ordering international relations. In the later years of the war, jointly with the ILP, it sponsored peace by negotiation candidates at by-elections against the 'knock-out blow' policies of the Conservative-dominated Lloyd George Coalition, which in December 1916 ousted Asquith's Coalition (which had governed since May 1915). Prominent in the UDC were Arthur Ponsonby and Ramsay MacDonald, now frequently working together.

On 26 September 1915 Keir Hardie died. Memorial notices included one of deep bleakness from George Bernard Shaw:

I do not see what Hardie could do but die [when] the Labour Party he had so painfully dragged into existence should snatch still more eagerly at the War to surrender those liberties and escape back into servility, crying: 'You may trust your masters: they will treat you well.'[11]

The misery was rubbed in when the ILP failed to hold the seat at the Merthyr by-election. Under the electoral truce at by-elections the parties stood aside for the party previously holding the seat. The ILP nominee for the seat was opposed by a Labour independent supporting conscription. This was Charles Stanton, who had wrecked Keir Hardie's meeting at the start of the war. Stanton won comfortably, a victory which sent the London jingo press into raptures. In Parliament the bellicose Stanton railed at peace promoters and defenders of civil liberty, readily using the word 'crank' and accusing dissenters of being traitors – on one occasion bragging in the House of Commons about (violently) breaking up a meeting at which several MPs were on the platform.[12]

Labour was now part of the Government. In January 1916 its leadership reversed its position on conscription and accepted the Government's compulsion bill, despite a big rank and file Labour conference having voted heavily against. The tame acquiescence in conscription of men when there was no conscription of wealth brought despair to Labour and Liberal dissenters. Ramsay MacDonald commented in his diary about his party's decision to keep its ministers in the Coalition, despite conscription:

> The men were very anxious to remain themselves. They are applauded by their enemies. Some of my colleagues were born to hew wood and with a little flattery they can be backed to fulfil their destiny.[13]

January 1916 was a time of especially low spirits for those opposed to war and conscription. On the 18th, as fog blanketed London, the arguments on the committee stage of the compulsion bill went on into the night. Arthur Ponsonby wrote to Dolly:

> We were up till 2 last night. It is very desperate. I long to speak on every amendment but have refrained. We are now discussing conscientious objectors and of course the Tories are convinced that such people are shirkers. The Tory officers look at one in the lobbies as if one was beneath contempt.[14]

It could be bitingly personal. On 10 January 1916 Leonard Outhwaite complained about the suppression of the Scottish weekly socialist newspaper *Forward*, for reporting the rough reception received by Munitions Minister Lloyd George when he addressed a Glasgow meeting of workers. (He was booed and told to get his hair cut and the 'Red Flag' was sung.) Only a heavily sanitised account of the event was allowed by the censors. Outhwaite's defence of the magazine's breach of the censorship provoked Captain Duncan Campbell (North Ayrshire) to comment:

> I tell the House frankly that if I had the Honourable Member for Hanley in my battalion at the front he would be strung up by the thumbs before he had been there half an hour.[15]

Captain Campbell then told Outhwaite that he would do it himself, 'even though I have the use of only one arm, having lost the use of the other in a task which the Honourable Member for Hanley would never dream of attempting to risk'. Campbell, a Canadian by birth, had been wounded severely at Ypres in November 1914. Later this year he regained the use of his arm and was promoted to colonel. He was injured by a mine on the Western Front and died of his wounds in September 1916. It was difficult to argue against soldier MPs who put their lives on the line. Outhwaite himself had expressed it the previous year:

> Let me say ... that it is very hard indeed for any member to criticise statements made by a soldier in this House. We are all full of sympathy with these men who come from what one might call the very antechamber of death.[16]

It had been predicted that opposition to conscription would melt away but this did not happen. The minority was small but it was determined and well organised, around forty MPs through the various stages of the Government's two 1916 bills. Afterwards the cross-party group stayed together to defend civil liberty.

The Liberal leadership's embrace of the twin tigers of war and conscription kept their party clinging to power or a (diminishing) share of it, but the abandonment of Liberal principles ultimately proved disastrous. The party never formed a government again. MPs such as Arthur Ponsonby, Charles Trevelyan, Leonard Outhwaite, Joseph King and Josiah Wedgwood were among the eventual torrent of migration from Liberal to Labour.

For the Irish Nationalists, support of British entry into the war (and in 1916 of conscription in return for Ireland being excluded) had equally calamitous results. John Redmond had hoped that partnership with the British Government in the war would lead to Home Rule for all Ireland. Instead there was the 1916 Dublin uprising and, following on the brutal treatment of its leaders by the British Government, there was the rise of Sinn Féin, which largely swept away the moderate Irish Parliamentary Party in the 1918 General Election. And Irish civil war would turn out not to have been averted by world war, merely delayed.

Arthur Ponsonby was physically attacked twice. His diary in July 1915 describes the experience when a mob, incited by a newspaper, broke up a UDC meeting which he had gone to address, and attacked him along with two colleagues:

> The actual fighting was the least bad part. I have never been in a scrap before and was surprised how little a blow on the face can hurt. But the faces of those awful brutes standing round and insulting us I can never forget. It was like some awful hideous nightmare.[17]

The hazards for dissenting campaigners in wartime are well shown by an episode of 1915. The UDC attempted to launch its peace by negotiation campaign in London on 29 November at the Memorial Hall in Farringdon Street. Among those billed to speak were Arthur Ponsonby, Ramsay MacDonald and Charles Trevelyan. On the day of the meeting there were newspaper headlines such as 'Mass Meeting of Peace Cranks: Insult to London'. The gathering was a very obvious target for wreckers.[18]

Present was Sir Hubert Parry, supportive of his son-in-law but not quite seeing eye to eye with him on the war. Parry's biographer has noted that, 'for the first time in their relationship arguments were less amicable in disagreement'. A few months after this Parry composed his 'Jerusalem' music to accompany William Blake's poem (at the request of Robert Bridges) for Sir Francis Younghusband's 'Fight for Right' organisation. This movement was meant to be of spiritual ideals and Parry lent his support. But it turned jingo and the composer resigned. The music instead became the anthem of women's suffragists, with the blessing of Parry, who was a keen supporter. In later years it became the song of the Women's Institute.[19]

Parry's 29 November 1915 diary description of what happened at the Memorial Hall records what was a common experience, the break-up of peace and civil rights meetings by vigilantes:

> We found a mob surrounding the hall and had great difficulty in getting in at a side door . . . We sat on the platform for half an hour. Arthur, Morel, Trevelyan came in. Just when the meeting was going to begin we saw a large body of soldiers forcing their way up the central alley in the hall and flinging people right and left. They clambered on to the platform and ousted everyone off it. I got Maud away safely and as we could not get out (the

doors being blocked by the mob) I deposited her ... in a waiting room and went back to the hall. It was almost entirely occupied by soldiers, and men on the platform were endeavouring to make fiery speeches. Maud was very frightened and pale as parchment.[20]

The *Daily Sketch* of 30 November described the events at Farringdon Hall in terms of a battle of soldiers against 'peace-crank speakers':

PEACE BANNERS TORN TO PIECES

WOUNDED CANADIANS, AUSTRALIANS, NEW ZEALANDERS AND
SOUTH AFRICANS SHOW LONDON THE WAY TO DEAL WITH
PEACE TRAITORS.

The rest of the account made it sound like an engagement on the Western Front:

Without a moment's warning a hundred or more soldiers swept up the narrow aisle. One or two stewards, more zealous than discreet, who tried to stem the tide, were badly mauled. The soldiers' triumph was achieved within a minute ...

The paper finally declared: 'To talk of peace now is treason, to question the justice of our cause is treason, to demand soft terms for Germany is treason.'[21]

There were furious protests in Parliament about the break-up of the meeting. Government minister Jack Tennant responded by reading out the account of an Assistant Provost-Marshal, who had reported to the Government on the incident. This included:

The meeting was perfectly quiet and orderly until one of the stewards apparently on the instruction of the Honourable Member for Leicester [Ramsay MacDonald] attempted to remove four or five colonial soldiers who were seated at the front of the hall. At the same time another person on the platform said in a voice sufficiently loud to be heard, 'let that accursed military element be got rid of before we start'. Similar remarks were audibly made in Teutonic accents by three or four of the stewardesses.[22]

It was clear from this farce that there would be no redress in Parliament.

The episode demonstrated the hopelessness of the dissenters' chances of getting serious major public debate.

Charles Trevelyan was also on the receiving end. The *Daily Express* had a report in December 1915:

NO ROOM FOR PEACE CRANKS
ELLAND CONDEMNS MR TREVELYAN TO BE SHOT!

The whole country is being aroused by the danger of the peace cranks. Elland has condemned Mr C. P. Trevelyan, its own representative in Parliament to be shot. Only one member offered an objection when the Elland District Council passed a resolution 'that Mr Trevelyan be taken out and shot'.[23]

Resilience was needed and Trevelyan had it. Ramsay MacDonald, who was thinner-skinned, suffered having his birth certificate paraded in *John Bull*: 'the illegitimate son of a Scotch servant girl', gleefully proclaimed the paper. (MacDonald's mother had been a housemaid and his father a ploughman.) With abuse went physical threats: before one meeting (in September 1918) a reward was offered 'to the first man who caused Mr Ramsay MacDonald to be taken away on a stretcher'.[24]

The personal consequences of a stand on the war could run deep. A letter of early October 1914 from Johnnie Ponsonby to his brother Arthur shows the family hurt that taking a dissenting line on the war could cause. Johnnie, leading his battalion, had been in the thick of the fighting in the British retreat from Mons, being wounded in the leg. He wrote to his brother:

You seemed the other day to be so enthusiastic and to agree when I said that one of the best things of this war terrible as it was, was that it brought out the whole country as one man. I can't help feeling that the *Nation* or some other paper has got a speech of yours all sideways . . . I do know that everybody now out in France believes that the whole Country is behind them – Conservatives, Home Rulers, Radicals, Socialists etc. I know in my heart of hearts that this is the same with you . . . I am very proud of Fritz going out and I hope soon to get out again so that the two of us in the family can do our small share and I know that as you can't very well make up the third you will back us up both . . . I know you would come out yourself with a rifle if you could and perhaps your country may want you if a lot of us get knocked out.[25]

The reference to the newspaper article is to a distorting version of a letter which Arthur had written to the *Nation* on 22 August, which had been run in a Swedish newspaper. It had come to Fritz Ponsonby who had asked Johnnie to get an explanation from Arthur. Arthur wrote in his diary:

> It has made me feel useless, impotent and almost criminal and yet in calmer moments I still feel most deeply that the future must be faced that my view of the war is right and that preparations for the future and the formation of a strong public opinion against these cruel brutalities and against the people being deceived, kept ignorant and then driven to the slaughter by their governments, is the most important thing of all.[26]

The apprehension with which Westminster lived during these years was recorded in diaries. On 19 June 1916 Richard Holt wrote: 'We are all expecting a big attack by the British on the West. Pray God if it comes, my brother Philip may get through safely. I fear terrible loss of life.'[27]

The Battle of the Somme, a joint British and French operation, was launched on 1 July 1916. The terrible story is well known. Allied troops were cut down in swathes as they walked, weighed down with their heavy equipment, towards the German lines, whose fortifications were largely intact despite the prolonged and massive artillery barrage which preceded the attack.

Charles Trevelyan wrote to Molly on 4 July:

> Certainly the great effort is proceeding. The figures of the casualties of the first day were given by Gulland [Liberal Chief Whip] at 42,000. What unimaginable horror! At least everyone determines not to imagine it.[28]

The figure given here is an underestimate. On the first day of the battle the British Expeditionary Force suffered 58,000 casualties, a third of them killed, more losses than on any other day in the history of the British Army.[29]

The parliamentary dissenters were in a difficult position. Newspaper presentation was of a successful advance. After two weeks of horrifying casualty lists, Arthur Ponsonby decided that it was time for a move in Parliament. He wrote to Charles Trevelyan on 13 July:

> I dined with [Francis] Hirst. Had a long talk. I followed up this yesterday morning by an hour with [Lord] Loreburn. Briefly he agreed that we could not sit with folded hands while the offensive went on for months. Because the idea seems to be that we cannot break through but we can massacre a sufficient number of Germans to make a difference. Therefore before the recess might not some simultaneous action be taken by both Houses?[30]

In his diary Ponsonby outlined the idea of a conference of members of the two Houses, 'with a view to seeing whether simultaneous action might not be taken in order to press for negotiations instead of waiting till this hideous massacre has exhausted itself'.[31]

But the move had to be abandoned. Ponsonby wrote to Trevelyan on 17 July: 'Now people's minds are concentrated on this advance and we should have to wait till the deadlock was more apparent.'[32]

One of the many households to suffer was Shulbrede. Arthur Ponsonby's diary for 21 July 1916 has:

> The present moment is almost the most unbearable that there has been. The advance is costing a terrible price. The enormous casualty lists give no idea of the real truth. Even here at Shulbrede our poor housemaid Gertie received a packet of her own letters back because the man she was engaged to has been killed. And the advance does not go on. It has stuck . . . It is useless saying anything – no one will listen.[33]

On 17 August the diary reports: 'I hear the casualties are well over 200,000. How this can be described as a victory I do not know. Johnnie has moved to Pozières.'[34]

Pozières was a ruined village on the Somme battlefield over which there was fierce fighting. Johnnie Ponsonby was now commanding the 2nd Brigade of the Guards Division. Serving under him was Lieutenant Raymond Asquith, son of the Prime Minister and prospective Liberal candidate for Derby, whose reputation was as one of the brightest of his generation. Johnnie kept Arthur informed about what was happening and gave him frank assessments. Arthur wrote to Charles Trevelyan on 12 September:

My eldest brother came over from the front and returned this morning for the big attack which takes place at the end of this week. The German trenches are to be to be taken whatever the cost. He anticipates a fearful massacre and says we do not know nearly all the casualties since July.[35]

The 'whatever the cost' attack took place on 15 September. The Allies used a new weapon – tanks. There was some territorial gain but the follow-up miscarried, and the advantage was squandered. The casualties were very heavy. Those killed included Raymond Asquith, who took part in one of the attacks, in which seventeen out of twenty-two officers were either killed or wounded. Raymond had given some hint in his last letter (to his friend Diana Manners) two days before the attack that his survival chances were poor.[36]

Arthur Ponsonby wrote again to Charles Trevelyan on 27 September:

I don't believe the push will develop much further. It is preposterous our not knowing what it costs. It would make a great difference to the most enthusiastic war-mongers if they knew how fearfully expensive these small advances were.[37]

Parliament resumed on 10 October. A Vote of Credit occupied the following two days. The Prime Minister reported: 'By these operations we have advanced a distance of some seven miles on a front of nine miles.'[38]

The shocking costs of the battle were becoming known. The late summer silence on the part of the dissidents was now broken. Charles Trevelyan protested in the debate:

It is not everybody who is blind to the real meaning of that abominable phrase, 'a war of attrition'. Part of the attrition is now hundreds of thousands of British men. I do not know what the casualties have been in the last three months. I am going to ask.

Leonard Outhwaite declared:

[The Prime Minister] did not tell us how many thousands of men have been killed and mutilated, but we can give a fair guess at what the total must be, when over a long period running into months, we have seen casualty lists of 5,000 a day. But surely it is obvious that if an advance of seven miles on a nine mile front entails the sacrifice of hundreds of thousands of lives, the total crushing of Germany and the Central Powers must inevitably take years and must amount to the loss of millions of men.[39]

The Potteries MP predicted: 'You will see the forces of revolution sweep through Europe after this war over who is to pay for this wild debauch of blood.'

Leonard Outhwaite had commented on the horror of the war in a small book called *The Ghosts of the Slain*, published towards the end of 1915, in the manner of an illustrated manuscript. It imagines the nations seeing the folly of the war:

> Womanhood demands her dead and the people rise up against
> the madness. For they have seen the Ghosts of the Slain go by,
> wailing, 'Woe, woe! For on earth we slew one another!'[40]

In the spectral procession British and German helmets are mingled. The two sides have merged in sorrowful regret.

Dissenting MPs faced a growing threat of prosecution. Among those whose political activities featured in Home Office and police files were Philip Snowden, Charles Trevelyan, Joseph King and Leonard Outhwaite. In October 1916 Joseph King was fined £100 under the Defence of the Realm legislation as a result of a letter to a friend in New York, extracts of which were sent to the *New York Times*, mentioning military details. King must have feared prison, given that as an opponent of conscription he could expect no favours.[41]

Peace campaigners did go to jail. In February 1916, an elderly former Liberal MP, Arnold Lupton, was sent to prison for six months in the brutal 'second division'. Edmund Morel, the driving force of the UDC, was jailed for six months for breach of the Defence of the Realm Act in sending a UDC pamphlet to someone in neutral Switzerland. The offence was trivial and Government motivation behind the charge and its outcome was plain. Morel was put in the second division at Pentonville and his health was broken. Bertrand Russell served six months for the publication of literature deemed to be subversive.[42]

The battle to protect ancient freedoms against the inroads of the war state drew together the backbench Liberal and Labour MPs of the civil rights group, with back-up from outside, including anti-war women's suffrage campaigners. The joint action which Arthur Ponsonby and Ramsay MacDonald had tried to bring about in the August 1914 days was now working. On 1 June 1916 Richard Holt came to the Commons for a debate on the Defence of the Realm Act, equipped with some useful quotations, thanks to the help of women's suffrage activist Catherine Marshall. Referring to the case of two women in Northampton who had been prosecuted for distributing a pamphlet entitled 'Repeal the [Conscription] Act', Holt quoted one of the leaflet's snippets – a passage from an article by Sydney Smith in the *Edinburgh Review* of 1813:

> If three men were to have their legs broken and were to remain all night exposed to the inclemency of the weather, the whole country would be in a state of the most dreadful agitation. Look at the wholesale death on a field of battle, ten acres covered with dead, and half-dead and dying; the shrieks and agonies of many thousands of human beings. There is more misery inflicted on mankind by one year of war than by all the civil peculations and oppressions of a century. Yet it is a state into which the mass of mankind run with the greatest avidity.[43]

The MP delivered more quotations from pamphlets which had fallen foul of the authorities. With Herbert Samuel, the Home Secretary, in attendance, he made particular play of one passage:

> If warfare continues it is largely because, even in an age of enlightenment, wars are popular. The fighting is welcomed for its own sake. There is still surviving much of the old barbaric delight 'in the merry days of battle'. If we are candid we are bound to confess that this spirit is not so different from that which led all Rome on a feast-day to flock to the Colosseum and sit crowding to see the gladiatorial shows; it is the thrilling joy of watching a game in which men's lives are at stake. And while war evokes these elemental passions among the masses of the people, the leaders of public opinion in the press, on the platform and even in the pulpit, are often found justifying war by elaborate and plausible sophisms.

Who was the author? Holt gave the answer:

... Let me see, I find that it was written by a gentleman called Herbert Samuel. The book from which I take it is called 'Liberalism: its Principles and Proposals'. It was published in 1902, shortly after we had emerged from a great war.

Holt remarked in his diary: 'On Thursday 1 June I made a speech in the H of C on the treatment of anti-conscriptionists. The best thing I have yet managed.'[44]

The records of the anti-conscription and defence of civil liberty group in the House of Commons have not survived, but in the papers of Catherine Marshall there is an attendance list of a meeting of 27 June 1916 at which Marshall was a visitor. About half of those present had been Members active in Arthur Ponsonby's pre-war foreign affairs group. The big change was the participation of Labour Members. The hopes of Arthur Ponsonby and Ramsay MacDonald, and their respective allies, of progressive political realignment were starting now to come to some fruition.[45]

Women provided a vital support role. Catherine Marshall was well to the fore in the successful battle to save forty conscription resisters who were shipped to France. The Army leadership wanted to shoot them (or some of them). Chilling drama occurred in the House of Commons on 22 June 1916 when Liberal Howard Whitehouse, MP for mid-Lanark, shouted across to the Minister Jack Tennant at the Despatch Box, 'Are you going to shoot them?' Marshall's things-to-do list on this occasion included ringing up the whole Cabinet. (Presumably a team would do this.) Ottoline Morrell helped by buttonholing Herbert Asquith when he and his family visited the Morrells' Oxfordshire home. It was Asquith who saved the men. He phoned Commander-in-Chief Douglas Haig to tell him that he must not shoot the objectors. Death sentences were delivered, with confirmation, but immediately commuted.[46]

Meanwhile on the international politics of war, Parliament was kept in the dark. What was not revealed included: the Allies' acceptance of Russia's claims to Constantinople (March 1915), which was the consequence of Britain's backing of Tsarist war aims; the Treaty of London (April 1915) which induced Italy into the war on the Allied side with large territorial promises; and the Sykes–Picot Agreement (May 1916) to partition the Ottoman Empire into spheres of interest among the Allies. As Douglas Newton has observed, the notion that 'the British and Empire dead were part of a great sacrifice for a new democratic Europe ... is a fairy tale'. The peace group set out its own agenda but had little chance of making headway in the House of Commons, as long as there was hope of military victory. When Radicals shouted 'Annexations!' about empire and power-block building, few listened.[47]

Of course there was very big aims-expansion on the other side too. For the Central Powers, the *status quo*, on which to conduct any negotiations, was not 1914 but 1916 including the swathes of territory which they had overrun, from which they aimed to take large advantage. And for both sides, especially Germany, it was a question of who was in charge of the war aims, the politicians or the military? For the peace group in the British Parliament perhaps the only real hope was a non-violent uprising of the peoples of Europe against their rulers' war in the manner of Outhwaite's *Ghosts of the Slain*.[48]

For a few months in 1917 the impossible dream seemed to be happening. On 15 March Tsar Nicholas Romanov abdicated. The Russian Provisional Government, with its mixture of liberals and socialists, was welcomed joyfully by British House of Commons campaigners for peace by negotiation. The new Russian government was continuing the war, but its policy was a negotiated peace on the basis of 'no annexations and no indemnity'. British peace group MPs looked particularly to Alexander Kerensky, the Minister of Justice (a socialist), who became Prime Minister in July; he had identified himself with the policy which the British parliamentary peace by negotiation group promoted.

On 4 April Leonard Outhwaite gave the House of Commons his views on Russia's spring revolution in an Easter adjournment debate:

> I feel certain myself that every belligerent country will be swept away by revolutionary movement; by these economic and social forces autocracies throughout Europe will fall, and it is because I am so confident that these economic forces will achieve the objects which we are stated to have in mind that it seems to be futile and useless to go on one day longer than is necessary fighting and sacrificing the lives of the young and brave of this country.[49]

Hansard records on the same day an Outhwaite question for Lloyd George:

Mr Outhwaite asked the Prime Minister whether his attention has been drawn to the fact that the Russian Government has abolished the death penalty in the case of military offences; and will he consider the question of taking similar action?[50]

The question was taken by Bonar Law:

The answer to the first part is in the affirmative, and the second in the negative.

The British firing squads would continue. The shooting of selected 'deserters' with the aim of beefing-up discipline, had an element of continuity with the pre-war eugenics bills against which Josiah Wedgwood protested in the Commons on the Wednesday before the war. There is some evidence that whether a 'deserter' or a 'coward' sentenced to death in the British Army was selected to perish (a minority) or had his sentence commuted (the majority) might be influenced by the perceived worth of his stock. Irish soldiers seem to have been at extra risk in this regard.[51]

Wedgwood, on his returns from the battle front to Parliament, spoke up for conscientious objectors and others in who were in trouble with the law for political campaigning. *Punch*, one of the papers which had a low opinion of those who raised concern for civil liberty in wartime, remarked in July 1917:

Commander Wedgwood, I am sorry to observe, has almost exhausted the store of common sense that he brought back with him from the trenches of Gallipoli. Otherwise he would hardly have championed the cause of Mrs ANNIE BESANT, upon whose activities the Government of Madras have imposed certain salutary restrictions.[52]

Annie Besant was a campaigner for Indian Home Rule.

There was some real belief that Russia would lead the way to peace and sanity. Leonard Outhwaite held a meeting in Hanley, with handbills inviting constituents to 'come in crowds' to celebrate the revolution. Philip Snowden was another inclined to romantic revolutionary dreaming, declaring at the ILP Easter Conference in Leeds: 'To Russia, so long the most persecuted and oppressed nation of the earth, has been given the proud privilege of leading the world revolution of the workers.'[53]

Meanwhile Britain saw change. A significant moment occurred in August 1917. Arthur Henderson, Labour Leader and in the Cabinet, had been sent on a visit to Russia by the British Government leaders, who along with other Allied governments were alarmed that some members of the new Russian regime were looking to make a negotiated peace. Henderson's job was to get his socialist friends in Russia back onside with the war. But the Labour Leader was converted to the peace negotiation aspirations of the Russian socialists. When he came back, he called for attendance by representatives of the Labour Party at an international socialist conference in Stockholm. The result was that he was forced out of the Cabinet. It was expected by the Government that he would resign also as Labour Leader and that Labour would select a compliant replacement. But Henderson stayed. His party subsequently adopted the foreign policy principles of the Union of Democratic Control. Labour continued to support the war but in June 1918 it withdrew from the wartime electoral truce. Labour's patience with the draining of lives and resources was on the brink in the final year of the war.[54]

By 1917 some Liberals were looking for new party arrangements. Arthur Ponsonby in June 1917 was working on the idea of a new Radical Party. It would need a leader. Winston Churchill, out in the cold politically at that time, the man of energy and charisma, albeit with baggage, the man of the Dardanelles disaster but with the drive to succeed in a new direction, could be the person. Ponsonby's diary records a long meeting with Churchill:

> He listened but was a curious mixture of shrewdness and stupidity. He does not believe in decisive victory but he still hopes the military situation may develop in such a way as to persuade Germany that she is to all intents and purposes beaten. On the causes of the war he actually admitted that diplomacy properly handled might have steered events into an avoidance of war. Anyway he is not prepared to come out yet awhile.[55]

The moment passed. Lloyd George, aware of the dangers of Churchill on the loose, shortly afterwards appointed him Minister of Munitions. Arthur Ponsonby eventually gave up on the new party of Radicals and, with Charles Trevelyan leading the way, moved in the direction of Labour.

Inevitably the peace by negotiation cause had internal differences. Ramsay MacDonald thought that Russia should not quit the war unilaterally. Most of the peace by negotiation group was happy for Russia to get on with negotiating terms. Persuading Ramsay MacDonald to join the peace by negotiation speech-makers in the House of Commons had not been easy. While Snowden, Ponsonby and Trevelyan led the way in the parliamentary campaign, MacDonald had to be dragged aboard. The power of the Scot's oratory was one of the group's most cherished assets, as was his standing in the Labour movement, but MacDonald was also sometimes the cause of exasperation, convoluted in position and Delphic in exposition. His caution makes his courageous stand in August 1914 the more remarkable. Sylvia Pankhurst, who led the anti-war women suffragists, wrote in her memoirs of the wartime MacDonald:

> He must always be travelling roundabout, with so much con-
> cession to the opposite pole, that unless rudely thrust on by a
> strong force behind him, he was apt to end to the rear of the
> point from which he started.[56]

MacDonald headed the infamy list in the patriot vigilante press and yet he managed to keep one foot engaged with the establishment. He was ready to come out more directly against the war when it became unpopular, but the swing of opinion was stubbornly slow to happen.

In November 1917 what had seemed to be Russia's democratic spring was squashed by the Bolsheviks. But the new regime pulled Russia out of the war (early in 1918) and this won some praise from the British parliamentary anti-war group. The consequences for the peace by negotiation campaign were damaging. In March 1918 Philip Morrell rashly delivered a vote of thanks to the Bolshevik ambassador in London, in which while speaking of Lloyd George and his War Cabinet as 'knowing nothing of freedom', he declared that people in Britain were 'beginning to see that it is time that we followed the example of the Russian workmen'. *Punch*, apparently nonplussed, commented that:

> Of all the Members of the House the last I should have suspected,
> prima facie, of sympathy with Bolshevism is Mr MORRELL,
> who is the brother in law of a duke and dresses the part to
> perfection ... But if he wants to be taken seriously he must grow
> a beard à la LENIN and eschew clean collars and soap.[57]

Philip Morrell was not the only MP in the British parliamentary peace group with a soft spot for the Bolsheviks. In a debate on 13 February 1918 on a peace negotiations amendment in the Debate on the Address following the opening of the year's parliamentary session, Charles Trevelyan declared:

> Be sure of this, that there are masses of working men outside this House who do not approve of the violence of the Bolsheviks but approve of the principle they have been trying internationally to assist.[58]

Trevelyan had privately enthused, 'Wonderful the force of ideas, wonderful the Bolsheviks. They have reversed the engines.'

And on 5 January 1918 Arthur Ponsonby wrote to Trevelyan: 'The Bolshevists are simply splendid and I hope they will teach the world that military victory is not necessary for a good settlement.'[59]

The Bolsheviks also opened the Russian state archives and published the Allies' secret treaties. This went down well in British anti-war circles. But good words about the Bolsheviks cost the peace cause support. The February 1918 motion, which had looked very promising, gained only twenty-eight votes, with some who had spoken for the motion abstaining or even voting against it. Richard Holt (who had taken the lead in the debate) put the disappointing result down to 'the folly of Charles Trevelyan who eulogised rantingly Trotsky and the Bolsheviks'.[60]

The peace negotiations campaign had been showing signs of making some progress. The later months of 1917 had seen the prolonged horror of Passchendaele, the name forever synonymous with Western Front carnage in the mud. There were now reactions on a number of fronts. There were the Liberal and Labour disillusioned, originally persuaded in on ethical grounds, but now seeing with dismay war being prosecuted for imperialist purposes. There was also the famous 'Lansdowne Letter'. Lord Lansdowne, who had been the Conservative Foreign Secretary in the Government which signed the Entente Cordiale had had enough of the war's plundering of Britain's lives and resources. He himself had lost a son, killed in Flanders in 1914. On 29 November 1917 he had a letter published in the *Daily Telegraph* (having been refused by the *Times*) calling for peace negotiations to save the civilised world from ruin. He brought some Conservative scorn on himself and the jingo press jeered, but he pressed on with his campaign, allying himself with Labour members of the peace by negotiation movement. Like the war, the peace movement made strange bedfellows. There were 'Lansdowne/Labour Conferences', at which MacDonald and Snowden spoke. Liberals were there too. Opposition to carnage without end broke all the normal rules of political association. It had to. In the first peace debate, in February 1916, Leonard Outhwaite had asked:

> What benefit will it be to the people of this country if it means that to win this war you have to kill off all the youths, and there are only the old and middle-aged left? Such a victory could only be gained by dragging in the last million men or the last hundred thousand to hoist the flag of victory over an international graveyard.[61]

Two years on, the theory of victory for the side with one million left after the mutual slaughter of millions seemed to working its way to its appalling conclusion. It is not surprising that there were unprecedented political alliances in the attempt to save some society to go back to.

In 1918 the negotiation cause did seem to be gathering some modest momentum in the House of Commons. On board (though guarding his war credentials) was Labour's pivotally influential railway union leader, J. H. (Jimmy) Thomas, MP for Derby. Thomas had been an active supporter of recruiting but had opposed conscription and, while continuing to give his backing to the war, had declined an offer to join the Cabinet of the Coalition Government. In the February 1918 debate Thomas protested about the subversion of British war aims: 'The 5,000,000 lads who volunteered, and who voluntarily offered their lives, did not do it for any Imperialist aims.'[62]

Active service Liberal Godfrey Collins, a publisher, delicately chided the Government's war rhetoric:

> I confess I am sometimes tempted to prefer the tone and ring of President Wilson's speeches to some of those nearer home, because we seem to catch in the former what we miss in the latter – the vibration of unselfish ideals and noble aspirations after world-wide liberty, humanity and justice.[63]

Woodrow Wilson was the hero of British parliamentary progressives. In one debate when Arthur Balfour as Foreign Secretary said that, 'The

President of the United States speaks of the motives which animate the great country of which he is the head', Josiah Wedgwood shouted, 'He speaks for us as well,' plainly meaning that the British Government did not. The 1917 entry of the United States into the war had been a blow for the parliamentary peace group but there were distinctly consoling aspects. America was keeping its distance, as an associate power rather than an ally. There was reason for hope that President Wilson would not join the European pursuit of annexations but would stick to his enunciated principles. In January 1918 he talked about 'peace without victory'.[64]

Speakers for the February 1918 peace negotiations motion included Conservative active service MP Colonel Aubrey Herbert. The Somerset MP, known for his daring bravery, had been wounded at Mons. He had a question:

> I want to know what it is that we are going to be killed for. For instance, there have been preposterous arguments in our own Hun papers – in the Northcliffe Press – as to what we intend to do to all the Allies of Germany. There were leaders in *The Times*, one of them suggesting making a fantastic mosaic of Austria. There may be some eccentrics who are ready to die for that leader in *The Times*. As far as I am concerned, it can go and shed its own ink.[65]

The peace by negotiation group's view on the Austro-Hungarian Empire was that the best way to self-determination was through devolution and federalism rather than regime change. The group was highly sceptical about creating an artificial new state to be called Czechoslovakia and the Allies' motives in pressing for it. MPs enquired who the 'Czechoslovaks' were? Leonard Outhwaite in February 1917 asked whether liberation of the Czechs would be followed by liberation of the Irish; and how the Government proposed to deal with the German minority which would be in the new 'Czechoslovakia' state and which wished to maintain the imperial connection with Austria, as Ulster with Britain.[66]

The setback of the disappointing February 1918 vote disheartened peace by negotiation supporters. There were recriminations between the original group and the new group led by Richard Holt. But in June there was a further peace debate. Philip Snowden related to the

Commons details of mounting collapse around the country during 1918 of Labour confidence in the war. He read out to MPs a resolution of the Birmingham Labour Party which had been handed to him that morning just in time for the debate:

> The Birmingham Labour Party has learned of the contents of the secret treaties entered into by the Allied Governments with the utmost dismay and indignation. It recalls the fact that the party almost unanimously consented, jointly with the Birmingham Trades Council, to participate in the recruiting campaign early in the war because it was led to believe that the war was being fought for the freedom of small nations and the sanctity of international law. The Labour Party now discovers that it has been utterly deceived and that while the above mentioned recruiting campaign was proceeding the Allied Governments commenced a series of secret conferences at which secret treaties were formulated. In the opinion of the party those treaties flagrantly violate every reason put forward by British statesmen in justification for the war and embody precisely those obnoxious and immoral principles of Junker Imperialism which they were led to believe they were fighting against.[67]

It was a damning indictment.

Snowden hammered the point home: 'That resolution was passed unanimously. There is not a labour organisation in the country which would not endorse that resolution.'

A journalist wrote of Snowden in action in 1918: 'As was remarked by a Tory member, held in fascination by Mr Snowden's eloquence, "he spits fire and brimstone at us".'[68]

With the United States in the war and Russia leaving it, the military deadlock was going to be broken eventually – either a German victory (with the help of forces redeployed from the Eastern Front) before the Americans could get their troops over and organised in numbers, or an Allied triumph with the help of the big military resources of the United States. But how would the war end and what hopes would there be for a lasting peace?

The British Government's consistent position was that Germany must be broken. Bonar Law had put it thus it on 20 February 1917:

What guarantees have we today, if the war ends today – with the Prussian military machine unbroken, and with all the prestige of victory still surrounding the power of Germany – that in the next two decades the same preparations will not be made again, or that we shall not once more have to defend ourselves under worse conditions?[69]

The peace by negotiation group presented the reverse of this argument – that if Germany was broken rather than negotiated with, the outcome would be an insecure peace and the eventual resumption of war. Richard Lambert, a Wiltshire Liberal member of the group, in the same debate, after reminding the Government that he had accepted the war at the start and had helped at many recruiting meetings, gave what would be a much reiterated warning from the group:

If anybody thinks a military success, even a triumphal entry into Berlin, is going to produce the end of all war, and to bring about a permanent peace, he is labouring under a most terrible delusion.[70]

During the last part of the war a bright spot for progressive MPs was the passage of the Representation of the People Bill, which enfranchised women and completed the enfranchisement of men. The metal grille in front of the Ladies' Gallery was removed to symbolise that change had come. But the bill suffered from the patronising characterisation of war work reward, when the reform would have happened anyway; and it excluded women under thirty, in order to keep down the female numbers on the voting roll. The war did no favours for the cause of women's suffrage. The story of the Representation of the People Act is a continuation of the electoral reform up to 1914. The great debates on the franchise had happened before the war started. The battle was all but won. Britain was edging towards full adult suffrage in 1914. The process was if anything slowed by the war years as a result of so many women being excluded in 1918. The women who had to wait another decade (until 1928) included many of those who had worked in the munitions factories.

Also, there was an ugly reverse-democratic aspect to the Representation of the People Bill. While it was going through, an amendment was inserted to disenfranchise conscientious objectors for five years. (Meanwhile some men under twenty-one who had been on active service were enfranchised). The disenfranchising clause, debated on 21 November 1917, was opposed by some of the most impassioned speeches of the war, including one by high Tory Hugh Cecil, which won much admiration. But the measure was approved, by 209–171. It set back the earlier progress made in establishing rights for conscientious objectors. Richard Holt recorded it: 'Tories with assistance of a few bad Liberals disenfranchised conscientious objectors – an abominable piece of persecution and intolerance.'[71]

During the war the Union of Democratic Control published prolifically, as it set out its alternative perspective. Arthur Ponsonby used the ironic title *The Crank* for one publication. This took the form of a play-script on the subject of UDC policy. A secretary is facing the sack from his employer, a merchant, for having UDC-type views. The employer invites a professor to judge whether the man is an unpatriotic pro-German. The secretary sails through the cross-examination, to the vexation of the merchant who says of the professor, 'something of the crank in him too', but then leaves the impression that perhaps he may keep his employee.[72]

On 8 August 1918 the House rose for its break following what would prove to be the last of the peace by negotiation debates. In it ILP Member for Sheffield Attercliffe William Anderson (who had had to go before a tribunal to make his case for exemption from conscription), leading for the peace by negotiation group, declared, 'I do not believe that the world has ever realised so clearly as it does now the meaning of war and the misery of war.' He quoted from the *Daily News* a grisly calculation:

> If we sat day and night and saw the ghostly procession of those slain file by in ranks of four, minute by minute, ten years would pass and still the tale of the world's sacrifice of its youth and strength would not have been told.[73]

Anderson, forty-one (who entered Parliament for Labour at the end of 1914 under the electoral truce), in the estimation of some, had he lived would have become leader of the Labour Party. But he is barely remembered. After losing his seat in 1918, he died the following year, a victim of the 1918–20 influenza pandemic, which was a product of the war and which accounted for 50 million deaths.

In the debate the anti-war group's case provoked the usual scorn. The following day Arthur Ponsonby wrote to Charles Trevelyan in a depressed state: 'For the moment I feel that I should not shed a tear if I never saw the inside of that infernal place again.'[74]

But later in the day he was joined at Shulbrede by his wife and son. His diary records the change:

> D. arrived from Rustington with M. Immediately my spirits began to go up and all the crowd of scoffers, the Butchers and the Balfours and their bloody cynical ideas began to fade away. Blazing sunshine.[75]

Conservative John Butcher had heckled Arthur Ponsonby's speech in the debate, accusing him of 'helping the Germans'. Ponsonby had said:

> Those who want to go on until the Hun is beaten to his knees perhaps will have their way, but the National Debt will be piled up higher and higher, cemeteries will extend, and the procession of maimed and wounded men will wander back here, their lives wrecked forever. I say to the Foreign Secretary that I desire just as much as he does an honourable peace and a just peace . . . I desire just as much as he does the destruction of militarism in Germany and the world over; but I ask, in all reason, after having attempted by force of arms to effect those objects, during four years in which civilisation has been brought to the verge of ruin, whether it is not worthwhile to follow another road, and by deliberation, by reason, by conference, and by negotiation, to secure what the sword by itself can never give us.[76]

A telling of Parliament's wartime story ought perhaps briefly to mention the House of Commons at the war's ending, Armistice Day, 11 November 1918. It is worth noting that the day was not what Prime Minister David Lloyd George had intended. The cessation of hostilities was originally intended to be at 2.30 p.m., so that Lloyd George could announce when Parliament met at its usual Monday time that the war had ended a few minutes earlier. But the Prime Minister's instructions were countermanded by the British representative at the 5 a.m. signing of the Armistice, Admiral Sir Rosslyn Wemyss, who saw the poetic possibilities of the eleventh hour of the eleventh day of the eleventh month, and also wished to save some lives. The Admiral provoked the fury of the Prime Minister but the procession of the slain was thereby a little shorter than it otherwise would have been. Arthur Ponsonby and his fellow campaigners did not know but they would have approved.[77]

At the General Election following the end of the war the Lloyd George Coalition's infamous 'coupon' for its approved candidates and jingo hysteria, with pro-Government election slogans like 'Hang the Kaiser', meant that the chances of putting a balanced presentation to the electorate and winning voter favour were poor. Nearly all the members of the peace by negotiation group, including Ponsonby, Trevelyan, MacDonald and Outhwaite, lost their seats.

The following year came the settlement of the war. The Ponsonby circle had hoped that Woodrow Wilson would knock some moral principles into the Europeans. They were disappointed. On the Treaty of Versailles, which worked out the settlement, Arthur Ponsonby wrote in his diary:

> Annexations, dismemberment, robbery and ruin. No faint pretence of justice or generosity. This after the war. This to finish it all. This is the culmination of all the massacres and horrors.[78]

The *Daily Herald* of 13 May 1919 has a cartoon of a child weeping behind a pillar as the statesmen are emerging from the conference: it is labelled '1940 class'.[79] Aubrey Herbert was in Paris as the settlement was completed. He reported on the black humour: 'the seeds of a just and durable war' and 'a peace to end peace'. Arthur Ponsonby was dismayed at the punitive treaty: Germany specified as the party with the responsibility for the war, heavy financial reparations, and the creation of frontiers for strategic purposes and of new super-states, Poland, Czechoslovakia and (as it became) Yugoslavia. There was a League of Nations but the United States was not in it. In the view of Ponsonby and his friends, it was as bad a settlement as could have been imagined.[80]

Thomas Burt's prediction of 'a welter of anarchy' indeed proved to be correct. With the best will in the world it would hardly have been possible to create out of the mass of violent conflicts, an international map with fairness and the roots of secure peace. In some areas the fighting did not stop with the November 1918 Armistice. Where it did, ambition, aggrandisement and imperialism loomed large in the negotiations and mostly defeated the more principled approach of President Wilson, who had given some hope to the British parliamentary peace by negotiation group. The wartime warnings of the group that military victory would not provide the basis for making a sound settlement were amply borne out.

The 1918 electoral wipe-out of those who had promoted peace by negotiation was fairly soon being reversed. The turnaround in fortunes was most remarkable for Ramsay MacDonald, who in 1924 became Labour's first Prime Minister. MacDonald's Chancellor of the Exchequer was Philip Snowden, who had been one of the most effective critics of the war policy. Snowden was physically incapacitated, walking with two sticks, but he was one of Parliament's most powerful orators. In the House of Commons in the 26 July 1917 debate he declared:

> With all the strength at my disposal, Mr Speaker, I protest against such a policy as that. In the name of our common humanity I say it is scandalous and I will raise my voice against it. I say in the name of humanity we must stop this war now.[81]

Snowden went down to hefty defeat at Blackburn in 1918, but the 15,000 votes which he received cheered him. He returned to Parliament in 1922 for Colne Valley.

The wartime UDC was well represented in MacDonald's 1924 administration, with Charles Trevelyan at Education among those who had campaigned for peace by negotiation who were now Cabinet ministers.

Some of the peace group did not reappear after 1918. Not all survived the war. Sir William Byles died in October 1917. The war had been painful for the veteran progressive campaigner. He told Arnold Rowntree in 1916 that all his hopes were shattered. His last parliamentary act was to oppose the sanction of whipping in Jamaica.[82]

Allen Baker died in July 1918, two days after suffering a heart attack in Parliament. With the arrival of the war, Baker had thrown his energies into the Quaker Friends' Ambulance Unit. He made many overseas trips. He suffered injury from shrapnel on one occasion. Trevor Wilson has written of him, 'In August 1914 his world collapsed about him.'[83]

Some anti-war Liberals left politics. These included Phillip Morrell. The Burnley MP was not one of those who led the way on the peace by negotiation campaign. He was the first MP approached by Siegfried Sassoon in 1917 but declined to read out the soldier's personal statement in the House of Commons, despite having been an influence in Sassoon's beliefs. However, Morrell threw himself into the work of looking after conscientious objectors. He represented their cases in Parliament and provided them with work, by arrangement with the tribunals, on his family's Garsington Manor estate in Oxfordshire. They were not grateful. Ottoline's diaries describe a collection of inexperienced and unwilling farm labourers, who made feeble attempts to chop up firewood and needed to be directed to hoeing with the village women. They included a Cambridge economist who tried to organise a trade union, despite the local labourers not wanting it. (Meanwhile the local vicar was ranting in the pulpit that 'to kill a German is Christ's work'.) Morrell, like most of the anti-conscription Liberals, lost his party nomination. After the breach with the Burnley Liberals he became prominent in the House of Commons in the campaign for peace by negotiation. But there were rattling skeletons in his closet. In March 1917 he revealed to Ottoline that he had made two mistresses pregnant. For several days he had a mental breakdown and he was in terror of discovery bringing publicity disastrous to the peace campaign. After 1918 Morrell withdrew from public life. He had worked hard without much credit. Many pages of Hansard bear testimony to his defence of British civil liberty at its time of greatest challenge.[84]

Arnold Rowntree, after defeat at York as a Liberal in 1918, did not stand for Parliament again. Those Liberals who did stay in the electoral fray in the changed post-war world faced an uphill struggle. Richard Holt, on the libertarian right wing of his party, was never likely to consider joining the migration to the Labour Party. His attempts to return to the Commons were unsuccessful. Edmund Harvey did better, with the label of Independent Progressive, for the constituency of English Combined Universities.

The big migration from Liberal to Labour rescued the political careers of some. These included Richard Denman, who became Labour MP for Leeds Central. But not all of those who made the move found a seat to see them back into the House of Commons. The voice of Joe King which fills so many columns of Hansard between 1910 and 1918 was silenced. One may think that Parliament was the poorer. He managed a good second place at York in 1923 and then called time. He pursued an active interest in the Peasant Arts movement and was Honorary Curator of the Haslemere Museum collection.

Leonard Outhwaite lost at Hanley in 1918 but as an independent Liberal had the satisfaction of taking nearly twice as many votes as the official Liberal. He had continued his land taxation activism through the war. In 1918 a war event had revised the way some previously scornful MPs viewed him. The night of 22/23 April saw the famous Zeebrugge raid, the attempt by the Royal Navy to block the German naval bases at Zeebrugge and Ostend, in which there were heavy British casualties. A member of the British force who distinguished himself with conspicuous gallantry, was Leonard Outhwaite's son. Motor-boat commander, Sub-Lieutenant Cedric Outhwaite, was awarded a DSC for his part in the engagement, in which he torpedoed a German destroyer. The news caused what a journalist called 'a distinct change' in the attitude towards Outhwaite senior on the part of the jingoes who sat on the bench behind. At the 1918 General Election Leonard Outhwaite's meetings were chaired by his son.[85]

After the war Leonard Outhwaite joined the Independent Labour Party. But state socialism did not sit easily with his vision of the land as the key to personal liberty. He was also unhappy to see 'the conscriptionists' restored to their places in the leadership of a re-united Labour movement. He left the Labour Party to concentrate on the land tax movement and on his writing. Outhwaite died in 1930. The *Manchester Guardian* obituary reflected on a career which might have been:

> Outhwaite was an able and zealous propagandist. A man of intense and sincere convictions, he was in turn convincing, but he condemned himself to the agitator's life, and did not reach the position to which his gifts might have entitled him. But he loved liberty and consistently fought on its behalf – his best title to remembrance.[86]

The last survivor of the thirty-nine who walked through the No lobby on conscription on 12 January 1916 was Charles Trevelyan, who died in 1958, aged eighty-seven. He had succeeded to his family's baronetcy in 1928. He continued to use his wealth for the politics of the left. Wallington Hall, which he inherited, made a good conference venue. Sir Charles served in Ramsay MacDonald's second Labour Government (again as Education Minister). But he and his UDC comrade of the war were by then politically far apart. Charles Trevelyan resigned from his Cabinet post in November 1930 (being succeeded by Bertrand Lees-Smith). He wrote to his constituents that 'the central need of the world is a better distribution of wealth'.[87]

Charles Trevelyan never lost his spirited energy. He was ever the romantic optimist. Meanwhile MacDonald's formation of the – largely Conservative – National Government in 1931 (including Philip Snowden and Jimmy Thomas as 'National Labour') completed his journey into the heart of the establishment. At the General Election of that year Trevelyan stood as an independent Socialist against the National Government candidate, losing heavily. His blind-spot regarding the Bolsheviks and their successors in Russia lingered. He was one of the many on the British left who entertained wishful delusions about Soviet Russia. He lived long enough to see the Russian invasion of Hungary and to be disillusioned. He stayed physically and intellectually vigorous into advanced years, always interested in ideas and finding reasons for hope. At the end of his life he was looking at Communist China as a possible model.

Arthur Ponsonby fought the 1918 General Election at Stirling as an independent Democrat (with money for his campaign borrowed from Charles Trevelyan). He came third, behind the successful Coalition candidate and Labour (whose candidature against him was a large setback), but he polled respectably. He returned to Parliament in 1922 as Labour Member for the Brightside division of Sheffield. He served in Ramsay MacDonald's 1924 Labour Government as Secretary of State at the Foreign Office. (MacDonald was his own Foreign Secretary.) Ponsonby was responsible for the introduction of what became known as the 'Ponsonby Rule', a significant step towards a more democratic foreign policy, since it established the practice that ratification of a treaty should be delayed for twenty-one days to allow debate.[88]

During MacDonald's second Labour Government, it was suggested that Ponsonby could have a voice for Labour on foreign affairs if he moved to the Lords. He strongly resisted the move but was persuaded. He was created Baron Ponsonby of Shulbrede. He was Parliamentary Secretary to the Ministry of Transport, a role involving little serious work. He became for a short period Chancellor of the Duchy of Lancaster but the office did not carry Cabinet status and had no political value. (He found himself interviewing parsons under the patronage of the Duchy.) When MacDonald formed his National Government, Ponsonby declined to follow him. He became Labour Leader in the Lords in opposition to the Government.[89]

Arthur Ponsonby's life took in without difficulty membership of both the aristocracy and the Labour Party. Though he had rejected Society, he never failed to attend its gatherings, such as the annual Eton reunion of his house. As his biographer observes, he saw no contradiction in singing The 'Red Flag' at Labour rallies and the 'Eton Boating Song' at his old school. He enjoyed society in its widest sense. There was no patronising in his affection for his working-class constituents. In a letter to Dolly when he left the constituency to move to the Lords, he declared: 'Real people ... I am certain that if weighed in the balance with a section of our class, the recording angel would pronounce them superior ... I am sorry to leave them – very.'[90]

Because Arthur Ponsonby appreciated people, he wanted to save them from war, which in his lifetime he had seen cause so much suffering. He developed his belief in peaceful means of resolving international disputes and strife. He disagreed with the League of Nations Covenant provisions to use force as a last resort. This seemed to him like the behaviour of a victorious alliance. He felt that conferences at Geneva and elsewhere were not going to succeed unless there was a real will for peace and disarmament: Britain, he argued, should take a lead by example. He was Chairman of War Resisters' International, with Albert Einstein as President. He was prominently involved in the Peace Pledge Union.[91]

He continued his writing. *The Priory and Manor of Lynchmere and Shulbrede* was illustrated with his own drawings. The book gives an idea of the comfort which the MP's homestead refuge must have brought during the snarling war years when he and his group in the Commons were called cranks and traitors. He described returning home:

> To walk down a steep pathway through the copse to the pale, mysterious, lonely country below is like breaking into an enchanted land. And to pass from the chill evening air to the welcome side of a fire of great blazing logs, to sit and watch its red-hot caves, its licking flames and smouldering ash is a moment of warm consoling peace.[92]

Sitting by the fire, he would 'dream of the past and conjure up the presence of those who have been here before me', during the building's procession of the centuries.

Ponsonby's writing canvas was broad, taking in history, biography, philosophy and politics. His greatest success was his 1928 *Falsehood in Wartime*, which was a best-seller. The first chapter deals with the British Government's commitment to France to fight in a European war. The analysis has a message for today:

> There can be no question, therefore, that the deliberate denials and subterfuges, kept up till the last moment and fraught as they were with consequences of such magnitude, constitute a page in the history of secret diplomacy which is without parallel and afford a signal illustration of the slippery slope of official concealments.[93]

In recent years *Falsehood in Wartime* has been attacked by historians, one calling it, 'a deliberate attempt to discredit the war against Germany which he [Arthur Ponsonby] had opposed throughout, an attempt to re-write history on behalf of the losers'. Ponsonby is characterised as 'deeply sympathetic to Germany in general and the Kaiser in particular'. Ponsonby actually derides the Kaiser as 'a tinsel figure-head of no account . . . his vanity, his megalomania and his incompetence'. The Kaiser chapter in *Falsehood* looks at the channelling of hate against an individual for propaganda purposes, culminating in the 'Hang the Kaiser' campaign. On the unfairness of making the Kaiser *personally* responsible for the war (however objectionable a person he was), Ponsonby quotes the memoirs of Sir Edward Grey: 'If matters had rested with him [the Kaiser] there would have been no European war arising out of the Austro-Serbian dispute.'[94]

Of course not everything in *Falsehood* stands up after three-quarters of a century and there are perhaps instances where the author was misled by post-war German propaganda. But the book is *not* about German or British or any other regimes as such but about something more timeless – the corruption of truth by war. Ponsonby's book is carefully documented and cites precisely its sources. The exposure of First World War atrocity fabrications had a very unfortunate consequence in the Second World War, when reports of the Nazi holocaust were doubted by some at first, but the inter-war promoters of honesty in reporting cannot be blamed for this.[95]

The history of Hitler, Stalin, the Second World War, the Cold War and the rest needs no summarising here but it does bear out the warnings of Arthur Ponsonby and his friends before and during the Great War. The history of our times has done plenty to confirm their rejection of the belief in 'war to end wars', which found such favour in 1914–18 and then let down its followers so badly. The two world wars of the twentieth century are now starting to be viewed as phases of 'the European civil war' which started in 1914 and did not finish until 1991. Eric Hobsbawm wrote in 2002 that, 'the 20th Century was the most murderous in recorded history' and that 'the world as a whole has not been at peace since 1914'.[96]

What if the advice of Arthur Ponsonby and his friends had been followed in August 1914? If the Ponsonby group had been listened to, Britain would have stood aside and used its neutrality in attempting to bring the warring sides to the conference table. This would in all probability not have succeeded, but who knows? In any case it would have set an example in promoting the values of conciliation, arbitration and rational settlement which had been developing promisingly with the international organisations at The Hague and elsewhere but which were knocked aside with the August 1914 recourse to brute force.

It is often said that had Britain stayed out of the war it would have had to accept the status of a vassal state of an all-dominant Greater Germany. This makes no sense. It is true that Germany would have defeated the alliance of France and Russia. It would have been a much shorter war than the one which actually took place, since without Britain in the conflict there would not have been the prolonged deadlock. There would undeniably have been some bad outcomes. Germany would have taken some territory from France and probably from Belgium and quite possibly would have turned Belgium into a client state. It should be remembered, however, that a Britain which had been neutral in the war would have been a strong moral position to defend the interests of France and Belgium at the end of it and undoubtedly would have done so. Germany did not plan to take Belgian territory in August 1914 – the aims of both sides changed during the war – and Britain would have hammered this point during the end of war settlement, in defending Belgian territorial integrity. Germany for a period would have been the dominant power in central and western Europe. But France would not have been destroyed as a power (as Ramsay MacDonald stressed on the eve of the war). And Germany emerging from the resource-draining war (of perhaps a year or a year and a half) would have been in no position, even if it had wanted to, to launch a second war against a still strong Britain with its resources intact, still supreme on the seas, still dominating the management of global finance and with its trade not having taken the damage of war participation. The claims that a neutral Britain would have had to bow at the end of the war before an all-controlling Greater German Reich, confuse the world of 1914 with the mad schemes a generation later of a fascist regime which was the product of a prolonged world war and the consequences of its outcome.

The results of the war are history not speculation. They include a twentieth-century catalogue of brutish tyrannies, genocide, slavery and repeating war. To say that 1914–18 with Britain in the war was necessary because the alternative with Britain standing aside would have been *worse* in its results surely defies reason.

This is not an account from the perspective of those who held power in Britain in 1914. It has looked at the viewpoint of those backbenchers who were dismayed by the revelations on 3 August 1914 of the position into which Government ministers had put Britain. These MPs did not previously know of the expectations which had been created that Britain would support France in a European war. For the British Government to have disappointed France and to have reneged on a pre-planned joint military strategy would indeed have seemed like a breach of honour and letting down a partner, but this situation had arisen behind the backs of a Parliament which had been falsely assured that British independence of action regarding European war was untrammelled. It turned out not be so. Britain's developing democracy had been deceived.

Given what was presented to the House of Commons in the terms that it was on 'the fatal afternoon', the backbench campaign was probably bound to fail. Sir Edward Grey's 'Let every man look into his own heart', carried the day, 'sharp practice' though it was, to use Alexander MacCallum Scott's phrase. But the failed neutrality campaign led on to the new one, which became the Union of Democratic Control, to try to create democratic safeguards on foreign policy, so that Parliament could not be duped again. The 'Ponsonby Rule' of 1924 enabling parliamentary scrutiny of prospective treaties was one step along the way towards the desired outcome. There is plainly still far to go. In the early years of the twenty-first century the suspicion of a pre-commitment at the top of British Government behind the backs of Parliament to another power to join it in going to war in Iraq had distinct echoes of ninety years earlier and seemingly left as much doubt as ever (whatever the truth or otherwise of the suspicions) as to whether democracy prevails in matters of peace and war. And yet just ten years later there was the quite remarkable vote on Syria in the House of Commons which saw MPs assert their constitutional power to overturn Government intentions on carrying out a military strike. Change is occurring and it is in the direction of accountability to Parliament. The debate which the Ponsonby group began on democracy, peace and war in 1914 is with us still and will continue.

During the Second World War Arthur Ponsonby largely withdrew from active politics but he was one of the opponents of aerial bombing of civil populations. He suffered a stroke in September 1943 and never fully recovered his previous good health. He died in 1946.

Arthur Ponsonby did his best in impossible times. In 1914 when the crisis arrived, he was a Member of Parliament whose aspirations were the removal of slums and making Britain a fairer and more democratic society, and the world a safer place. Then along came the July/August days, which ushered in a world of war dreams, with governments and armies squandering blood and treasure in the march towards the glorious tomorrow. All the war visions took a heavy toll of lives and none delivered the millennium.

Arthur Ponsonby did not believe in a glorious millennium of any hue. He believed in step by step progress, and the preciousness of all life. He put his own belief thus in his 1936 book *Life Here and Now*:

> A 'life to be' which will be Here, here in this world of ours which we know; a life to which we may feel full satisfaction that we are actually contributing by our efforts . . . Now, even now.[97]

December 1916 saw the de-selection of Arthur Ponsonby by his constituency Liberal Party. The official snub was despite the rousing success of a public meeting which he had just held at Dunfermline. At this, Ponsonby talked about his own dreams. A local newspaper carried a report of the speech. The MP concluded:

> I have been told that I am not a patriot and that I am an anti-patriot. All I can say is that I have had my country's welfare

in my mind first and foremost and on the whole I prefer my particular type of patriotism to that louder and more violent type represented by those whose object is vengeance and hatred ... I have been told that I am a dreamer of dreams. (Laughter) A dreamer of dreams. I take down that taunt with gladness, knowing that:

> God, beyond the years you see,
> Hath wrought dreams that count with you for madness
> Into the substance of the life to be.

(Loud applause during which Mr Ponsonby resumed his chair.)[98]

Arthur Ponsonby's dreams were not of some imagined future deemed worthy of the sacrifice of today's lives. They were dreams of here and now, and in them all lives mattered.

Notes

Prologue
1. Bodleian Library, MS Eng. Hist, c. 661, ff. 60–6 (Arthur Ponsonby's copy of the letter); *Stirling Observer*, 17 October 1914.
2. 'Dragon's teeth': David Stevenson, *1914–1918: The History of the First World War*, pp. 587–8.
3. Jo Vellacott, *From Liberal to Labour with Women's Suffrage*, p. 363.

1 Spectators Only?
1. House of Commons ventilation: Christopher Silvester, *The Pimlico Companion to Parliament*, pp. 457–62, quoting Henry Lucy's *Memories of Eight Parliaments*.
2. Hereditary Titles (Termination) Bill: Ponsonby Papers c. 660; discussion of a possible bill: Arthur Ponsonby: *The Decline of Aristocracy*, pp. 132–4.
3. Shulbrede MSS: A. Ponsonby Diary, 27 April 1914.
4. A. Ponsonby Diary, 27 July 1914.
5. A. Ponsonby Diary, 19 February 1914.
6. Sir Richard Denman, *Political Sketches*, p. 20.
7. Geoffrey Marcus: *Before The Lamps Went Out*, p. 182.
8. Michael Howard, *The First World War*, pp. 16–17.
9. Lloyd George speech: A. J. A. Morris, *Radicalism Against War 1906–1914*, p. 376.
10 Michael and Eleanor Brock (eds), *H. H. Asquith Letters to Venetia Stanley*, pp. 122–3.
11. Sir Frederick Ponsonby: Peter Snow, *To War with Wellington*.
12. Quoted, Raymond A. Jones: *Arthur Ponsonby: The Politics of Life*, p. 3; Henry Ponsonby at Sevastopol, William M. Kuhn: *Henry and Mary Ponsonby*, pp. 45–7.
13. Herbert Samuel meeting: Jones, p. 8.
14. Jones, p. 8; Francis W. Hirst, *In the Golden Days*, pp. 252–3; Sir Frederick Ponsonby, *Recollections of Three Reigns*, p. 51.
15. Kuhn, pp. 65–6; Kate Hubbard, *Serving Victoria*, Chapter 11.
16. Ponsonby, *Recollections of Three Reigns*, p. 234.

17. A. Ponsonby Diary, 6 August 1908; Jones, p. 57
18. Arthur Ponsonby, *The Camel and the Needle's Eye*, p. 12.
19. Shulbrede MSS: A Ponsonby to D. Ponsonby, 27 July 1914.
20. A Ponsonby to D. Ponsonby, 27 July 1914; Ponsonby at Eton: Jones, pp. 5–6; information on Matthew Ponsonby's schooling in Haslemere: thanks to Laura Ponsonby.
21. House of Commons chamber pre-WW1: Earl Winterton, *Orders of the Day*, p. vii.
22. Sir Courtney Ilbert, *Parliament: Its History, Constitution and Practice*, pp. 236–8.
23. Christopher Addison, *Four and A Half Years*, p. 29.
24. Newcastle University, Robinson Library, C. P. Trevelyan MSS [hereafter C. P. T.], Ex 106: C. Trevelyan to M. Trevelyan, 27 July 1914.
25. A. J. A. Morris, *C. P. Trevelyan 1870–1958: Portrait of a Radical*, p. 14.
26. Edwardian Radicals: A. J. A. Morris, *Edwardian Radicalism*.
27. John Keegan: *War and Our World*, The Reith Lectures, 1998, p. 33; Morris, *C. P. Trevelyan*, pp. 112–13.
28. *Brighouse Echo*, 31 July 1914.
29. *The Times*, 27 July 1914.
30. Marvin Swartz, 'A Study in Futility', in Morris, *Edwardian Radicalism*, p. 252.
31. Sir Harry Hamilton Johnston, *Common Sense in Foreign Policy*, p. 2; *The Times* and the Government: Zara S. Steiner, *The Foreign Office and Foreign Policy 1898–1914*, pp. 186–7.
32. Social and economic composition of the House of Commons: Thomas; Parliament as like a school: Rowland Prothero (Lord Ernlie): *Whippingham to Westminster*, pp. 38–9.
33. Johnston, p. 6.
34. Johnston, p 2.
35. Lawyers in the House of Commons: Thomas, p. 22.
36. Adam Riches, *When the Comics Went to War*, pp. 64–5; Jeremy Paxman, *Great Britain's Great War*, p. 19.
37. Hirst, pp. 263–5.
38. Michael Waterhouse: *Edwardian Requiem: A Life of Sir Edward Grey*, p. 109.
39. Nicolson and the Entente: Christopher Clark, *The Sleepwalkers*, p. 539.
40. Jones, pp. 56–7.
41. Haldane mission to Germany: Margaret MacMillan, *The War That Ended Peace*, pp. 508–9.
42. Sir Edward Grey and Germany: T. G. Otte, 'Detente 1914: Sir William Tyrrell's Secret Mission to Germany', *Historical Journal* 56 (2013), pp. 175–204.
43. Asquith at the Despatch Box: *Illustrated London News*, 14 February 1914; Violet Asquith birthday party: A. Ponsonby Diary, 15 April 1914.
44. Hansard, Parliamentary Debates, House of Commons, Series 5, Vol. 65: 919.
45. Hansard, 65: 912.

46. Snow, p. 99.
47. A. Ponsonby to D. Ponsonby, 27 July 1914.
48. Hansard, 65: 936.
49. C. P. Trevelyan Papers: C. P. T. 59, 'Personal Record' (an account of this time written by Trevelyan several months later).
50. Hansard, 65: 937.
51. C. P. T., Ex. 106, C. Trevelyan to M. Trevelyan, 27 July 1914.
52. A. J. P. Taylor, *The Troublemakers*, p. 115.
53. Adam Hochschild, *To End All Wars*, pp. 62–3; Ponsonby speech: Hansard 22: 1896 (13 March 1911).
54. Beresford cartoon: *Punch*, 19 February 1913.
55. Quoted by Francis Neilson, *The Churchill Legend*, p. 231.
56. Beresford: Koss, p. 66; Tyrrell on Splendid Isolation: Otte.
57. Hansard, 63: 457 (11 June 1914).
58. Otte; Waterhouse: pp. 319–21; MacMillan, pp. 501–2.
59. The manifesto of the federalist group is in Arthur Ponsonby's papers (c. 660); Ponsonby's Diary entry for 23–28 March 1914 mentions the federalist group.
60. Peter Rowland, *The Last Liberal Governments: Unfinished Business, 1911–1914*, pp. 267–8.
61. Morris, *Radicalism Against War*, pp. 362–3; Hansard 63: 1174 (17 June 1914).
62. Addison, p. 29.
63. Lichnowsky and the proposed conference: Brock and Brock, pp. 129–30.
64. David J. Dutton (ed.), *Odyssey of an Edwardian Liberal: The Political Diary of Richard Durning Holt*, p. 33.

2 A Balkan War Begins

1. A. Ponsonby to D. Ponsonby, 28 July 1914.
2. A Ponsonby to D. Ponsonby, 27 July 1914, 28 July 1914; D. Ponsonby to A. Ponsonby 29 July 1914, 30 July 1914.
3. Jeremy Dibble, *C. Hubert H. Parry: His Life and Music*, pp. 463–4.
4. School feeding bill: Addison p. 30; Ian Packer (ed.), *The Letters of Arnold Stephenson Rowntree to Mary Katherine Rowntree 1910–1918*, p. 152.
5. F. Ponsonby to A. Ponsonby, 30 July 1912; Ponsonby and the newspaper articles: Jones, p. 78.
6. Alfred Havighurst, *Radical Journalist: H. W. Massingham*, pp. 152–3; A. Ponsonby to D. Ponsonby, 28 July 1914.
7. Hansard, 50: 12–70.
8. Cameron Hazlehurst: *Politicians at War*, p. 21.
9. *Punch*, 29 July 1914; 5 August 1914.
10. On Arthur Ponsonby's mother and William Harcourt: Kuhn. For Lewis Harcourt, see Patrick Jackson, 'Lewis Harcourt: The life and career of Lewis "Loulou" Harcourt', *Journal of Liberal History* (Autumn 2003), pp. 14–18. (Harcourt's nickname was both 'Loulou' and 'Lulu', Ponsonby used the latter.)

11. Hansard, Series 4, Vol. 25: 196, 1 June 1894.
12. Hochschild, pp. 18–19.
13. Hansard, 65: 1154.
14. Hansard, 65: 1123.
15. Addison, p. 30.

3 'Close the Ranks'

1. Steiner, p. 126; *Punch*, 22 November 1911.
2. Morris, *Radicalism Against War*, pp. 274–5.
3. Arthur Ponsonby and 1914 Select Committee: Steiner, p. 198 n.
4. A. Ponsonby Diary, 29 July 1914.
5. The timing of the meeting is indicated in a letter of Arnold Rowntree to his wife: Packer, p. 153.
6. *The Times*, 29 July 1914.
7. Hansard, 65: 1324.
8. *The Times*, 30 July 1914.
9. R. J. Q. Adams, *Bonar Law*, p. 169.
10. Hansard, 65: 1319.
11. Hansard, 50: 1316–17.
12. Violet Bonham-Carter, *Winston Churchill as I Knew Him*, p. 44.
13. Brock and Brock, p. 139 n.
14. Hansard, 170: 325.
15. Hansard, Series 4, Vol. 185: 765.
16. Rowntree diary for 28 July 1914: Packer, p. 152.
17. Philip Morrell's early life and his marriage: Miranda Seymour, *Ottoline Morrell: Life on a Grand Scale*.
18. Hansard 63: 1217–18.
19. Seymour, p. 265; marriage of Philip and Ottoline Morrell: Katie Roiphe, *Uncommon Arrangements*, pp. 181–213.
20. Ponsonby on his speech in the Persian oil debate: A. Ponsonby Diary, 18 June 1914.
21. A. Ponsonby Diary, 18 June 1914.
22. Ponsonby Papers, c. 660.
23. Viscount Grey of Fallodon, *Twenty-Five Years*, Vol. II, p. 337–8.
24. Ponsonby Papers, c. 660, f. 49.
25. Shulbrede MSS.
26. Nicolson on the Cabinet: Otte.
27. C. P. T., Ex. 106, C. Trevelyan to M. Trevelyan, 29 July 1914.
28. Edward David, *Inside Asquith's Cabinet: From the Diaries of Charles Hobhouse*, p. 179.
29. Clark, p. 540; Steiner, pp. 198–200; Grey comment (20 February 1906): quoted by Rowland, p. 362.
30. Alexander MacCallum Scott Diary, 12 February 1914: MSS 1465/5.
31. Ponsonby Papers, c. 660, f. 43.

32. Douglas Newton, *British Labour, European Socialism and the Struggle for Peace*, pp. 322–4.
33. 'Bores of Supply': Silvester, pp. 359–61.
34. Hansard, 65: 1491.
35. Hansard, 65: 1520.
36. Wedgwood's opposition to eugenics: Paul Mulvey, *The Political Life of Josiah C. Wedgwood*, pp. 38–40; Gerald Oram, *Worthless Men*, pp. 77, 79.

4 'That Hateful Medieval Survival'

1. Harvey quoted by Hazlehurst, p. 39.
2. Jones, p. 80.
3. Flying: Mark Bostridge, *The Fateful Year*, Chapter 2; Churchill remark: Brock and Brock, p. 129.
4. Ponsonby Papers, c. 660.
5. *The Times*, 30 July 1914.
6. Hazlehurst, p. 42.
7. Seymour, p. 256.
8. Alexander MaCallum Scott Diary, 30 July 1914: 1465/5.
9. Packer, p. 153.
10. *The Pall Mall Gazette*, 30 July 1914.
11. *The Times* editorial of 31 July 1914.
12. Hansard: 25: 791, 5 May 1911.
13. Bonham-Carter, p. 321–2.
14. C. P. T., Ex. 106, C. Trevelyan to M. Trevelyan, 30 July 1914.
15. Addison, p. 31; Packer: p. 154; Ponsonby Papers, c. 660, f. 64.
16. Ponsonby Papers, c. 660, f. 64.
17. Ponsonby Papers, 660, f. 50.
18. Hope Costley White, *Lord Dickinson of Painswick A Memoir*, p. 136.
19. C. P. T., Ex. 106, C. Trevelyan to M. Trevelyan, 27 July 1914; Morris, *Radicalism Against War*, pp. 353–5; Paul Laity, *The British Peace Movement 1870–1914*, p. 210; Packer, p. 128 (Rowntree letter, 20 September 1913).
20. *The Times*, July 31st 1914.
21. David Marquand, *Ramsay MacDonald*, p. 131.
22. *An Autobiography of Philip Snowden*, Volume I, p. 332.
23. Trevor Wilson (ed.), *The Political Diaries of C. P. Scott*, pp. 92–3.
24. Ponsonby Papers, c. 660, f. 58; Churchill, *The World Crisis*, pp. 111–12.
25. Scott as inquisitor of the Government: *Punch*, 15 August 1917.
26. Hansard, 65: 1693; MacMillan, p. 569; Brock and Brock, p. 133.
27. Max Hastings, *Catastrophe: Europe Goes to War 1914*, pp. 103–4.
28. Brock and Brock, p. 136.
29. Keith Robbins: *Sir Edward Grey*, pp. 293–4; Waterhouse, pp. 341–2.

5 'Many People Seem to Have Gone Crazy'

1. C. P. T., Ex 106, C. Trevelyan to M. Trevelyan, 31 July 1914.
2. *The Times*, 31 July 1914.

3. Britain's dependence on imported foodstuffs: Howard, *The First World War*, pp. 3–4.
4. *Pall Mall Gazette*, 31 July 1914.
5. C. P. T., 59: Personal Record.
6. Addison: p. 31.
7. ILP anti-war meetings: Laity, pp 220–1.
8. Sir Norman Angell, *After All*, pp. 179–85, Swartz, pp. 254–9.
9. C. P. T., 59, Personal Record.
10. MacCallum Scott MSS: 1465/5.
11. Addison, p. 32.
12. Ponsonby Papers, c. 660, f. 56.
13. Tyrrell's projected trip to Germany: Otte.
14. Otte, citing H. W .V. Temperley's 28 March 1918 diary comment.
15. Marcus, p. 239; Charles Emmerson, *1913: The World Before the Great War*, pp. 28–9.
16. Cabinet meeting: Clive Ponting, *Thirteen Days: The Road to the First World War*, p. 243; Pease Diary quoted by Hazlehurst, p. 84.
17. Ponting, p. 243; Robbins, *Sir Edward Grey*, pp. 294–5.
18. Denman, pp. 20–1.
19. *Punch*, 4 May 1910; E. A. and G. H. Radice, *Will Thorne: Constructive Militant*, p. 71; Hansard, 65: 1729.
20. Hansard, 65: 1737.
21. *The Times*, 30 July 1914.
22. Marcus, p. 240.
23. C. P. T., 59: Whyte's Notes about the Crisis, August 1914.
24. Ponting, p. 244.
25. A Ponsonby to D. Ponsonby, 28 July 1914.
26. Committee meeting: Ponsonby Papers, c. 660, f. 64.
27. On below the gangway areas in more recent times see: John Biffen: *Inside Westminster*, pp. 165–6.
28. C. P. T., 59: Personal Record.
29. Cambon's view of Grey's attitude: Ponting, p. 243.
30. Shulbrede MSS: Diary of Sir Hubert Parry, 31 July 1914.

6 'The Crime and Folly of Joining in'
1. Josiah C. Wedgwood, *Memoirs of a Fighting Life*, p. 88; Wedgwood: Hansard, Fourth Series, HC, 32: 2625 (14 December 1911).
2. *Whitaker's Almanac*, 1914, p. 104; Ferguson, p. 442.
3. *Pall Mall Gazette*, 1 August 1914.
4. House's comment: Morris, *Radicalism Against War*, p. 381.
5. Parry Diary, 1 August 1914.
6. For Parry and *The Acharnians* see Dibble, pp. 467–8.
7. White, p. 136.
8. C. P. T., 59: Personal Record.
9. *Manchester Guardian*, 1 August 1914 (quoted by Swartz, p. 256).

10. Dutton: Richard Holt Diary, 9 August 1914.
11. Hardie letter: Caroline Benn, *Keir Hardie*, pp. 323–4.
12. C. P. T., Ex. 106, C. Trevelyan to M. Trevelyan, 31 July or 1 August 1914.
13. C. P. T., Ex. 106, C. Trevelyan to M. Trevelyan, 31 July or 1 August 1914.
14. F. L. Carsten, *War Against War*, pp. 13–18; V. P. Berghahn, *Germany and the Approach of War in 1914*, pp. 215–18; David Fromkin, *Europe's Last Summer*, p. 221.
15. Waterhouse, p. 325.
16. Liverpool University, Sydney Jones Library, Glasier Papers, GP/2/1/21.
17. Ponting, pp. 254–5; Brock and Brock: p. 140; MacMillan, pp. 577–9; J. Paul Harris, in Richard F. Hamilton and Holger H. Herwig (eds), *The Origins of World War 1*, p. 284.
18. Clark, pp. 540–1; MacMillan, pp. 579–80.
19. *Manchester Guardian*, 1 August 1914; *Nation*, quoted in Marcus, p. 266.
20. John Charmley, *Lord Lloyd and the Decline of the British Empire*, p. 33–5; *The Leo Amery Diaries, Volume One 1896–1929*, John Barnes and David Nicholson (eds), pp. 103–6; David Faber, *Speaking for England*, pp. 83–6; Nigel Keohane, *The Party of Patriotism: The Conservative Party and the First World War*, p. 13.
21. Churchill, pp. 111–12.
22. Francis Hirst, *Alexander Gordon Cummins Harvey A Memoir*; George Kelsall and Keith Parry, *Looking Back at Littleborough* (Rochdale Local Studies Library).
23. Progress of anti-militarism: Niall Ferguson, *The Pity of War*, p. 442.

7 'The War Fever Beginning'

1. C. P. T., 59: Personal Record.
2. Brock and Brock, p. 146; *Leo Amery Diaries* (5 August 1914): 'Hamar [Greenwood, Liberal MP] told me that a majority of the Cabinet had agreed to war on condition that no Expeditionary Force was sent abroad.'
3. Macmillan, pp. 498–500.
4. Cambon on the British Navy move: Hastings, p. 88.
5. Runciman quoted by Clark, p. 543.
6. Conservative leadership letter to Asquith: Morris, *Radicalism Against War*, p. 397.
7. Shulbrede MSS: 'Fellow Travellers on the Road: Brief Glimpses', pp. 2, 3.
8. William Kent, *John Burns Labour's Lost Leader*, pp. 187, 205, 207–8.
9. Dibble, p. 469; Hubert Parry Diary, 1 August, 1914.
10. Parry Diary, 2 August 1914.
11. Thomas Pakenham, *The Scramble For Africa*, pp. 336–8.
12. Johnston, p. 20.
13. Jonathan Schell, *The Unconquerable World*, p. 41; Poincaré statement: T. G. Otte, 'the Great Carnage', *New Statesman*, 13 December 2012; France in 1914: Howard, *First World War*, pp. 4–5.

14. Herbert Gladstone, *William G. C. Gladstone: A Memoir*, pp. 100–4. (Herbert Gladstone, Will Gladstone's uncle was a former Cabinet Minister.)
15. C. P. T.: Ex. 106, C. Trevelyan to M. Trevelyan, 2 August 1914.
16. C. P. T., 59, Personal Record.
17. Marcus, p. 264; *The Times*, 3 August 1914; Emmerson, p. xiv; MacMillan, pp. 509–10.
18. White, p. 136.
19. Glasier Papers, GP/2/1/21 (3 August 1914).
20. Ramsay MacDonald Diary, 23 September 191, PRO 30/69 1753/1.
21. *The Times*, 3 August 1914.
22. Brock and Brock, p. 148.
23. Telegram to Richard Denman: Denman 1C; *Carlisle Journal*, 4 August 1914.
24. Denman, pp. 82–7.
25. Swartz, pp. 157–258.
26. Swartz, pp. 255–6; Kate Courtney Diary, 1 August 1914, Courtney /36.
27. *Manchester Guardian*, 4 August 1914.
28. Angell, p. 182; John Howes Gleason, *The Genesis of Russophobia in Great Britain*.
29. Alexander MaCallum Scott Diary: MSS 1465/5.
30. Ponting, pp. 280–1; *Leo Amery Diaries*, I, p. 106 (2 August 1914).
31. Hansard 24: 538, 12 April 1911, quoted by Steiner, p. 199.
32. *Punch* depiction of King with question numbers in hat: for example 17 April 1912.
33. King letter: *Manchester Guardian*, 3 August 1914.
34. Fromkin, pp. 279–80.
35. C. P. T., 59: Whyte Notes.
36. D. Ponsonby to A. Ponsonby, 4 August 1914.
37. A. Ponsonby to D. Ponsonby, 3 August 1914.
38. Philip and Ottoline Morrell and Burnley: Seymour, p. 263.
39. Clark, p. 543; Ramsay MacDonald Diary, 23 September 1914, PRO 30/69 1753/1.
40. C. P. T., 59, Personal Record.
41. A. Ponsonby to D. Ponsonby, 3 August 1914.

8 'Hideous and Terrible'

1. Francis Neilson, *My Life in Two Worlds*, p. 334.
2. A. Ponsonby to D. Ponsonby, 3 August 1914.
3. C. P. T., Ex. 106, C. Trevelyan to M. Trevelyan, 3 August 1914.
4. MacMillan, p. 578.
5. *Pall Mall Gazette*, 3 August 1914; Marcus, pp. 275–6.
6. *The Times*, 3 August 1914.
7. David, p. 180: Hobhouse Diary, August 1914.
8. Whyte notes, C. P. T., 59.
9. *The Leo Amery Diaries*, I, pp. 104–5.
10. *The Autobiography of Bertrand Russell*, Vol II, pp. 15–16.

11. MacDonald Diary, 23 September 1914, National Archives, 30/69 1753.
12. White, p. 137; Elizabeth Balmer Baker and P. J. Noel-Baker, *J. Allen Baker*, p. 227.
13. A. Ponsonby to D. Ponsonby, 4 August 1914.
14. On 'crusading' see Laity, pp. 6–7 (citing Martin Ceadel's definitions).
15. T. G. Otte and Paul Readman (eds), *By-Elections in British Politics 1832–1914*, pp. 221–3; John Saville in article on R. L. Outhwaite in *Dictionary of Labour Biography*, Vol. 8, pp. 188–9; Duncan Tanner: *Political Change and the Labour Party 1900–1918*, p. 302.
16. Outhwaite described the effect viewing the Boer War graveyards had on him at a constituency meeting (*Staffordshire Sentinel*, 18 April 1918).
17. Morrell on Wedgwood: Mulvey, p. 207.
18. Marcus, p. 294.
19. On Morel, see Catherine Cline, *E. D. Morel*; on Morel's switch of focus from the Congo to the Anglo-French Entente, see Catherine Cline: 'E. D. Morel: from the Congo to the Rhine', in Morris, *Edwardian Radicalism*, and Cline, *E. D. Morel*, pp. 68–97.
20. C. P. T., 59, Personal Record.
21. Hansard, 65: 1794.

9 'The Fatal Afternoon'
1. J. R. Clynes, *Memoirs*, p. 168.
2. Neilson, *My Life in Two Worlds*, pp. 334–5.
3. Neilson, *My Life*, p. 334.
4. Sir Edward Grey's speech: Hansard, 65: 1809.
5. Hazlehurst, p. 45.
6. Roy Jenkins, *Asquith*, p. 329.
7. *Daily News*, 4 August 1914.
8. Waterhouse, p. xiv.
9. Marcus, pp. 295–6; *Westminster Gazette* on cheers: 4 August 1914.
10. Viscount Ullswater: *A Speaker's Commentaries*, Vol. II, p. 167.
11. *Westminster Gazette*, 4 August 1914.
12. Morris, *C. P. Trevelyan*, p. 118.
13. A. Ponsonby to D. Ponsonby, 4 August 1914.
14. Clynes, p. 169.
15. David French, *British Economic and Strategic Planning, 1905–1915*, p. 51.
16. C. P. T., 59: Personal Record.
17. Packer: Arnold Rowntree to Mary Rowntree, 3 August 1914.
18. Neilson, *My Life*, p. 335.
19. Applause for Grey's speech in the public galleries: Nigel Jones, *Peace and War: Britain in 1914*, Chapter 10 ('Descent into the Dark').
20. *Northampton Daily Echo*, 7 August 1914.
21. Marcus, p. 299; Hansard 65: 1874.
22. *Leo Amery Diaries*, I, p. 106 (3 August 1914).
23. The Burns Papers: British Library, 46336 LVI (3 August 1914).

24. Herbert Samuel to Beatrice Samuel, 3 August 1914, Herbert Samuel MSS: Houses of Parliament, Archives, A/157/698ff.
25. Taylor, p. 129.
26. C. P. T., 59, Personal Record.
27. *Leo Amery Diaries*, I, p. 106 (3 August 1914).
28. Clynes, p. 169.
29. Stephen Gwynn, *John Redmond's Last Years*, quoted in Silvester, p. 281.
30. Hansard, 65: 1828.
31. Llewelyn Williams, "'A proved and Loyal Friendship": The Diary of W. Llewelyn Williams MP, 1906–15'.
32. Thomas Hennessey, *Dividing Ireland: World War 1 and Partition*, pp. 42–79.
33. C. P. T., 59, Personal Account.
34. MacDonald's Commons nerves: Diary for 6 November 1917, MacDonald MSS, 30/69/1753.
35. MacDonald speech: Hansard, 65: 1829–33.
36. On MacDonald's thinking at this time, see Christopher Howard, 'MacDonald, Henderson and the Outbreak of War', *Historical Journal*, 20, 4 (1977), pp. 871–91.
37. Hansard, 65: 1831.
38. *The Early Memoirs of Lady Ottoline Morrell*, ed. R Gathorne-Hardy, p. 260.
39. C. P. T., Ex. 106, C. Trevelyan to M. Trevelyan, 3 August 1914.
40. Leonard Outhwaite on 3 August 1914 as 'the fatal afternoon': Hansard 74: 276, 16 September 1915.

10 'The House that Jack Built'

1. Neilson, *My Life in Two Worlds*, pp. 327–8.
2. Addison, pp. 32–3.
3. Ponsonby Papers, c. 660, f. 66.
4. *Daily News*, 4 August 1914.
5. Addison, pp. 32–3.
6. A. Ponsonby to D. Ponsonby, 4 August 1914.
7. Pringle speech: Hansard 65: 1879; *Westminster Gazette*, 4 August 1914.
8. Alexander MacCallum Scott Diary, 3 August 1914: Glasgow University Library, MSS 1465/5.
9. Hansard, 65: 1834
10. Ullswater, Vol. II, p. 167.
11. Hansard 65: 1876; Ullswater, II, p. 168.
12. Hansard 65: 1873.
13. See Avner Offer: 'Going to War in 1914 – A Matter of Honour?', *Politics and Society*, June 1995.
14. Hansard, 65: 1860.
15. Unemployment and Army recruiting: Ferguson, p. 444.
16. On Russia, see Howard, *The First World War*, pp. 5–7.
17. Hansard, 65: 1863.
18. Hansard, 65: 1837.

19. French, p. 63; Gerard DeGroot: *Blighty: British Society in the Era of the Great War*, pp. 54–6.
20. Ponsonby on Wedgwood speech: A. Ponsonby to D. Ponsonby, 4 August 1914; Josiah Wedgwood and the European crisis, see Mulvey, pp. 55–6.
21. J. C. Wedgwood MSS: JCW 1/1.
22. Ponsonby speech: Hansard 65: 1841.
23. *Westminster Gazette*, 4 August 1914.
24. A. Ponsonby to D. Ponsonby, 4 August 1914.
25. Hansard, 65: 1848.
26. Hansard, 65: 1838.
27. Packer: Rowntree letters, p. 155; Hansard 65: 1845.
28. Johnston, p. 37.
29. Germans in Britain: Emmerson, p. 18.
30. Moltke: Fromkin, pp. 36–8.
31. MacMillan, p. 64.
32. Germany and South-West Africa: see Casper Erichsen and David Olusoga, *The Kaiser's Holocaust: Germany's Forgotten Genocide and the Colonial Roots of Nazism*; King Leopold and Congo exploitation and E. D. Morel's campaign against it: Cline, *E. D. Morel*.
33. German students at Oxford and *Times* letter on German scholarship: Bostridge, Chapter 2.
34. Hansard, 65: 1845
35. Hansard, 66: 1019.
36. Hansard, 65: 1869.
37. Newton, *British Labour*, p. 340; Keith Robbins, *The First World War*, p. 17; Marcus, p. 293.
38. Hansard, 65: 1856.
38. Hansard, 65: 1874.
40. *Leo Amery Diaries*, I, p. 106 (3 August 1914).
41. First World War emotions and the twentieth century: DeGroot, p. 333
42. Ponsonby Papers, 600, ff. 68–71.

11 'More Like a Book by Conan Doyle'

1. *Manchester Guardian*, 4 August 1914.
2. Leaflets: Ponting, p. 185.
3. London School of Economics and Political Science, Graham Wallas Papers: Wallas 4/4 (British Neutrality Committee).
4. A. Ponsonby to D. Ponsonby, 4 August 1914.
5. *Manchester Guardian*, 5 August 1914.
6. Emmerson, p. 5; MacMillan, pp. 281–2.
7. Rowntree letter: Packer: Arnold Rowntree to Mary Rowntree, 4 August 1914.
8. Havighurst, p. 229.
9. F. Ponsonby to M. Ponsonby, 4 August 1914.
10. D. Ponsonby to A. Ponsonby, 4 August 1914.
11. C. P. T., 59, M. Trevelyan to C. Trevelyan (5 August 1914).

12. *Manchester Guardian*, 4 August 1914.
13. *Daily News*, 4 August 1914.
14. *The Times*, 4 August 1914.
15. *Westminster Gazette*, 5 August 1914.
16. Biography of Gordon Harvey written and published by Keith Parry, Rochdale Alternative Press, p. 14.
17. A. Ponsonby to D. Ponsonby, 5 August 1914.
18. Wallas 4/4.
19. Dutton: Richard Holt Diary, 9 August 1914.
20. On liberal attitudes to war across Europe: Michael Howard, *War and the Liberal Conscience*, p. 73.
21. *Westminster Gazette*, 4 August 1914.
22. The Territorial Force: Philip Warner, *Kitchener*, p. 173.
23. *The Times*, 5 August 1914.
24. Hansard, 65: 1925; Ferguson, p. 162; Brock and Brock, p. 150.
25. Arthur Ponsonby, *Falsehood in Wartime*, pp. 51-2, quoting Hansard, 150: 199.
26. Ponsonby, *Falsehood in Wartime*, p. 56.
27. Gathorne-Hardy, *Early Memoirs*, p.260.
28. Newspaper boys: Marcus, p. 308.
29. The electorate at this time: Martin Pugh, *Electoral Reform in War and Peace 1906-18*, Chapter 1.
30. Josiah Wedgwood to daughter Helen, 5 August 1914, J. C. Wedgwood MSS: Keele University Library, JCW 1/1.
31. *Staffordshire Sentinel*, 5 August 1914.
32. Jo Vellacott, 'Anti-war Suffragists', *History*, 62 (1977).
33. A. Ponsonby to D. Ponsonby, 5 August 1914.
34. On war and the mood of ordinary people, see Adrian Gregory, *The Last Great War*, pp. 9-39.
35. *Dunfermline Express*, 4 August 1914.
36. C. P. T., 59.
37. A. J. P. Taylor, *English History, 1914-1945*, pp. 2-3; Ponsonby sleeplessness: A. Ponsonby to D. Ponsonby, 5 August 1914.

12 'Protest is Futile'

1. A. Ponsonby to D. Ponsonby, 5 August 1914.
2. *Daily News*, 5 August 1914.
3. *Punch*, 12 August 1914; Asquith's *'les braves Belges'* comment in his 4 August letter to Venetia Stanley (Brock and Brock, p. 150) contrasts interestingly with his public tone on Belgium.
4. On the Labour movement and the speed of events, Newton, pp. 349-50; Bruce Glasier Diary, 4 August 1914, Glasier Papers, GP/2/1/21.
5. Decision on the BEF: Taylor, *English History*, pp. 6-8.
6. Offer to MacDonald of a Cabinet place: Newton, p. 352.
7. J. M. Winter, *Socialism and the Challenge of War*, pp. 184-5.
8. Newton, p. 331.

9. Wallas MSS, 4/4.
10. Kate Courtney Diary, 9 August 1914, London School of Economics and Political Science, Courtney MSS 36.
11. A. Ponsonby to D. Ponsonby, 5 August 1914.
12. Lord Elton, 'The Role of Ramsay MacDonald', in Peter Stansky (ed.), *The Left and the War: The British Labour Party and World War I*, p. 62; Winter, p. 185; Newton, pp. 331–2.
13. Newton, p. 332; Bruce Glasier Diary, 5 August 1914, Glasier Papers, GP/2/1/21.
14. Packer, p. 156 (A. Rowntree to M. Rowntree, 5 August 1914).
15. Hazlehurst, p. 114.
16. Hansard, 65: 1963.
17. Hansard, 65: 1987
18. Taylor, *English History*, p.3.
19. A. Ponsonby to D. Ponsonby, 6th August 1914; Denman 4/3; Packer (A. Rowntree to M. Rowntree, 5 August 1914), p. 157.
20. *Manchester Guardian*, 6 August 1914.
21. C. P. T., 59, Personal Record.
22. Newton, pp. 332–3.
23. A. Ponsonby to D. Ponsonby, 6 August 1914.

13 'I do not Want my Country to be Beaten"

1. A. Ponsonby to D. Ponsonby, 6 August 1914.
2. Parry, *Gordon Harvey*, pp. 14–15.
3. Bodleian Library, Sir Richard Denman Papers, Denman 4/3.
4. Benn, pp. 326–7.
5. Hansard, 65: 2065.
6. *Punch*, 12 August 1914.
7. Vote of Credit debate: Hansard 65: 2073–2100.
8. Warner, p. 174; Howard, *The First World War*, p. 48.
9. Neilson, *My Life*, p. 344.
10. Hansard, 65: 2083.
11. Hansard, 65: 2089.
12. A. Ponsonby to D. Ponsonby, 6 August 1914.
13. Dickinson speech: Hansard, 65: 2090.
14. Hansard, 65: 2092.
15. Hansard, 65: 2095.
16. Harry Patch, with Richard van Emden, *The Last Fighting Tommy*, pp. 55, 201–3.
17. Rowntree speech: Hansard, 65: 2096.
18. Baker speech: Hansard, 65: 2098.
19. J. Scott Duckers, *Handed Over*, pp. 5–6.
20. Packer: A. Rowntree to M. Rowntree, 6 August 1914.

14 Afterwards

1. Mulvey, p. 59, 63.
2. Denman, pp. 26–9; newspaper extract: cutting dated 23 April 1916, Denman MSS, Cuttings, Box 1.
3. Denman, pp. 26–9.
4. Ponsonby Papers, c 665; Denman MSS 4 (2).
5. *Cumberland Evening Mail*, 10 March 1917.
6. Hansard, 88: 1725, 21 December 1916.
7. *Bradford Pioneer*, 23 February 1917.
8. A. Ponsonby Diary, 31 December 1914.
9. D. Ponsonby Diary, 8 December 1914, Shulbrede MSS.
10. D. Ponsonby Diary, June 1915 (indications of 5th or 7th).
11. Quoted in Sylvia Pankhurst, *The Home Front*, p. 235.
12. On the break-up of the meeting by Charles Stanton, see Brock Millman, *Managing Domestic Dissent in First World War Britain*, Chapter 6 ('the Battle of Corey Hall'). The meeting was in Cardiff on 11 November 1916. The MPs on the platform included Ramsay MacDonald. Stanton made his boast in Parliament on 14 November 1916 (Hansard, 87: 722).
13. Ramsay MacDonald Diary, 13 January 1916, National Archives 30/69/1753/1.
14. A. Ponsonby to D. Ponsonby, 19 January 1916; on the foggy weather: *Punch* 'Essence of Parliament', 26 January 1916.
15. Hansard, 77: 1419.
16. Hansard 74: 276, 16 September 1916.
17. A. Ponsonby Diary, 23 July 1915.
18. Jones, *Arthur Ponsonby*, pp. 104–5.
19. Dibble, pp. 475, 483–5.
20. Parry Diary, 29 November 1915.
21. *Daily Sketch*, 30 November 1915.
22. Hansard, 76: 1007, 2 December 1915.
23. *Daily Express*, 3 December 1915.
24. Marquand, pp. 189–91; Millman, p. 260.
25. J. Ponsonby to A. Ponsonby, 4 October 1914.
26. A. Ponsonby Diary, 9 October 1914; Jones, *Arthur Ponsonby*, p. 94.
27. Dutton, p. 44.
28. C. P. T., Ex 110 (1), C. Trevelyan to M. Trevelyan, 4 July 1916.
29. Stephen Pope and Elizabeth-Anne Wheal, *The MacMillan Dictionary of the First World War*, p. 440.
30. C. P. T., 77, A. Ponsonby to C. Trevelyan, 13 July 1916.
31. A. Ponsonby Diary, 13 July 1916.
32. C. P. T., 77, A. Ponsonby to C. Trevelyan, 17 July 1916.
33. A. Ponsonby Diary, 13 July 1916.
34. A. Ponsonby Diary, 17 August 1916.
35. C. P. T., 77, A. Ponsonby to C. Trevelyan, 12 September 1916; John Jolliffe, *Raymond Asquith, Life and Letters*, p. 208.
36. Jolliffe: p. 296.

37. C. P. T., 77, A. Ponsonby to C. Trevelyan, 27 September 1916.
38. Hansard, 86: 95.
39. Hansard, 86: 325.
40. R. L. Outhwaite and Joseph Southwell, *The Ghosts of the Slain*.
41. Report on prosecution of Joseph King, *New York Times*, 21 October 1916.
42. Imprisonment of Lupton: Millman, pp. 186–7. (The reference to Arnold Lupton as an MP is incorrect: he was the former MP for Sleaford.) Caroline E. Playne, *Britain Holds On*, p. 303; on imprisonment of Morel: Cline, *E. D. Morel*, pp. 111–13.
43. Hansard, 82: 2977.
44. Dutton, p. 44 (Richard Holt Diary, 7 June 1916).
45. Carlisle Record Office, Catherine Marshall Papers: D/Mar/4/7.
46. Hansard, 83: 490; Marshall Papers, D/Mar/4/7, 1 June 1916; Robert Gathorne-Hardy (ed.), *Ottoline At Garsington*, pp. 102–3. For the story of the transported conscientious objectors see: Felicity Goodall, *A Question of Conscience*, pp. 19–26.
47. On British war aims: Douglas Newton, *British Policy and the Weimar Republic 1918–1919*, pp. 6–7; charge of 'annexations': for example Leonard Outhwaite: Hansard, 103: 229, 13 February 1918.
48. On the problems of compromise peace, see A. J. P. Taylor, *The Struggle for Mastery in Europe 1848–1918*, pp. 551–7.
49. Hansard, 92: 1467.
50. Hansard, 92: 1278.
51. See Oram: *Worthless Men*.
52. *Punch*, 4 July 1917.
53. *Forward*, 14 April 1917.
54. G. D. H. Cole and Raymond Postgate, *The Common People*, pp. 525–6; F. M. Leventhal, *Arthur Henderson*, pp. 64–73.
55. A. Ponsonby Diary, 14 June 1917.
56. MacDonald on Russia and the war: *Forward*, 5 May 1917; Sylvia Pankhurst on MacDonald: *The Home Front*, pp. 319–20.
57. *Punch*, 13 March 1918.
58. Hansard, 103: 218.
59. C. P. T., 79, A. Ponsonby to C. Trevelyan, 5 January 1918.
60. Dutton, p. 54 (Holt Diary, 21 February 1918).
61. Lansdowne/Labour conferences: Keith Robbins, *The Abolition of War*, pp. 156–8; Outhwaite speech: Hansard, 80: 766, 23 February 1916.
62. J. H. Thomas, *My Story*, pp. 43–5; Hansard, 103: 212
63. Hansard, 100: 1993.
64. Wedgwood shout: Hansard, 100: 2008, 19 December 1917.
65. Hansard: 103: 161.
66. Outhwaite questions on Germans, Czechs and Irish: Hansard, 90: 1341, 21 February 1917; 91: 705, 12 March 1917.
67. Hansard, 107: 561, 20 June 1918.
68. Harry Jones (see note 85, below).

69. Hansard, 90: 1230.
70. Hansard, 90: 1230.
71. Debate on disenfranchisement of conscientious objectors: Hansard, 99: 1209–1282; Richard Holt on the vote: Diary, 3 December 1917 (Dutton, p. 51).
72. Arthur Ponsonby, *The Crank* (1916).
73. Hansard, 109: 1578
74. C. P. T., 79, A. Ponsonby to C. Trevelyan, 9 August 1918.
75. A. Ponsonby Diary, 9 August 1918.
76. Hansard, 109: 1597.
77. The changing of the time of the end of hostilities was revealed in a 2000 Armistice Day BBC Television programme.
78. A. Ponsonby Diary, 10 May 1919.
79. For the *Daily Herald* cartoon, see David Reynolds, *The Long Shadow The Great War and the Twentieth Century*, introductory pages.
80. Margaret Fitzherbert: *The Man Who Was Greenmantle*, pp. 219–20; on the peace group and expectations regarding Woodrow Wilson, see for example Packer, pp. 252–3 (Arnold Rowntree letter of 18 October 1918).
81. Hansard, 96: 1527.
82. Byles and Rowntree: Packer, p. 206 (A. Rowntree to M. Rowntree, 18 January 1916).
83. Trevor Wilson, *The Downfall of the Liberal Party*, p. 28.
84. Roiphe, pp. 181–5; Seymour, p. 383; Gathorne-Hardy, *Ottoline at Garsington*, pp. 124–7.
85. Information on Cedric Outhwaite at Zeebrugge: thanks to Mark Outhwaite, his grandson; reactions in the House of Commons: Harry Jones, 'Pacifists in Parliament', *U.D.C.* magazine, September 1918. (Jones was a *Daily Chronicle* journalist.)
86. *Manchester Guardian*, 10 November 1930.
87. Charles Trevelyan's later years: Laura Trevelyan, *A Very British Family: The Trevelyans and their World*, pp. 142–5.
88. Jones, *Arthur Ponsonby*, pp. 133–5, 143.
89. Jones, *Arthur Ponsonby*, pp. 178–89.
90. Jones, pp. 158, 179.
91. On Arthur Ponsonby's inter-war peace campaigning, see Jones, *Arthur Ponsonby*, pp. 164–225.
92. Arthur Ponsonby, *The Priory and Manor of Lynchmere and Shulbrede*, p. 194.
93. Ponsonby, *Falsehood in Wartime*, p. 42.
94. Gregory, pp. 41–4; Ponsonby, *Falsehood in Wartime*, pp. 71-–7.
95. Gregory, pp. 41–4; Arthur Ponsonby, 'The Criminal Kaiser', in *Falsehood in Wartime*, pp. 71–7.
96. Eric Hobsbawm: *London Review of Books*, 21 February 2002.
97. Arthur Ponsonby, *Life Here and Now*, p. 289.
98. *Dunfermline Journal*, 9 December 1916

Bibliography

Primary Sources
Carlisle Record Office
   Catherine Marshall Papers
Glasgow University Library
   Alexander MacCallum Scott Diary
Hull University Library
   U.D.C. Papers
Kew, The National Archives
   Ramsay MacDonald Diary
Keele University Library
   Josiah Wedgwood Papers
Liverpool University, Sydney Jones Library
   Bruce Glasier Papers
London, The British Library
   John Burns Diary
London, Houses of Parliament, Parliamentary Archives
   Herbert Samuel Papers
London School of Economics Library
   Catherine (Kate) Courtney Diary
   Graham Wallas: British Neutrality Committee Papers
Oxford University, Bodleian Library
   Arthur Ponsonby, 1st Baron Ponsonby of Shulbrede: Political Papers
   Richard Denman Papers
Newcastle University, Robinson Library
   Charles P. Trevelyan Papers
Shulbrede Priory MSS (Ponsonby family papers)
   Arthur Ponsonby Diary and Papers
   Dorothea (Dolly) Ponsonby Diary and Papers
   Frederic (Fritz) Ponsonby Papers
   Sir Hubert Parry Diary

Printed Sources
Hansard, Parliamentary Debates, 4th, 5th Series
Annual Register
Dod's Parliamentary Companion
Who's Who
Whitaker's Almanack

Newspapers and Journals
Bradford Pioneer
Brighouse Echo
Carlisle Journal
Cumberland Evening Mail
Daily Express
Forward
Daily Sketch
Daily News
Dunfermline Express
Dunfermline Journal
Illustrated London News
Manchester Guardian
Northampton Daily Echo
Pall Mall Gazette
Punch
Staffordshire Sentinel
Stirling Observer
Times
U.D.C. Magazine
Westminster Gazette

Secondary Sources
Adams, R. J. Q.: *Bonar Law,* John Murray (1999)
Addison, Christopher: *Four and a Half Years,* Hutchinson (1934)
Angell, Sir Norman: *After All,* Hamish Hamilton (1952)
Baker, Elizabeth Balmer, and Noel-Baker, P. J.: *J. Allen Baker,* Swarthmore Press
    (1927)
Barnes, John, and Nicholson, David: *The Leo Amery Diaries: Volume One
    1896–1929,* Hutchinson (1980)
Benn, Caroline: *Keir Hardie,* Richard Cohen Books (1997)
Berghahn, V. P.: *Germany and the Approach of War in 1914,* MacMillan (1993)
Biffen, John: *Inside Westminster,* André Deutsch, (1996)
Bonham-Carter, Violet: *Winston Churchill as I Knew Him,* Pan Books (1967)
Bostridge, Mark: *The Fateful Year: Britain 1914,* Viking (2014)
Brock, Michael and Eleanor: *H. H. Asquith Letters to Venetia Stanley,* Oxford
    University Press (1982)
Brockway, Fenner: *Towards Tomorrow,* Hart-Davis (1977)
Carsten, F. L.: *War Against War,* University of California Press (1982)
Charmley, John: *Lord Lloyd and the Decline of the British Empire,* Weidenfeld
    and Nicolson (1987)
Churchill, Winston: *The World Crisis,* Penguin Classics (2007)
Clark, Christopher: *The Sleepwalkers,* Allen Lane (2012)
Clark, Ronald W.: *The Life of Bertrand Russell,* Penguin Books (1978)
Cline, Catherine: *E. D. Morel,* Blackstaff Press (1980)
Cole, G.D.H. and Postgate, Raymond: *The Common People,* Routledge (re. edn,
    1992)
Clynes, J. R.: *Memoirs,* Hutchinson (1937)

David, Edward: *Inside Asquith's Cabinet: From the Diaries of Charles Hobhouse*, John Murray (1977)

DeGroot, Gerard: *Blighty: British Society in the Era of the Great War*, Longman (1996)

Denman, Sir Richard: *Political Sketches*, Charles Thurnam, (1948)

Dibble, Jeremy: *C. Hubert H. Parry: His Life and Music*, Clarendon Press (1992)

Dictionary of Labour Biography

Duckers, J. Scott: *Handed Over*, C. W. Daniel (1917)

Dutton, David J. (ed.): *Odyssey of an Edwardian Liberal: The Political Diary of Richard Durning Holt*, Alan Sutton Publishing (1989)

Emmerson, Charles: *1913: The World Before the Great War*, The Bodley Head (2013)

Ensor, R. C. K.: *England 1870–1914*, Clarendon Press (1936)

Erichsen, Casper and Olusoga, David: *The Kaiser's Holocaust: Germany's Forgotten Genocide and the Colonial Roots of Nazism*, Faber and Faber (2010)

Faber, David: *Speaking for England*, Pocket Books (2007)

Ferguson, Niall, *The Pity of War*, Allen Lane (1998)

___: 'It was the Biggest Error in Modern History', *History Today*, February 2014

Fitzherbert, Margaret: *The Man Who Was Greenmantle*, Oxford University Press (1983)

French, David: *British Economic and Strategic Planning, 1905–1915*, Allen and Unwin, (1982)

Fromkin, David: *Europe's Last Summer*, Vintage (2005)

Gathorne-Hardy, R. (ed.): *The Early Memoirs of Lady Ottoline Morrell*, Faber and Faber (1963)

___: *Ottoline at Garsington*, Faber and Faber (1974)

Gladstone, Herbert: *William G. C. Gladstone: A Memoir*, Nisbet (1918: reproduced by Ulan Press)

Gleason, John Howes: *The Genesis of Russophobia in Great Britain*, Harvard University Press (1950)

Goodall, Felicity, *A Question of Conscience*, Sutton Publishing (1997)

Gregory, Adrian, *The Last Great War: British Society and the First World War*, Cambridge University Press (2008)

Grey of Fallodon, Viscount: *Twenty-Five Years*, Hodder and Stoughton (1925)

Grigg, John: *Lloyd George: From Peace to War 1912–1916*, Methuen (1985)

Hamilton, Richard F., and Herwig, Holger H.: *The Origins of World War 1*, Cambridge University Press (2003)

Hastings, Max: *Catastrophe: Europe Goes to War 1914*, HarperPress (2013)

Havighurst, Alfred: *Radical Journalist: H. W. Massingham*, Cambridge University Press (1974)

Hazlehurst, Cameron: *Politicians at War*, Jonathan Cape (1971)

Hennessey, Thomas: *Dividing Ireland: World War 1 and Partition*, Routledge (1998)

Hirst, Francis: *Alexander Gordon Cummins Harvey: A Memoir*, Cobden-Sanderson (1925)

____: *In the Golden Days*, London: Frederick Muller (1947)

Hobsbawm, Eric: in *London Review of Books*, 21 February 2002

Hochschild, Adam, *To End All Wars*, Pan (2012)

Howard, Christopher: 'MacDonald, Henderson and the Outbreak of War', *Historical Journal*, 20, 4 (1977), pp. 871–91

Howard, Michael: *The First World War*, Oxford University Press (2002)

____: *War and the Liberal Conscience*, Hurst (2008)

Hubbard, Kate: *Serving Victoria*, Chatto and Windus (2012)

Hynes, Samuel: *A War Imagined*, Pimlico (1992)

Ilbert, Sir Courtney: *Parliament: Its History, Constitution and Practice*, Williams and Norgate (1911)

Jackson, Patrick, 'Lewis Harcourt: The life and career of Lewis "Loulou" Harcourt', *Journal of Liberal History*, Autumn 2003

Jenkins, Roy: *Asquith*, Collins (1966)

Johnston, Sir Harry Hamilton: *Common Sense in Foreign Policy*, Smith, Elder (1913: Nabu Public Domain reprints)

Jolliffe, John: *Raymond Asquith: Life and Letters*, Collins (1980)

Jones, Nigel: *Peace and War: Britain in 1914*, Head of Zeus (2014)

Jones, Raymond A.: *Arthur Ponsonby: The Politics of Life*, Christopher Helm (1989)

Keegan, John: *War and Our World*, The Reith Lectures, 1998, Hutchinson

Kent, William: *John Burns: Labour's Lost Leader*, Williams and Norgate (1950)

Keohane, Nigel: *The Party of Patriotism: The Conservative Party and the First World War*, Ashgate (2010)

Kuhn, William M.: *Henry and Mary Ponsonby*, Duckworth (2002)

Laity, Paul, *The British Peace Movement 1870–1914*, Clarendon Press (2001)

Leventhal, F. M.: *Arthur Henderson*, Manchester University Press (1989)

McMeekin, Sean: *July 1914: Countdown to War*, Icon Books (2013)

MacMillan, Margaret, *The War That Ended Peace*, Profile (2013)

Marcus, Geoffrey: *Before the Lamps Went Out*, Allen and Unwin (1965)

Marquand, David: *Ramsay MacDonald*, Richard Cohen Books (1997)

Millman, Brock: *Managing Domestic Dissent in First World War Britain*, Frank Cass (2000)

Morris, A. J. A.: *Radicalism Against War 1906–1914*, Longman (1972)

____: *Edwardian Radicalism*, Routledge and Kegan Paul (1974)

____: *C. P. Trevelyan 1870–1958: Portrait of a Radical*, Blackstaff Press (1977)

Mulvey, Paul, *The Political Life of Josiah C. Wedgwood*, Boydell Press: Royal Historical Society (2010)

Neilson, Francis: *My Life in Two Worlds*, Nelson (1952)

____: *The Churchill Legend*, Nelson (1954)

Newton, Douglas: *British Labour, European Socialism and the Struggle for Peace*, Clarendon Press (1985)

____: *British Policy and the Weimar Republic 1918–1919*, Clarendon Press (1997)

Nicolson, Harold: *Sir Arthur Nicolson, Bart, First Lord Carnock* (1930)

Offer, Avner: 'A Matter of Honor?', *Politics and Society*, June 1995

Oram, Gerald: *Worthless Men: Race, eugenics and the death penalty in the British Army during the First World War*, Francis Boutle (1998)

Otte, T. G.: 'Detente 1914: Sir William Tyrrell's Secret Mission to Germany', *Historical Journal* 56 (2013), pp. 175–204

Otte, T. G., and Readman, Paul (eds), *By-Elections in British Politics 1832–1914*, Boydell Press, (2013)

Outhwaite, R. L., and Southall, Joseph, *The Ghosts of the Slain*, National Labour Press (1915)

Packer, Ian (ed.): *The Letters of Arnold Stephenson Rowntree to Mary Katherine Rowntree 1910–1918*, Cambridge University Press, Royal Historical Society (2002)

Pakenham, Thomas: *The Scramble For Africa*, Abacus (1992)

Pankhurst, E. Sylvia, *The Home Front*, Cresset Library (1987)

Patch, Harry, with van Emden, Richard, *The Last Fighting Tommy*, Bloomsbury (2007)

Paxman, Jeremy: *Great Britain's Great War*, Viking (2013)

Playne Caroline E., *Britain Holds On*, Allen and Unwin (1933)

Ponsonby, Arthur: *The Camel and the Needle's Eye*, A. C. Fifield (1909)

____: *The Decline of Aristocracy*, Unwin (1912)

____: *The Crank*, Headley Brothers (1916)

____: *The Priory and Manor of Lynchmere and Shulbrede*, Wessex Press (1920: openlibrary.org)

____: *Falsehood in Wartime*, Allen and Unwin (1928)

____: *Life Here and Now*, Allen and Unwin (1936)

Ponsonby, Sir Frederick: *Recollections of Three Reigns*, Eyre and Spottiswoode (1951)

Ponting, Clive: *Thirteen Days: The Road to the First World War*, Chatto and Windus (2002)

Pope, Stephen, and Wheal, Elizabeth-Anne: *The Macmillan Dictionary of the First World War*, MacMillan (1995)

Porter, Bernard: *The Lion's Share*, Longman (2012)

____: 'Cutting the British Empire Down to Size', *History Today*, October 2012

Prothero, Rowland (Lord Ernlie): *Whippingham to Westminster*, J. Murray (1938)

Pugh, Martin, *Electoral Reform in War and Peace 1906–18*, Routledge and Kegan Paul (1978)

Radice, E. A. and G. H.: *Will Thorne: Constructive Militant*, George Allen and Unwin (1974)

Reddy, E. S.: 'Parliaments and the Struggle against Apartheid', http://www.anc.org.za/ancdocs/history/aam/Parliaments.html

Reynolds, David, *The Long Shadow: The Great War and the Twentieth Century*, Simon and Schuster (2013)

Riches, Adam: *When the Comics Went to War*, Mainstream (2009)

Robbins, Keith, *The Abolition of War*, University of Wales Press (1976)

____: *The First World War*, Oxford University Press (1984)

____: *Sir Edward Grey*, Cassell (1971)

Roiphe, Katie: *Uncommon Arrangements: Seven Portraits of Married Life in London Literary Circles 1910–1939*, Virago (2008)

Rowland, Peter: *The Last Liberal Governments: Unfinished Business 1911–1914*, Barrie and Jenkins (1971)

Russell, Bertrand: *The Autobiography of Bertrand Russell*, Allen and Unwin (1968)

Schell, Jonathan: *The Unconquerable World*, Allen Lane (2004)

Seymour, Miranda: *Ottoline Morrell: Life on a Grand Scale*, Hodder and Stoughton (1992)

Silvester, Christopher: *The Pimlico Companion to Parliament*, Pimlico (1997)

Snow, Peter: *To War with Wellington*, John Murray (2010)

Snowden, Philip: *An Autobiography*, Nicholson and Watson (1934)

Stansky, Peter (ed.): *The Left and the War: The British Labour Party and World War I*, Oxford University Press (1969)

Steiner, Zara S: *The Foreign Office and Foreign Policy 1898–1914*, Cambridge University Press (1969)

Stevenson, David: *1914–1918: The History of the First World War*, Penguin (2005)

Swartz, Marvin, 'A Study in Futility', in A. J. A. Morris, *Edwardian Radicalism*, op. cit.

Tanner, Duncan: *Political Change and the Labour Party 1900–1918*, Cambridge University Press (1990)

Taylor, A. J. P: *The Troublemakers*, Hamish Hamilton (1957)

____: *The Struggle for Mastery in Europe 1848–1918*, Oxford University Press (1971)

____: *English History, 1914–1945*, Clarendon Press (1965)

Thomas, J. A.: *The House of Commons 1906–1911*, University of Wales Press (1958)

Thomas, J. H.: *My Story*, Hutchinson (1937)

Trevelyan, Laura, *A Very British Family: The Trevelyans and their World*, I. B. Tauris, (2006)

Ullswater, Viscount: *A Speaker's Commentaries*, Edward Arnold (1925)

Vellacott, Jo: *From Liberal to Labour with Women's Suffrage*, McGill-Queen's University Press (1993)

Warner, Philip: *Kitchener*, Orion (2006)

Waterhouse, Michael: *Edwardian Requiem: A Life of Sir Edward Grey*, Biteback (2013)

Wedgwood, Josiah C: *Memoirs of a Fighting Life*, Hutchinson (1940)

White, Hope Costley: *Lord Dickinson of Painswick: A Memoir*, John Bellairs (1956)

Williams, Llewelyn: '"A Proved and Loyal Friendship": The Diary of W. Llewelyn Williams MP, 1906–15', http://www.llgc.org.uk/fileadmin/doc

Wilson, Trevor: *The Downfall of the Liberal Party*, Collins (1966)

____ (ed.): *The Political Diaries of C. P. Scott*, Collins (1970)

Winter, J. M.: *Socialism and the Challenge of War*, Routledge and Kegan Paul (1974)

Winterton, Earl: *Orders of the Day*, Cassell (1953)

Index